The Last Sweet Bite

The Last Sweet Bite

*Stories and Recipes
of Culinary Heritage
Lost and Found*

MICHAEL SHAIKH

CROWN
NEW YORK

CROWN
An imprint of the Crown Publishing Group
A division of Penguin Random House LLC
1745 Broadway
New York, NY 10019
crownpublishing.com
penguinrandomhouse.com

Grateful acknowledgment is made to the following for permission to reprint
previously published material:
Mayyu Ali: "No Place On Earth" by Mayyu Ali. Reprinted by permission of the author.
Joy Harjo & W. W. Norton & Company, Inc.: "Perhaps the World Ends Here" from
The Woman Who Fell From the Sky by Joy Harjo, copyright © 1994 by Joy Harjo.
Reprinted by permission of the publisher and Joy Harjo.

Library of Congress Cataloging-in-Publication Data is on file with the publisher.

Hardcover ISBN 978-0-593-44284-5
Ebook ISBN 978-0-593-44285-2

Editor: Madhulika Sikka | Assistant editor: Fariza Hawke | Production editor: Sohayla
Farman | Text designer: Aubrey Khan | Production: Dustin Amick and Phil Leung |
Copy editor: Hilary Roberts | Recipes copy editor: Sharon Silva | Proofreaders: Janet
Renard, Robin Slutzky, Tess Rossi, Nancy Inglis, Jacob Sammon, and Eldes Tran |
Recipes proofreader: Rachel Markowitz | Publicist: Mary Moates | Marketer: Mason Eng

Broken plate art by MyImages_Micha via gettyimages.com
Plate design art (clockwise from top) by prmustafa and avika via gettyimages.com,
Lroy via shutterstock.com, and imageBROKER/Daniel Vonwiller via alamy.com

Manufactured in the United States of America

9 8 7 6 5 4 3 2 1

First Edition

The authorized representative in the EU for product safety and compliance is
Penguin Random House Ireland, Morrison Chambers, 32 Nassau Street,
Dublin D02 YH68, Ireland, https://eu-contact.penguin.ie.

For my parents—
my successes are all yours,
the mistakes all mine;

and Dominique,
who never doubted the whole thing
(or, if you did, never let it show).

The world begins at a kitchen table. No matter what, we must eat to live.

The gifts of earth are brought and prepared, set on the table. So it has been since creation, and it will go on.

We chase chickens or dogs away from it. Babies teethe at the corners. They scrape their knees under it.

It is here that children are given instructions on what it means to be human. We make men at it, we make women.

At this table we gossip, recall enemies and the ghosts of lovers.

Our dreams drink coffee with us as they put their arms around our children. They laugh with us at our poor falling-down selves and as we put ourselves back together once again at the table.

This table has been a house in the rain, an umbrella in the sun.

Wars have begun and ended at this table. It is a place to hide in the shadow of terror. A place to celebrate the terrible victory.

We have given birth on this table, and have prepared our parents for burial here.

At this table we sing with joy, with sorrow. We pray of suffering and remorse. We give thanks.

Perhaps the world will end at the kitchen table, while we are laughing and crying, eating of the last sweet bite.

—"Perhaps the World Ends Here,"
JOY HARJO

CONTENTS

AUTHOR'S NOTE

THIS IS A BOOK that celebrates food and the people who make it. But it is also a book about how violence changes our treasured food cultures. Most people I've written about in these pages felt safe and comfortable sharing the details of their lives and personalities; others did not. Yet they still wanted their stories told without putting them at greater risk. Therefore, I've occasionally changed names, dates, and locations, as well as other details, to give cover to people I've written about. We are talking about violence, after all, and some of the people you will meet are still at risk, even those in exile. For example, as recently as 2023, the Chinese government has been operating undeclared police stations in New York, London, Rome, Tokyo, and Toronto to harass and silence critics, such as the Uyghur activists you'll meet later in this book. It's not just the Chinese Communist Party that is guilty of this. Dozens of other governments have targeted their critics living abroad.

Second, I have limited the book to only a handful of cases where violence changed cuisines. I chose those that I thought were the clearest examples of the phenomenon to make the strongest case (at least to me) for why the world should be more proactive in protecting our culinary heritage during war. Moreover, I chose them because they involve people whom the world seems to have forgotten. There are, unfortunately, countless examples, old and new, of violence wreaking havoc on our food cultures. In fact, new wars broke out every few months while I was writing this: the civil wars in Myanmar and Sudan; the Russian invasion of Ukraine; the attacks on Israel by Hamas, Hezbollah, and Iran; and Israel's assaults on Gaza, the West Bank, and Lebanon. And each day, a ceasefire in Kashmir feels more fragile. Food traditions are at risk in all these conflicts. I wish I could have included many more chapters.

Finally, there are recipes at the end of each chapter. I endeavored to keep them as close as possible to the original versions provided to me. That said, I did make a few adjustments with the help of the skilled editors at Crown to adapt the recipes—some of which were developed in restaurants—for home kitchens.

The Language of Food

MY FATHER HAD MAGIC POWERS. At least, that's what I thought when I was a small child, growing up in Cleveland, Ohio. My mother, my brother, my sister, and I all spoke one language, English. But my father, who was born in what is today Pakistan, spoke three: English, Urdu, and Sindhi. Whenever I heard my dad speak these other two languages with my aunts or uncles or at parties with family friends, it was as if he crossed an invisible boundary into another world where I couldn't follow. I wanted my father's magic powers; they felt like my birthright.

I didn't know how to ask for those powers until I was about seven, maybe eight years old. I remember feeling slightly sullen when I did. We had just come home after a long trip to Larkana, a city on the banks of the Indus River where my grandmother lived in Pakistan. For those two weeks in Larkana, I was relentlessly teased by cousins in a language I couldn't understand, and I wanted to even the playing field before I saw them next. More so, I wanted that magic key that unlocked that part of who I was and where I came from.

I don't remember when I asked my father to teach me Sindhi, but I probably had to corner him somehow. His work as a doctor demanded long, often unpredictable hours. As a kid, I could go days without seeing him. What I do remember clearly is his reply. He said no, explaining that there was no need, that I was American and wouldn't use it, and that my mother didn't speak it and he was too busy to teach me on his own. The brush-off was compassionately parental but firm, and logically, I couldn't argue with his reasoning. It stung, but it made sense.

. . .

As I got older, my desire to acquire my father's linguistic powers never really abated. It just found other expressions. In high school, I tried Spanish; I enjoyed it, but it didn't take. In college, I learned why: My high school Spanish teachers approached learning a language as a grammatical equation to be solved, whereas my college Japanese professor taught me to see past the language and into the culture. Japanese was more than a means of communication. Its intonations and pen strokes were crucial elements of Japan's history, politics, art, and spirituality; in short, it was a way of being in their world.

In 1999, after college, I got a job teaching English in southern Japan. I was posted to a small town called Takanabe, an old-timey working-class town in Miyazaki Prefecture on the Pacific Ocean known locally for its oyster reefs and surfing scene. Looking for a place to eat one warm summer evening, I came upon the town's tiniest but best-known izakaya, a bar called Kimamaya. I heard the bar before I saw it. To keep the peace, bars in Japan have unusually heavy doors to shut the noise in and police out. When those doors open as drinkers come and go, the revelry and karaoke pour out, breaking the calm like thunder. The laughter echoing down the block toward me from Kimamaya that night was magnetic.

Kimamaya was a romanticized slice of Japan: small and pristine in that *wabi-sabi* way, with only five stools along a well-worn cypress-wood counter. As soon as I walked in, Keiko, the owner, signaled me with her eyes to take the last empty seat at the bar, and placed an ice-cold beer down in front of me with a sloppy thud. Attractive and tiny, Keiko was also loud, vulgar, and uncompromising, a chain-smoker and heavy drinker. She constantly battled town officials over mysterious rules that, curiously, seemed to affect only her bar. An attentive single mother *and* successful female business owner in one of the world's most patriarchal societies, Keiko was unafraid and unapologetic about trampling the stereotype of the diminutive and placating Japanese woman. I quickly realized it was her irreverence toward officialdom—and her incredible cooking—that never failed to attract a similarly brash and unconventional clientele.

I spent a lot of time at Kimamaya over those two years—on both sides of the bar. On busy weekends, it wasn't uncommon for Keiko to summon me into the kitchen to wash dishes or shuck oysters. On slow nights, Keiko would teach me the essentials of Japanese cooking and the mainstays of the local Kyushu cuisine, like *kara-age,* succulent pieces of ginger-, sake-, and soy-marinated chicken deep-fried with a perfect, shattering crust, or how to perfectly grill *pachi ebi,* the sweet and tangy fan lobsters that plied Kyushu's coastal waters. She was troubled that I was single and living alone—this could only mean that I wasn't eating well.

During one of our impromptu cooking classes, I unexpectedly felt a cold wave of guilt wash over me: Here I was learning to cook Keiko's old family recipes, like her grandmother's *karaage;* yet I knew only vague details about my own grandparents, and almost nothing about their cuisine. Here I was trying to establish fluency in her society's language and culture while I couldn't speak a word of Sindhi, the language of half my family. I was certainly familiar with and proud of my Sindhi heritage. But without the language I felt cut off, partitioned from a truer self.

· · ·

Aside from the occasional phone call home, my father and I hadn't talked much while I was in Japan. After I returned to the United States for graduate school, we shared a bottle of Johnnie Walker Black Label over the course of several summer evenings, and the alcohol helped us to reconnect. The conversations eventually found their way to Pakistan—family gossip, weddings, funerals, old friends. But the evening before I left for school, we discussed Partition. It was the first time I had heard his memories in any detail. As my father revealed them, it became clear that they were ever present, like a mountain range on the horizon.

For most of my life, I was unaware of the effects Partition of the Indian subcontinent had on my family. During my time in Pakistan, even when I was living there as an adult, my aunts and uncles never discussed it, despite how profoundly it had altered their lives. My father disclosed only recently that he was the first Muslim born in his family. Shortly before his birth in 1935, the idea of a Muslim-only Pakistan was gaining ground. His family had been Hindu forever. But my great-uncle, the patriarch of the family, perhaps predicting the precariousness Hindus would face in a future sectarian country, converted everyone to Islam. My father was born a few months later into a family still struggling to call one another by their new Islamic names.

In August 1947, two months before my father's twelfth birthday, after three hundred years of colonization, the British cleaved the Indian subcontinent into two independent nation-states: Hindu-majority India and Muslim-majority Pakistan. In what is perhaps the greatest migration in human history, Partition sent millions of Muslims into West Pakistan (now Pakistan) and East Pakistan (now Bangladesh) and millions of Hindus and Sikhs into India. What should have been a triumphant moment in the struggle for independence turned horrifically dark. Communities that had co-existed across the subcontinent for millennia launched genocidal campaigns of violence: Hindus and Sikhs on one side, Muslims on the other.

My uncle was living in New Delhi then and was forced to cross a new and disorienting international border to Pakistan to escape a mob attacking trains, cars set ablaze with refugees still in their seats. My father recalls feeling helpless that summer as anti-Hindu violence enveloped the province for months, emptying his village of his childhood friends and their families. Until Partition, Hindus and Muslims had remained relatively close in Sindh. By the time the violence subsided in 1948, nearly fifteen million people had been forced into new countries. Nearly two million never made it. The legacy of this violence is central to the identity of the people of the Indian subcontinent. As the historian Aanchal Malhotra writes, "Partition is not yet an event of the past."[1]

My father left Pakistan for the United States in 1965 to continue his medical career, nearly twenty years after Partition. But as I listened to him recount his experience, it was clear Partition had dislocated him from his home long before he left. "Partition was a tragedy," he told me. "The Hindus were Sindhis. They were our neighbors." Then my father revealed a deeper truth: "Even if I had a way to teach you Sindhi—I still couldn't." The violence of Partition, he said, had attached itself to almost everything he associated with Pakistan, including his language, preventing him from passing it on. Partition's violence had changed him profoundly. More recently, he told me: "I think about it every day. How can I not?"

It's not uncommon for cultural identity to fade across generations as immigrant connections fall away. But in my family, Partition's ugly reach came across the generations to steal part of our culture. Violence persists after the atrocities are over. It can pass almost undetected from one generation to another, menacing us, changing who we are. That is why I don't speak Sindhi.

. . .

A few years later, in the summer of 2007, I was in Kabul, Afghanistan. I was scheduled to fly out of Kabul early in the morning, and I was tired, the kind of exhaustion that penetrates your bones and soul. My body ached from packing my life into bags and boxes. I just wanted to sleep. Just then, my friend Tamim called to invite me to dinner. I hesitated to accept. Tamim, however, was less of a friend and more of an elder brother, so his dinner invitation was really an order.

Still, my body resisted. Afghanistan had been a tough assignment. I worked for Human Rights Watch as its lead researcher in the country. My job was to document war crimes and persuade the warring parties to stop killing civilians. It was exhilarating and heartbreaking, and it had taken its toll. I had been briefly held by the Taliban, nearly killed by a suicide bombing carried out by its fighters, and chased out of Kabul by an Afghan warlord whose abuses I had reported on. By the summer of 2007, it was time to head home.

Much of my time in Afghanistan had been spent crisscrossing the country to interview victims of violence. Most Afghans I met on these trips served me a meal as part of the interview; this kind of hospitality was hardwired into Afghan culture. It also made talking about tragedy a little less painful.

The meal was almost always Afghanistan's national dish, *qabuli palaw:* dark brown lamb shanks buried in spiced basmati rice, topped with carrots, raisins, and slivered almonds and pistachios.[2] I ate mountains of it. Even the Taliban, when I was briefly in their "care," fed me *qabuli palaw.* Other times, I was offered *ashak* and *mantu,* dumplings filled with minced lamb or leeks and herbs, topped with a face-puckering garlicky yogurt.

I found a greater variety of dishes in restaurants and roadside stalls. Fatty lamb kebabs were what those stalls did best. The *kebabis* sprinkled the lamb with *ghoreh-angoor,* dried sour grapes pulverized into powder that gave the grilled meat a rich, lemony, sumac-like tang. The *kebabis* slid the meat off the skewer onto long pieces of naan that captured the juices. This tangy, fat-soaked bread wrapped around the meat was also a delicacy. Second only to the kebab itself, it is scandalously referred to as the *khwhare-aaros,* or the "bride's sister."

The repetition that I experienced of only a handful of dishes gave me pause. There are a dozen ethnic groups in the country, each with a distinct culture, and microclimates for growing everything from olives to the most intoxicating melons. Afghanistan is wedged between Iran, Pakistan, and China, culinary powerhouses whose influences permeate many other aspects of their smaller neighbor's culture. Surely, Afghan ingenuity combined with these ethnic, topographic, and geographic realities ought to be a recipe for a broader cuisine. Why hadn't I tasted it?

It was dark when I arrived at Tamim's house in Taimani, the closest thing war-torn Kabul had to an upscale neighborhood. Tamim lives by the old Afghan saying that you can tell a man's generosity by the length of his tablecloth, so I wasn't at all surprised to find a half-dozen other guests sipping cocktails in the living room when I arrived. I said my hellos before sneaking to the kitchen to glimpse what we'd eat for dinner. Tamim, an accomplished cook, has a street-smart culinary wisdom born of a life of exile. But he wasn't cooking that night.

Reza, the shy cook, didn't look up from the simmering pot as I opened the screen door. As in many old houses in Kabul, the kitchen was separate from the main house, nestled in a garden behind. It was spacious, painted a soothing shade of sweet-potato orange. The kitchen appliances were numerous but all manual rather than electric, in deference to regular disruptions of the power grid by Taliban bombings. For Reza, the kitchen was a respite from his country's troubles, and he was protective of it. When I asked what he was cooking—what my final meal in the country would be—he barely looked up from the stove, narrowed his eyes, and whispered, "Afghan."

What he meant was "Get the fuck out of my kitchen!"

Later that night, when I saw that Reza had served dinner, placing a variety of stews in earthenware pots in the center of the dinner table, I was thrown. All my years of eating in Afghan homes had conditioned me to expect large platters of lamb and rice.

I had the honor of serving myself first. I ignored the pot of plain rice and went right for the first unfamiliar dish, a thick golden stew of whole chickpeas and sour yogurt, what Tamim called *saland-e nakhod*. I ladled it onto my plate, tore a piece of naan, and soaked it in the chickpeas for a few seconds. The taste was familiar but disorienting, like the moment you step out of an airport into a country that you are visiting for the first time. The punch of ginger, chili, and black pepper and the electric tang of the sour yogurt were both mellowed by the earthy starch of the soft chickpeas. I asked Tamim if the dish was an Afghan recipe, thinking it was something influenced by Iran or Pakistan next door. "Yes, it's ours," he replied. Then with a touch of melancholy he added, "But it's a dish some Afghan families have forgotten."

A forthright and calm man, Tamim has an imposing yet warm and hospitable demeanor. In his mid-thirties then, he had already lived several lives, as refugees often have. Tamim was born in 1963 in Shahr-e Naw in downtown Kabul. When his family was forced to flee Afghanistan during an earlier phase of the country's never-ending violence, Tamim was the first to leave. Desperate for man-power, both the mujahideen and the communists were forcing children to fight in the early 1980s; to keep his son off the battle-field, Tamim's father smuggled him across the border to Pakistan and eventually to the United States, where he received asylum.

Two decades later, after the American invasion in 2001, Tamim and many Afghans returned to Kabul to rebuild their country, dev-astated by a generation of war. He and his circle started small busi-nesses and nonprofits focused on nurturing the talent of young Afghan artists, architects, cooks, and entrepreneurs. Tamim set up two information technology companies and the country's first ca-tering business.

Like Tamim and his family, many Afghans took with them their financial, intellectual, and cultural capital when they fled, stripping away decades of professional experience and knowledge. Artists and musicians escaped the war, hid their work, or stopped practic-ing their trade. It was the same for Afghanistan's chefs and cooks, Tamim explained. Their generationally ingrained recipes, like *saland-e nakhod,* were an essential yet diminishing part of the country's culture. "The wars have strangled Afghan culture," Tamim told me recently. "They have narrowed our language of food."

Imagine this: a favorite family recipe taken to the grave by a grandmother, and the longing and consternation of her children and their children and all the family friends who had for so long come to dinner just for that dish. That night at Tamim's dinner table, he helped me see that the violence I'd spent the past three years investigating had robbed Afghans of their rich culinary culture, one recipe at a time. At that moment, I saw the same tentacles that had reached across generations in my family to steal part of our culture doing that to Tamim's.

But in tasting *saland-e nakhod* that evening, I also experienced a small but crucial act of culinary restoration and resistance.

•   •   •

For a decade, I chronicled the human cost of war. I investigated war crimes in Afghanistan, Pakistan, and Sri Lanka; genocide in Myanmar; deadly coups in Bangladesh and Thailand; and civilian casualties in Mali and Syria for organizations like Human Rights Watch (HRW), the International Crisis Group (ICG), the Center for Civilians in Conflict (CIVIC), and the UN's Office of the High Commissioner for Human Rights (OHCHR). Then, for nearly five years, I worked for the New York City Office of the Mayor to integrate human rights principles into the city's climate change programs. I saw how violence—and climate change is also a form of violence—alters human culture. I saw the impact of violence on art, music, and politics. Most surprising, I saw its impact on food—how it changes, even erases, centuries-old recipes and traditions.

Cuisine is more than an expression of what society eats on any given day; it's a repository of people's history handed down from generation to generation. Cuisine is akin to language. In its most rudimentary form, a cuisine is a way of one society communicating to another where its cultural, and in some cases territorial, boundaries begin and end. And like a language, a cuisine can change or even disappear when a community comes under intense pressure to integrate with another, more powerful group and is forced to surrender its identity. The Holocaust, the Partition of India, the Cambodian genocide, the civil wars in Afghanistan and Sri Lanka, the centuries of subjugation of Native Americans, and the mass internment of the Uyghurs underway in western China are the exact types of violent pressure that alter or dismantle a society's food culture. While this culinary phenomenon is not uncommon in countries that have experienced extreme violence, how the story unfolds is unique in each instance.

As a human rights investigator, I have witnessed how vital the seemingly quotidian facets of human culture, such as what and how we eat, are to a community's sense of history, identity, and security. When a community's food culture is attacked, it can have cascading and devastating implications not only for its emotional and spiritual well-being but also for its physical existence. At the time of this writing, in the spring of 2024, almost all the fishing fleets in Gaza have been destroyed by Israel following the Hamas-led attacks in southern Israel on October 7, 2023. Fishing is more than just a livelihood for Gazans; it is an identity, a way of life. For millennia, Gazans have been a seafaring people. If that is destroyed, then those people have been destroyed.[3]

When I talk about food throughout this book, I am referring to something far more than just basic sustenance, the daily accumulation of enough calories to keep a person alive. I am referring to food and the culture that surrounds it. The recipes, written and oral. The specific way of organizing, cooking, serving, and eating a meal. The ingredients and flavor profiles, which are almost always indicative of, and connected to, a specific geography, ancestral stories, and the spirituality of a people. Even the structures (like homes and kitchens) and the societal infrastructure (like bakeries, farms, fishmongers, *masalawalas*, and seed savers) that enable it. In other words, a cuisine.

Our cuisines are among the most important aspects of human culture, perhaps more important than language in some circumstances: I still don't speak Sindhi, yet the way I access that part of my heritage is through cooking Sindhi food. Eating *our* food is not only comforting but also dignifying and life-affirming; it reminds us of who we are. I have heard women and men who fled genocide in Myanmar recount how they survived in the jungle on grasses and leaves for weeks. They described to me feeling like animals forced to forgo their humanity. When they got to the safety of the refugee camps in Bangladesh and had their first meal of lentils and rice, staples of their cuisine, they told me they "became Rohingya again." For these people, and many others you will meet, and perhaps even for you, food was and is an umbilical connection to our cultures and their world-orienting philosophies. In the most basic sense, our cuisines ground us.

Yet there is little international sympathy for attacks on culinary heritage. Governments and global institutions like the UN have historically prioritized the protection and restoration of tangible treasures like the Raubkunst, the Jewish art looted by the Nazis; the Old Mostar Bridge in Bosnia and Herzegovina, destroyed during the Balkan Wars; and, more recently, the ancient Timbuktu mausoleums in Mali, razed by Ansar Dine and Al Qaeda. These types of heritage should absolutely be protected, but so should other parts of culture with the same enthusiasm. But they aren't. This is mostly because a Global North elitist male perspective determines which aspects of culture should be elevated above others and are therefore worthy of preservation. As a domestic chore done primarily by women, home cooking is not valued in the same way as other aspects of heritage.

This sexism partly explains why the international community recognizes neither war's impact on culinary culture nor the value of culinary culture as something to be protected from violence. In 2003, the UN adopted the Convention for the Safeguarding of the Intangible Cultural Heritage, a voluntary and very flawed treaty that leaves it up to a state, so often led by men, to determine what's worthy of protection. Why would a country such as China sign up to safeguard a minority culture like that of Uyghurs when it is hell-bent on destroying it? But there are some small changes afoot. In 2010, UNESCO began designating certain culinary traditions, like baking lavash in Armenia and making kimchi in North and South Korea, both traditionally done by women, as intangible cultural heritage, but it offered no legal protections and scant financial support.

At its core, this book is an attempt to disturb this gendered inequality that limits our lens on food and its cultural importance. As a young girl growing up in Ohio, my mother was estranged from most of her extended family. At Thanksgiving and Christmas, it was just my grandparents, my mother, and her younger brother at the dinner table in the small dine-in kitchen in their two-story brick farmhouse on the outskirts of Cleveland. Birthday parties were tiny affairs too, no aunts, uncles, or cousins coming for cake with presents. Disputes between my grandparents and their parents had split the families. My mother's cousins lived only four miles away. She met them only as an adult.

My mother's childhood was isolating at times, but she ensured mine was different. Despite a full-time career in public health and philanthropy, and later as a ceramic artist, she did everything she could to keep her kids close to our relatives in both Ohio and Pakistan. At holidays and birthdays, the dinner table was loud and crowded. Every empty space was filled with family. It still is: It seems we're always cramming more chairs around her dining room table at Christmas or finding a bigger room to fit ever more family and friends. For nearly fifty years, my mother has persisted in building a new family culture, which has been a powerfully stabilizing force getting us through major life events like births, deaths, divorce, and adoptions. And she's imbued it with new food traditions too: Depending on the price of king crab legs at Costco, she might serve them steamed in butter and miso next to the Thanksgiving turkey.

Throughout history, women and girls have been at the forefront of building and protecting families and food culture. The story of wars changing cuisine is also a story of violence against women. Wars disproportionately impact women. To be serious about protecting food culture means to be committed to better protecting women and girls during war. Among the most urgent things we can do is to end domicide, the wartime tactic of systematically destroying homes and leveling entire neighborhoods, as has been done in Aleppo, Mariupol, Maungdaw, Gaza, and Khartoum. Home is where women from many cultures spend most of their time. The protection of women, food, and homes is simply part of the same equation.

Perhaps the best thing we can do to protect a cuisine during violence is just pay attention. Later in the book, I'll cover how the intentional attacks on a community's food culture may presage more violence. In some cases, an attack on culture may become an attack on a people. Indeed, attacks on heritage are often intended to demoralize and intimidate a community or weaken and erase it altogether. This was the case with the genocide of the Indigenous peoples in the Americas and is the case today with the Uyghurs in western China. Human rights activists, academics, and policymakers often use a tool called the Ten Stages of Genocide to monitor an unfolding genocide. Incorporating attacks on cuisine into this tool could be useful for determining genocidal intent.

Even outside of war, in peacetime, culinary traditions are manipulated to inflict political and racial violence. A century ago, British colonists derided Indian Hindus for their vegetarianism to justify their subjugation of the subcontinent. Today, populist movements like Germany's Alternative für Deutschland (AfD) politicize culinary practices like alcohol and pork consumption to pursue anti-immigration policies against Muslims. An AfD ad has featured baby pigs with the caption "Islam? It doesn't fit in with our cuisine," a reference to Muslims abstaining from eating pork. In the United States, the Republican Party has similarly used racist memes, not only blaming the Covid-19 pandemic on Chinese eating habits, calling the disease the "Chinese virus" and the "Kung flu," but also demonizing Haitian immigrants by absurdly claiming they were eating house pets in Ohio. And both Republicans and Democrats now want to sanction human rights investigators (and their families) for reporting on people culpable for the violence that often destroys a community's food culture.[4]

Food can also tell stories of heroic persistence. I've met rebel and civilian cooks in Sri Lanka forced by war to create new dishes with fewer ingredients, like the *mithivedi,* or "land mine": a dense, samosa-like pastry named after the weapon. The *mithivedi* is still being eaten by Sri Lanka's northern Tamil community years after the civil war. I've met chefs using food to actively resist violence, like those in the Czech Republic revitalizing a cuisine nearly killed by decades of communist rule and those in Bolivia cooking with coca leaf, an ancient Andean plant stigmatized by the drug war. And I've met Rohingya writers, photographers, and poets forced to live as refugees in squalid camps, painstakingly documenting their cuisine to keep their food culture from disappearing.

As we watch the globe's three most important and trendsetting countries—China, India, and the United States—embrace, to varying degrees, violent cultural authoritarianism, I believe we have a responsibility to interrogate what's on our plate, not just from the perspectives of health, carbon emissions, and ethics but also from the standpoint of political violence, to fully understand why it's there and why it might not be in the future.

Everything humans do is connected to just about everything else, and that is especially true of violence. Violence in one form or another has shaped what humans eat since we first started hunting for food or fending off invaders. When it comes to cuisine, violence (or the absence of it), of course, is not the sole determinant of what shapes a society's food culture, but it is an incredibly influential force. But I believe a community should be able to decide on its own terms, not on the terms of an invading army, how its cuisine changes.

This is not your typical food book and I am not a traditional food writer. I'm not a restaurant critic or a chef. I am neither an anthropologist nor a culinary historian. Rather, I'm a longtime human rights investigator who loves cooking, who has often found himself at the intersection of food and war. I've found that I can get to know someone differently when I eat and drink with them. I understand another culture better when I cook with someone trying to defend it from destruction. I've seen how individuals who have suffered through war use food to connect to their cultures, communities, and histories. You'll find at the close of each chapter, the people I write about—the activists, refugees, and rebels on the battlefield, the home cooks and professional chefs and survivors of all stripes—have shared their recipes not only as a means of preservation but also as a way to understand their lives, their people, and, simply, what brings them so much joy.

Keiko's Karaage

(Japanese Fried Chicken)

Makes 2 to 4 servings

Karaage is the first dish Keiko taught me to cook in her *izakaya*. Although *karaage* is the name for a cooking technique in which different meats or vegetables are marinated and then deep-fried, it is now most closely associated with chicken. Legend has it that the chicken version originated in Ōita Prefecture on Kyushu in southern Japan, up the coast from Keiko's *izakaya* in Miyazaki Prefecture. It's a relative newcomer to Japanese cuisine, less than one hundred years old. After World War II, Japan introduced industrial chicken farming to make up for postwar food shortages. Suddenly faced with a glut of chicken, cooks did the obvious and fried it. Today, *karaage* is right up there with the best fried chicken recipes around the world. What's more, this is communal food. In my experience, *karaage* is meat to be eaten with friends, plenty of ice-cold beer, and a bottle of sake.

This recipe calls for two unique ingredients. The first is *yuzu kosho,* a traditional Kyushu condiment made from fresh green chilies, yuzu (a type of East Asian citrus), and salt, which come together to add a citrusy tang and a touch of spicy heat to the marinade. If you can't find it, *togarashi,* a common chili powder seasoning used in Japanese cuisine, is a good substitute. The second is *katakuriko,* Japanese potato starch—not to be confused with potato flour—which gives the chicken a wonderfully crunchy coating. Look for both of these ingredients in Japanese markets and online.

¼ cup soy sauce

2 tablespoons sake

Thumb-size piece fresh ginger,
peeled and grated

4 garlic cloves, grated

1 tablespoon sugar

½ teaspoon yuzu kosho or
togarashi (see Note),
plus more for serving

4 or 5 boneless, skinless
chicken breasts, cut into
strips about 2 inches long and
1½ inches wide

Peanut, canola, or sunflower oil
for deep-frying

1 cup potato starch
(katakuriko)

½ teaspoon white pepper

Fine sea salt

Lemon wedges for serving

Kewpie mayonnaise for serving
(optional)

1. In a bowl large enough to hold the chicken, stir together the soy sauce, sake, ginger, garlic, sugar, and yuzu kosho to dissolve the sugar. Add the chicken and toss to coat evenly. Cover the bowl and marinate the chicken at room temperature for 1 hour. For best results, marinate in the refrigerator for 24 to 48 hours.

2. Pour the oil into a large, deep pot to a depth of 3 to 4 inches and heat until a deep-fry thermometer registers between 325° and 335°F.

3. While the oil heats, in a medium bowl, stir together the potato starch, pepper, and ½ teaspoon salt. Set a wire rack over a sheet pan and place the sheet pan near the potato starch mixture.

4. Working with one or two pieces at a time, toss the chicken pieces with the potato starch mixture, coating them evenly. Be sure to work the mixture into the little crevices. Gently shake off the excess, and place the coated pieces on one side of the rack and let them rest for a few minutes before frying.

5. When the oil is ready, add three or four chicken pieces to the hot oil and fry until the crust is a light golden brown, 3 to 4 minutes. (There will still be patches of white potato starch, but don't worry, you're going to fry them again.) Using a wire skimmer or slotted spoon, place the chicken on the clean side of the rack to drain. Repeat until all of the chicken is fried, always letting the oil return to 325°F before adding the next batch.

6. After all the chicken is fried, increase the heat of the oil to 375°F. Working in batches, fry each piece again until golden brown, 1 to 2 minutes. Using the skimmer or slotted spoon, return the chicken to the rack to drain again. Sprinkle with yuzu kosho or togarashi. Serve the chicken hot with lemon wedges and with Kewpie mayonnaise, if desired.

NOTE

There are three types of *togarashi: ichimi, shichimi,* and *nanami. Ichimi togarashi* is simply red chili powder, while *shichimi* and *nanami togarashi* also contain ingredients like sansho pepper, hemp seeds and/or poppy seeds, sesame seeds, ginger, citrus peel, and nori. *Nanami togarashi* usually contains more citrus than *shichimi togarashi.* Bottom line: Any *togarashi* will work in this recipe if you can't find *yuzu kosho.* What's more, you might find yourself sprinkling this stuff on just about everything you eat.

Tamim's Saland-e Nakhod

(Afghan Chickpea Stew)

Makes 3 to 4 servings

This is Tamim's recipe for *saland-e nakhod*, the richly spiced chickpea dish I ate at his Kabul home in the summer of 2007 that sparked the idea for this book. Here I am serving it with rice, but on that evening, I scooped up the stew with pieces of Afghan naan. Wheat is among Afghanistan's largest cereal crops, and stacks of wheat naan appear at nearly every local baker and sit alongside dishes at nearly every Afghan meal. Although Afghan naan is made in a tandoor like other versions in Central and South Asia, it differs in shape, texture, and taste. Afghan naan is long, sometimes up to two feet, and slightly thicker than most other versions in the region. It's crusty on the outside and chewy inside with a delicate smoky flavor from the masala of salt, sesame seeds, and nigella seeds. Most Afghans purchase naan from their local baker. Rice is the second most important cereal crop and is the basis of not only the national dish, *qabuli palaw,* but of many other rice dishes, from orange-scented *narenj palaw* to sweet-and-sour *zereshk palaw.* Basmati rice goes really well with Tamim's *saland-e nakhod,* but feel free to substitute it with naan; a good Afghan restaurant will have fresh stacks on hand. And if you live near San Diego, Kabul Kabob House in El Cajon has the best naan (and Afghan food) I've tasted outside Afghanistan. However, if you'd really like to make your own bread to go with this dish, there's a recipe for an incredibly delicious Afghan sourdough (see page xxxiv).

2 cups dried chickpeas	2 or 3 garlic cloves
1 cup plain full-fat Greek yogurt	Kosher salt

2 tablespoons vegetable oil
1 red onion, finely chopped
1 fresh green chili (such as Thai or serrano), stemmed and finely chopped, plus a few whole chilies for serving
1 tablespoon ground coriander
1 teaspoon ground cumin
1 teaspoon ground turmeric
1 teaspoon freshly ground black pepper
1 small tomato, very finely chopped
Fresh cilantro, whole leaves or chopped, for serving
Cooked basmati rice for serving

1. Pick over the chickpeas and discard any with shriveled or broken skin and any bits of grit. Place the chickpeas in a large fine-mesh sieve and rinse well under cold running water. Transfer to a large bowl, add water to cover generously, and let soak overnight.

2. The next day, put the yogurt into a small bowl. Finely grate two garlic cloves over the yogurt and add a pinch of salt. Stir well and then taste. You want to taste the garlic, so don't hesitate to grate the remaining clove if it is needed. Cover the bowl and refrigerate the yogurt.

3. In a medium, heavy pot, warm the oil over medium-high heat. When the oil is shimmering, add the onion and chopped chili and cook, stirring often, until the onion is lightly golden and the chili is softened, 10 to 15 minutes. Add the coriander, cumin, turmeric, and pepper and cook, stirring, for 1 minute. Add the tomato and 1 teaspoon salt and mix well.

4. Drain the chickpeas, add to the pot, and add water to cover by 1 inch. Stir well and bring to a boil, then turn down the heat so the mixture is at a gentle simmer. Cover partially and cook, stirring occasionally, until the chickpeas are tender and the liquid has reduced to a thick soup consistency, 45 minutes to 1 hour (but start checking at 30 minutes).

5. Remove from the heat, taste, and adjust the seasoning with salt if needed. Stir in 2 tablespoons of the garlic yogurt. Taste and add more yogurt if desired. Transfer the stew to a serving bowl and top with cilantro. Serve immediately, accompanied with the remaining garlic yogurt, warm rice, and whole chilies to nibble on for extra heat.

Timur's Halfghan Sourdough

Makes 2 loaves

This is Timur Nusratty's Afghan-inspired sourdough bread. Timur lived with Tamim in Kabul, and as is true with Tamim, I consider Timur more of an older brother than a friend. Timur is also known as the "Halfghan Chef," a play on his half-Afghan, half-Western heritage. But it's also because his cooking bridges those two worlds, like this bread recipe. It combines aspects of a classic sourdough with a *khameer torsh,* a starter for Afghan naan, which Timur learned from bakers in Kabul. What makes this sourdough truly shine is rolling the tops of the unbaked loaves in a *masala* of salt, nigella seeds, and sesame seeds. This gives the loaves a toasty, earthy, and savory crust characteristic of great naan found on the streets of cities like Kabul, Kandahar, and Herat.

Timur's family has played a central role in protecting and promoting Afghanistan's cuisine and culture in the United States. In 1968, Mohammed Hasan Nusratty, Timur's father, opened the Khyber Pass in Oakland, California—America's first Afghan restaurant. In 1979 when the Soviets invaded Afghanistan and ignited a generation-long war, millions of Afghans were forced from their homes. Some came to the Bay Area, where they found safe haven with people like Timur's family, who sheltered and supported them with jobs at the Khyber Pass. Those jobs supported families, which in turn fostered the development of California's vibrant Afghan diaspora, the largest in the United States.

Timur is a lawyer by trade, but his heart belongs in the kitchen. For years, he ran the Flower Street Café, his family's restaurant in Kabul. His cooking, as I have come to learn, is as big and generous as his personality, a trait that allowed Flower Street, like the Khyber Pass, to also function as a safe haven of sorts, though not for refugees, but for young progressive Kabulis to temporarily free themselves from the confines of a conservative society. Both Flower Street and the Khyber Pass have closed, but the legacy of their generosity lives on in recipes like this one and many others which Timur shares online.

800g unbleached all-purpose flour, plus more for dusting	150g Timur's Khameer Torsh (recipe follows)
200g stoneground whole wheat flour	3½ tablespoons kosher salt
650g warm water	3 tablespoons nigella seeds
	3 tablespoons white sesame seeds

1. In a large mixing bowl, combine both flours and the water, and mix thoroughly until a craggy dough with a firm consistency forms.
2. When the khameer torsh (sourdough starter) has peaked, place the dough mound on a floured work surface and pour it in the middle of the dough. Stretch and fold the corners of the mound over the starter to combine it into the dough. Repeat the stretching and folding five to six times. Add 2½ tablespoons salt and continue to stretch and fold thoroughly until a well-combined, smooth, and cohesive dough forms.
3. Lift the dough and slap it down onto a flat, floured work surface to help accelerate the yeast fermentation process. Repeat this step two to three times over the course of 1 hour. Alternatively, you can continue to stretch and fold the dough four to five times over the course of 2 hours. After each slap or fold, shape the dough into a ball, place it in a bowl, and cover it until the next round. After the final slap or fold, shape the dough into a ball, return it to the bowl, cover, and let it rest on your counter for at least 6 hours or (ideally) overnight until the dough has doubled in size.
4. Using a bench scraper, pour the dough out onto a lightly floured work surface and cut it into two equal parts. Lightly flour your hands and shape each half of the dough into a mound. Let both rest on the work surface for 15 to 30 minutes.
5. Make the naan masala. In a small bowl, combine the nigella seeds, sesame seeds, and 1 tablespoon salt. Stir until combined, pour the

mixture onto a large plate, and spread it evenly across the surface. Set aside.

6. Dust two proofing baskets with flour. Shape each dough mound to fit the baskets. Using the bench scraper, pick up one dough mound from the bottom and carefully invert it, lowering the top of the dough into the plate containing the naan masala. Roll the top of the dough over and into the masala so that the dough is properly crowned with as much of the masala as possible. Then carefully lower the dough into one of the proofing baskets with the masala side facing the bottom of the basket. Cover the basket with a tea towel, and let proof for 2 to 3 hours. Repeat with the second loaf. Any leftover masala can be stored in a sealed glass jar for up to 3 months in the pantry.

7. Thirty minutes before the dough is finished proofing, preheat the oven to 500°F, with two empty Dutch ovens and their lids inside.

8. Once proofing is complete, carefully remove the dough from the basket and place it on a piece of parchment paper, masala side facing up. Repeat with the second basket. Using a very sharp knife, give each of the loaves a long score across the top to create an "ear," that nice, defined ridge that peels back and away from the main loaf.

9. Carefully remove the hot Dutch ovens from the oven and place them on the stovetop or a trivet. Gently lift the parchment paper, set it inside the Dutch oven, and cover with the lid. Repeat with the second dough mound. Bake for 30 minutes until the loaves rise and increase in volume, and the "ears" open up. After 30 minutes, remove the lids, lower the temperature to 435°F, and bake the loaves for an additional 10 to 15 minutes, until sufficiently browned and crusty. Remove from the oven and let the loaves rest uncovered in the Dutch ovens for about 30 minutes. Then lift the loaves from the pots by the parchment paper and place them on a wire rack to continue cooling.

Timur's Khameer Torsh

(Sourdough Starter)

This is the recipe for Timur's *khameer torsh* or Afghan sourdough starter. When your starter lives in your refrigerator, simply keep it healthy by feeding it weekly and it will last you years (see Notes, page xxxviii). You can use your *khameer torsh* for any type of sourdough. Remember, it's a living thing; it requires vigilance. But the reward is well worth it.

| All-purpose flour | Water |
| Stoneground whole wheat flour | |

1. **DAY 1:** Using a scale, weigh a clean 1-quart glass jar without its lid. Record the weight in grams and write the number on the lid using a Sharpie. In the glass jar, combine 100g all-purpose flour with 150g of lukewarm water, approximately 85°F. Stir until a thick, smooth paste forms. Scrape down the sides of the jar. Loosely cover the jar with the lid, but don't seal it completely, and leave at room temperature for 24 hours. After 24 hours, you should see some bubbles or a slight increase in volume.

2. **DAY 2:** You now need only 70g of the jar's current contents (i.e., the empty jar weight written on the lid plus 70g of starter). Weigh the starter in its jar and discard the excess. Add 50g all-purpose flour, 50g whole wheat flour, and 115g lukewarm water to the jar and stir until thoroughly combined. Loosely cover the jar with the lid. Leave at room temperature for another 24 hours.

3. **DAY 3:** Repeat this process on Day 3. Observe your starter closely. You should see more bubbles forming, and the starter may rise and fall slightly. It should have a slightly sour smell.

4. **DAY 4:** You now need only 70g of the jar's current contents (i.e., the empty jar weight plus 70g of starter). Weigh the starter in its jar and discard the excess. Add 50g all-purpose flour, 50g whole wheat flour, and 100g lukewarm water to the jar and stir until thoroughly

combined. Loosely cover the jar with the lid and leave at room temperature for another 24 hours.

5. **DAY 5:** Repeat this process on Day 5.

6. **DAY 6:** You now need 50g of the jar's current contents (i.e., the empty jar weight plus 50g of starter). Weigh the starter in its jar and discard the excess. Add 50g all-purpose flour, 50g whole wheat flour, and 100g lukewarm water to the jar and stir until thoroughly combined. Loosely cover the jar with the lid and leave at room temperature for another 24 hours.

7. **DAY 7:** Repeat this process on Day 7. As the starter gets stronger, you'll notice it rising more predictably and becoming more active.

8. **DAY 8:** You now need 100g of the jar's current contents (i.e., the empty jar weight plus 100g of starter). Weigh the starter in its jar and discard the excess. Add 100g all-purpose flour and 100g lukewarm water to the jar and stir until thoroughly combined. Loosely cover the jar with its lid and leave at room temperature for another 24 hours.

9. **DAY 9:** Repeat this process on Day 9. Meet your new sourdough starter. By Day 9, it should be active and rising and falling after each feed. To make bread on Day 9, feed it according to the Day 8 instructions and leave it out on the counter. After a few hours or overnight, the starter will peak and be ready to use in Timur's Halfghan Sourdough.

NOTES

Store unused starter in the refrigerator, where it will last for years if you feed it properly. Some people advise feeding a starter every day, but Timur believes that's excessive. An active starter, he says, is very resilient, but don't starve it for weeks. He advises that feeding it every 4 to 7 days is enough when you are not baking bread. Just feed it according to the Day 8 instructions, and it will be happy.

On baking days, activate your starter by feeding it about 10 to 12 hours in advance. Speed things up a little by placing the starter in a warm environment, such as a bowl of warm water.

1

The Czech Republic

How the Communists Tried to Kill a Cuisine

IN THE SUMMER OF 2023, I found myself in a house in the hills of Prague that may contain the most comprehensive collection of Czech cookbooks in the world. In a kitchen filled with sunlight, there were four dozen old cookbooks and menus spread across the surface of a massive white oak dining table. One of the books was open to a recipe for *šišky s mákem*, a Czech equivalent of gnocchi where long, cylindrical, thumb-sized potato dumplings, dressed in melted butter, are dusted with powdered sugar and poppy seeds soaked in vanilla. It's an old Czech dish that to a non-Czech tastes and feels seductively new. It's eaten as a main course just as often as a dessert.

The archivist of this precious repository—more than fourteen thousand cookbooks and menus in all, from various periods of

Czech history—is a physically imposing man named Roman Vaněk. His clipped gray hair, which angles forward into a steep, Dracula-like widow's peak, insinuates a rather cold and serious temperament, but in conversation he is warm and hilarious and sizzling with curiosity about life. Many of these culinary artifacts Roman bought, some were gifts, and others he rescued from estate sales or trash cans. Roman's rarest books are stored in banks, in safe-deposit boxes, because they are the only copies still in existence. Most, however, are now resting comfortably on bookshelves in various rooms in Roman's home, or in cardboard boxes in his daughter's bedroom—a source of family friction he acknowledged apologetically.

Roman explained that the cylindrical poppy-seed dumplings were originally shaped that way to fit down a goose's neck to fatten the bird. But coated in warm butter, powdered sugar, and poppy seeds, these long, rich, pillowy dumplings become a luxurious human treat. The recipe exemplifies the style of cooking that flourished during the First Czechoslovak Republic, often called the First Republic, the first independent version of Czechoslovakia, which existed from 1918 to 1938. For many cooks, the First Republic remains the highwater mark for Czech culture and cuisine, when Czechs were spinning old Italian dishes like gnocchi in new and delicious ways.[1]

In the centuries leading up to the world wars, the Czech regions of Bohemia and Moravia were important cultural centers for both the Holy Roman and Austro-Hungarian empires. For centuries, Czech and Slovak culture had been suppressed, sometimes viciously. After Czechoslovakia became independent, Prague soon earned a reputation among European travelers as an exotic and romantic place "where life," Peter Demetz, the renowned Czechborn intellectual, once wrote, "seems to happen on stage."[2] The city's bars, cafés, and restaurants were electric, each trying to outdo its competition in luxury and splendor. Czech café society, arguably among the best in Europe at the time, buzzed with the intellectual and political fervor of the era. At Café Arco and Café Louvre in Prague, artists, scientists, and writers like Franz Kafka pondered the state of human affairs over coffee and cool *věneček*, a choux-like pastry shaped like a wreath and filled with cold, sweet, yolky cream.

Others disappeared into dark, wood-paneled taverns like U Zlatého Tygra and U Pinkasů, writing their novels between glasses of the city's freshest beer. Perhaps no other place in Prague epitomized the creative and optimistic fizz of the First Republic more than the Grand Café Orient. Here intellectuals ate and drank while they debated the direction of their new nation in a stunning, light-filled building on Celetná Street that feels like a cubist painting leaped off the canvas into an architectural form. Today, the Grand Café Orient still stands as a timeless masterpiece of cubist art.

This period of Czech cooking is best captured in *Velká kuchařka* (The Great Cookbook). The Czech equivalent of *The Joy of Cooking* or *An Invitation to Indian Cooking*, *Velká kuchařka* was written by Vilém Vrabec, a man widely adored as a godfather of contemporary Czech cooking, a cultural icon akin to Julia Child or Madhur Jaffrey. While his book was published in 1968, well after the First Republic years, Vrabec's recipes reflect much of what he learned as a young cook during that pivotal era. Vrabec died in 1983, the day after he submitted the manuscript of his last cookbook to the publisher.[3] Arguably, Roman Vaněk is the most important food person in the Czech Republic today. But before I could truly understand Roman's contribution to Czech cooking, I had to understand Vilém Vrabec.

· · ·

Vrabec was born in 1901. When he was a child, his teachers quickly recognized his artistic talent, and his parents sent him to Berlin to attend an industrial arts school. Short on cash, Vrabec worked at a deli, organizing its display cases. His artistic attention to detail, and probably his good looks, got him noticed, earning him a spot in the kitchen, where he learned the art of cold cuisine. The experience changed him; he left art school and returned to Prague to work in delis, both to beautify display cases and to introduce recipes he had picked up in Berlin. Then he set off across Europe. Working for room and board, he found jobs under chefs at some of the best hotels from England to Switzerland.

Vrabec is something of a hero to Roman. Vrabec, he explained, didn't leave the art world so much as he saw cooking as an alternative way of being in it. The same thing can be said for the First Republic's attitude toward Czech food, Roman observed. In the 1920s, while the young, vibrant Vrabec was finding his footing as a chef, the government of the First Republic was also looking to shake things up. Czechs and Slovaks were looking to break Austria's cultural grip on their new country. Chefs were encouraged to travel to broaden their culinary horizons. Some went to Italy and England like Vrabec; others went to France, which, in particular, was seen by Czechs then not only as the pinnacle of cooking but also as a "strong counterpoint to Austrian influence."[4]

When these chefs returned, they helped make Prague a place for first-rate food, on par with Paris and Vienna, drawing inspiration from French and Italian cooking techniques and blending them with those redolent of the city's German, Czech, and Jewish communities. Quoting Franz Kafka, Ivan Klíma, the renowned Czech novelist and playwright, once said: "Inside every citizen of Prague, there is a Czech, a Jew and a German."[5] During this period, the writer Elizabeth Smith points out, "Czechs were roasting goose better than Germans, using gnocchi in ways the Italians never thought of, and incorporating French techniques that made their meat sauces even richer."[6] In turn, Czech chefs were in high demand on the Continent; many were lured to Vienna, helping to turn that city into an epicurean destination.[7]

In Prague, the city's well-to-do would dine in opulent restaurants like the Golden Star and the Hotel Paris, an art nouveau panorama of tall windows, soaring ceilings, and sparkling crystal chandeliers, or in the intricately designed Café Imperial, ordering delicacies such as roast pheasant, duck, and *španělské ptáčky* (Spanish birds), a Czech roulade made from beef or veal.[8] Inside these grand, ballroom-sized dining rooms, light danced on immaculately set tables of polished glass and sterling silverware. Waiters in tight black tuxedos and starched white-collared shirts stood watch like generals surveying a battlefield, ensuring that their beautifully dressed guests remained carelessly enveloped in the sounds of laughter and clinking champagne glasses.

Soon Vrabec became a celebrity: He published a couple of books and spent years traveling Czechoslovakia holding pop-up cooking classes. Then, in 1929, Vrabec opened Prague's first cooking school in a beautiful baroque building at the corner of Štěpánská and Řeznická in New Town. Everyone from housewives to politicians to movie stars booked classes, Roman said. "He was an unpretentious guy, a cook for the people," Roman explained. Just as Julia Child and Madhur Jaffrey introduced Americans to French and Indian cuisine respectively, Vrabec brought the cooking and culture of high-class Prague restaurants to everyday Czechs. More than forty thousand people went through his cooking school.

• • •

All of this, however, was shattered by the Nazis. In the back corner of a Prague tavern late one July afternoon, I sat with Dr. Martin Franc, a Czech food historian at Charles University, who cohosts a popular YouTube show with Roman Vaněk called *Zmlsané dějiny* (*Once Upon a Craving*), which digs deep into the often-bizarre origin stories of old Czech food recipes. An affable and bespectacled man with wispy hair, Dr. Franc is often seen around town wearing his trademark white button-down shirt, black waistcoat, and bow tie. We were eating and drinking in Lokál, a chain of newish pubs known locally for its fresh beer as well as provoking nostalgia for the cooking of the communist years after World War II, a time, ironically, that many Czechs consider the low point of their cuisine.[9] Cutting into a square of *smažený sýr*, a fried semihard cheese evocative of the communist period, Dr. Franc said matter-of-factly, "The communists did a lot of damage to Czech gastronomy. But it really started with the Nazis."

In 1938, Adolf Hitler invaded Austria without objection from France and Britain, major European powers at the time. Emboldened by this policy of appeasement, Nazi Germany occupied and annexed the Sudetenland—the region of Czechoslovakia bordering Germany. It did so with the support of many ethnic Germans, who at the time were the second-largest ethnic group in Czechoslovakia. In the Munich Agreement in 1938, both Britain and France approved this annexation. Czechs had always seen themselves as culturally a part of the West, but now they felt abandoned by the Western European powers—a resentment that would linger for decades.

Then, in March 1939, Nazi troops marched into Prague, turning the remainder of the Czech lands into the Protectorate of Bohemia and Moravia, while the Slovak regions declared independence, becoming a fascist state aligned with Nazi Germany. "Hitler's real reason for the offensive was food," Franc said. Germany was the second-largest economy in the world but had more people than it could feed. Czechoslovakia, the seventh-largest economy in the world then, was both an agricultural and an industrial powerhouse. Seizing it, Hitler reasoned, would prevent Germany from going hungry during the next war. Others would have to starve instead.[10]

Jews, who had played a prominent role in Prague's cultural life for centuries, immediately faced stringent limits on what, when, and where they could eat in the new Nazi colony. Nazi storm troopers, unflinchingly cruel, dragged Jews out of restaurants, bars, and cafés, like the stately Café Louvre, where Albert Einstein often worked while teaching in Prague. Allowed to shop only during specified two-hour periods, Jews were also prohibited by anti-Semitic rules from buying foods such as fruit, cheese, and meat.[11] During their occupation, the Nazis sent 120,000 Jews to Terezín, a concentration camp thirty miles north of Prague, where 30,000 of them died of disease and intentional starvation.[12]

Coffee, the fuel of Prague's cultural life, disappeared, in part because of high import costs but also because the Nazi cult viewed caffeine as an unhealthy evil that could poison the Aryan race.[13] Meat, eggs, and cooking fats like lard were increasingly hard to come by.[14] Some Czechs could go to the black market for food, but Gestapo checks on homes made it risky, and prices were often out of reach. In turn, cooking at home soon became an effort to stretch out meager rations.

Restaurants made up for the lack of meat on their menus by serving fish imported from the North Sea, but the culinary change didn't catch on.[15] The same restaurants often had two menus, one for the occupier and another for the occupied. When I visited Roman, he occasionally disappeared upstairs in search of boxes of a few of these menus in his collection. One shows how Germans could order a variety of meat dishes, while Czechs had to make do with flour dumplings and thin, watery sauces. "Menus are mirrors of the public mood of a time," Roman said. "They're a way to see what a society values, what they are thinking, their creativity, as well as their darker sides."

In 1946, after World War II, the Czech lands and Slovakia reunited into Czechoslovakia. The quality and quantity of food improved, but the Nazi plunder of food during the occupation had led to skyrocketing rates of infant mortality and malnutrition, particularly among children. At the war's end, the theft of the Sudetenland and the Munich Agreement still cast an ugly shadow over much of the country; the Czech authorities saw all ethnic Germans as Nazi collaborators and sanctioned their forcible expulsion with an official order of ethnic cleansing that was also green-lit by the Allied powers.[16] About sixteen thousand ethnic Germans were killed by Czechs during the expulsions, with the killers granted amnesty, which, shamefully, remains in place today.[17]

Czechoslovakia emerged from war unaligned; both the Soviets and the Americans had liberated it. But in 1948, the Communist Party of Czechoslovakia (KSČ) came to power in a coup, cementing its Soviet hold over the country for the next half century.[18] The new communist government suspended imports of luxury ingredients while quietly buying food from capitalist countries to feed its people. Food shortages prevailed, and eating out for pleasure became an indulgence few could afford, as well as out of step with socialism, which was fast becoming the sole acceptable ideology of postwar Czechoslovakia.

The Hotel Alcron in Prague, perhaps the pinnacle of fine dining during the First Republic, was now a symbol of bourgeois life and erased from the city's cultural landscape. Café Louvre was also destroyed and its furniture tossed out the windows onto the street below. The KSČ leaders conspicuously shied away from dining out in flashy places, shifting their eating habits to emphasize a connection with the working class.[19] Martin Franc's research points out that the KSČ went so far as officially changing the names of dishes considered elitist. Irish stew was renamed "mutton braised with vegetables." *Minestra,* a popular Italian soup served in Czechoslovakia, became "beef soup with cabbage and rice." And soufflé was simply called "mild puffy cake."[20]

Culinary culture at all levels took a hit. The political isolation of Czechoslovakia by the West meant fewer people like chefs and their ideas entered the country. Domestically, the KSČ pulled skilled workers out of private restaurants and into public jobs in sectors prioritized in the new planned economy, like agriculture and mining. For four decades, the Communist Party dictated not only what could be grown but also what could be eaten. After the Second World War, once-common ingredients like broccoli and fennel faded from Czech culinary memory because of rigid and often violently enforced farming and cooking standards.[21] Creativity even in casual restaurants and home kitchens was culled by the KSČ to establish a singular national culinary identity in service of a socialist utopian ideal. The communists reduced almost everything to the lowest common denominator; for Czech cuisine, that denominator was calories.

Vilém Vrabec attempted to keep his cooking school going during these dark times. People continued to take his classes, which he paired with lessons on mixing cocktails. But Vrabec became frustrated that his students were too shit-faced to cook. He couldn't cut cocktails from his classes or he'd lose income. Instead, he had special cocktail glasses made. Roman had one among his cookbook collection. Made from Bohemian crystal, it was shaped like an ice-cream cone with a ball at the point. Roman gave the glass to me to hold. It immediately induced anxiety; the ball at the bottom made this fragile thing impossible to put down. That was the point, Roman explained: "Vrabec reasoned that if he made his students continuously hold their drinks, they'd stay sober enough to cook." I asked him if it worked. "No idea," Roman replied, "but aren't they beautiful glasses?"

Eventually the communists came for Vrabec too. In 1953, the KSČ took over his culinary academy and nationalized it. Vrabec was immediately demoted and banned from distributing his books; newspapers were ordered to stop printing his articles and recipes. By the late 1950s, however, the Communist Party's censors had allowed several of his books and articles to be republished, but in a heavily modified form.[22] Despite his demotion, Vrabec remained committed to the culinary arts, staying on at his institute as an ordinary employee until his retirement in 1961.[23]

. . .

"Communism killed our cuisine." It's hard to exaggerate how often I heard that from Czech chefs. Under the KSČ, many told me, ingredients that had once been staples of Bohemian and Moravian cooking disappeared. For most people, regular game dishes like Bohemian rabbit practically went extinct under communist rule, since the regime retained almost all such products for export to earn hard currency. Fresh Moravian asparagus, both the white and green varieties, nearly vanished as well. Ivančice, just outside Brno, the Moravian capital, was once renowned across Europe for its asparagus; for a time, it was even the official "chief court supplier" of the vegetable for the Austro-Hungarian emperor in Vienna. The KSČ, however, had no taste for it, deriding its consumption as a sign of bourgeois decadence, and took great pleasure in plowing under asparagus fields.

Thousands of small, privately owned farms, such as those growing "bourgeois" foods like asparagus, were forcibly confiscated and merged into sprawling, state-owned, collectivized industrial farms. Collectivization, as this period is often called, had as much to do with flexing political control over the countryside as it did with boosting farming productivity.[24]

Raised in Los Angeles but fluent in Czech, Anna West is a Czech American writer and academic living in Prague. Anna spent much of her career delving into the history and culture of Central Europe through the aperture of her family. Like many Czechs, Anna spent summers at her family's *chata*, their small countryside cottage, outside Prague. Surrounded by fruit trees, the cottage had been in her family for five generations. Her great-grandparents, Anička (whom Anna is named after) and František, built their *chata* in 1912 next to their family farm as a retirement home. "It's a beautiful place. But I always knew the *chata* was connected to the violence of collectivization," she told me.

Anna, who has written about her family's experience with collectivization, said that at first, the KSČ made joining the national farming cooperatives voluntary.[25] Many farmers signed up, believing it was a way to build a better society. However, many others, like Anna's great-grandparents, refused to forfeit lands and livelihoods that had been part of their families for generations. "That act of political courage," Anna said, "had disastrous consequences for people like my great-grandfather." In 1951, the KSČ launched "Operation Kulak," targeting the holdouts. (*Kulak* is Russian for "fist" but was used derisively by Czechs to refer to "tight-fisted" private landowners at the time.) Thousands of farmers who resisted collectivization were accused of treason and jailed as "class enemies" or sent to labor camps, and their children were denied jobs and education. When František refused, the KSČ confiscated his farm and sent him to Prague's Pankrác Prison, notorious for torture. František wasn't tortured, Anna explained, but many other Czechs and Slovaks were.

Almost overnight, collectivization transformed Czech food. On these new, sprawling farms, production was reduced to a handful of foods: cattle, pigs, wheat, and potatoes. Even so, food production dropped because experienced farmers were either in jail or had quit out of fear or disgust, leaving the least knowledgeable to work the land. Many of the novices couldn't cut it, abandoning not only the land but also the livestock. Countless animals died from starvation and neglect. In turn, a humiliated KSČ was forced to import vital foods—like cereals, lentils, onions, garlic, and caraway and mustard seeds—from both Soviet and capitalist countries for the next decade.

A legacy of this time is *smažený sýr,* the fried cheese Martin Franc was eating while we were talking in Lokál, the pub in Prague. It's still a popular food, eaten at home, in restaurants, or in the street. Also called *smažák,* this deep-fried guilty pleasure can be eaten with a knife and fork or held between two slices of bread with ketchup or tartar sauce. It is a dish tied closely to the communist era because it was incredibly inexpensive—the dairy industry was collectivized and heavily subsidized—and easy to make. A half-inch-thick slice of hard cheese like Edam or Gouda is coated with flour, dipped in a beaten egg, coated again with seasoned breadcrumbs, and fried in oil. Another reason for the dish's enduring popularity is that for years it was the only vegetarian option available in restaurants. During collectivization, the KSČ ordered restaurants to go meat-free one day a week to help relieve country-wide shortages. In the 1960s, on what in effect were communist Meatless Mondays, Martin Franc said, *smažený sýr* "went from being a starter to a main course."

Though the process was painful for countless families like Anna's, the KSČ ultimately secured a measure of food security through collectivization. While Czechoslovakia escaped the famines that accompanied collectivization in other Stalinist states, it was nevertheless a catastrophe with an enduring impact on Czech culture. As Anna pointed out, the eviction of more than four thousand families from their farms, including hers, severed deep bonds between people and their land, changing their lives forever: "Before collectivization, [family] farms were passed between generations. Farming was an important aspect of family and community identity. Because of collectivization, entire generations left farming for good." That displacement, she said, caused families to lose touch with old food traditions carried out only in the countryside, like the *zabijačka,* a cherished wintertime village pig slaughter dating back to medieval times that makes use of the whole animal to tide families over until the spring.

· · ·

The misery of collectivization was felt everywhere in Czechoslovakia. In Prague and other cities, private businesses were nationalized and food shortages fed inflation, which spiked to 30 percent. To bring it down, the KSČ devalued the currency. Overnight, Czechs and Slovaks saw their savings shrink, in some cases by 5,000 percent. "The communists tried to make everyone equal by impoverishing them," Roman Vaněk told me. "My grandfather just threw money out of the window because it had no value after the communists devalued the currency. We were lucky that's all my grandfather did; others committed suicide. It was not a good time to be alive then."

Something of a respite came in 1953, when a new leader of the

Soviet Union, Nikita Khrushchev, came into power and embarked on a project of liberalization known as the Khrushchev Thaw, which, according to the author Slavenka Drakulić, "sparked a cultural revival of sorts across the Soviet Bloc."[26] In Czechoslovakia, the openness that began in the late 1960s, known as the Prague Spring, allowed TV debates between politicians and space for filmmakers such as Miloš Forman and writers like Milan Kundera to critique the communist government more openly.

It also created space for Vrabec to publish his masterwork, *Velká kuchařka,* in 1968. But like other forms of public cultural expression at the time, commentary on Czech gastronomy had to be managed carefully so as not to be seen as celebrating life in the democratic First Republic with too much enthusiasm, which could be read as an implied critique of the regime.[27] Though given *Velká kuchařka*'s enthusiastic tone, as some point out, Vrabec appears to have escaped the wrath of censors.[28]

Cooking became an arena for peaceful competition between the Soviet bloc and the West during the era of détente.[29] Czech and Slovak people increasingly competed in international cooking competitions in cities such as Brussels, Montréal, and Osaka. Czechoslovak food was a highlight of Expo 58, the world's fair held in Brussels in 1958. Chefs, miles away from prying eyes of the Communist Party in Prague, discreetly served food from the First Republic that also paired with the free pilsner beer at the Czechoslovak pavilion. That changed at Expo 68, the world's fair held in Montréal in 1968, with Czechoslovakian chefs entering cooking competitions with less appealing but decidedly more imaginative dishes like *Loreta,* a veal filet sautéed with cognac and topped with almonds, bananas, and whipped cream, and *tournedos Hradčany,* a beef filet flambéed with vodka, stuffed olives, and truffles and dressed with tomato ketchup.[30]

In Czech homes, creativity tried to break free, but cooks were still constrained by what was available in the shops. Butchers seldom had high-quality meat. Fresh fruit and vegetables were hard to come by during the winter; tropical fruit like oranges and bananas (and that other household staple, toilet paper) was scarce all year. New food shows like *Vaří šéfkuchař* (*The Chef Is Cooking*) attempted to get people into cooking but were more or less propaganda, promoting canned foods that weren't selling well in government shops and educating people on how to get through food shortages.[31]

Something of restaurant culture reemerged in the 1960s but mostly for the Czech elite. Foreign chefs were imported from Communist Bloc countries to cook at places with names evoking a gulag-like austerity, like the Moscow Restaurant, the Sofia Restaurant, and the Chinese Restaurant (they were later joined by the Cuban Restaurant and the Vietnamese Restaurant, both of which opened in the 1970s).[32] For decades, the Chinese Restaurant was by far the most popular and fashionable, frequented by local celebrities and politicians. It was hard to get a table; you'd have to book at least a month in advance.[33] The Chinese Restaurant reportedly served sea cucumbers and shark-fin soup. Both Roman and Martin told me that one of the chefs might have cooked for Mao Zedong, but neither was absolutely sure.

•   •   •

In 1968, a reform-minded communist named Alexander Dubček took the reins of the KSČ. A shy and optimistic man, Dubček wasn't known for impulsiveness, but he almost immediately ushered in the Prague Spring. In some ways an extension of the Khrushchev Thaw, the Prague Spring aimed at ending the stringent

Stalinist socialism that had defined political life in Czechoslovakia to create what the writer Slavenka Drakulić describes as a more relaxed, "free, modern, and profoundly humane society."[34]

Dubček's "socialism with a human face," as he called it, was an attempt to transform rather than overthrow the communist regime. But soon the Soviets began to worry about his loyalty. Late in the evening on August 20, 1968, hundreds of Warsaw Pact tanks rolled over the Czechoslovak border. By morning, three hundred thousand soldiers were occupying Prague.

That day, Dubček was arrested and flown to Moscow, where he was forced to make humiliating concessions that ended the Prague Spring and, while saving many from firing squads and deportation to Siberia, also formalized the stifling twenty-three-year Soviet occupation of Czechoslovakia.[35] Soviet soldiers shot and killed more than fifty people on the first day of the occupation alone. Another eighty-seven were killed in the days and months that followed, while thousands of other innocent Czechs and Slovaks would eventually be arrested and sent to "reeducation" camps. By some estimates, hundreds of Czechoslovaks were killed during the Soviet occupation from 1969 to 1990.

Among the artifacts in Roman's collection are two volumes called *Gastronomy of the Nations of the Soviet Union* and *How to Prepare Cuban Citrus Specialties,* both from the 1970s. Roman told me that the Soviet invasion ushered in an era called *normalizace* (normalization). The Soviet's goal, Roman explained, was to standardize Czechoslovak life by eliminating all expression of independent ideas. "Everything had to be homogenized and put into the service of the state. Even what we ate," Roman explained. "To build their bullshit communist dream they had to flatten the Czech people and Slovak people into a singular lifestyle."

It would also require a singular cuisine.

Roman sat quietly, surveying dozens of cookbooks strewn across his kitchen table. He stood suddenly and bent over, plunging his large hands into a khaki cardboard box on the floor beside his chair. A few moments later, he hauled up two heavy books, one in each hand, like a grizzly bear pulling salmon out of a river. One book was called *Receptury teplých pokrmů* (*Standards for Warm Meals*) and its counterpart called *Receptury studených pokrmů* (*Standards for Cold Meals*). The books, Roman said, were collectively called the *Standards* but mockingly nicknamed *normičky*, or the "puny book of standards," by cooks in the post-1968 period for their dreary and unimaginative approach to eating. The *Standards* were books that restaurant chefs during normalization couldn't ignore, and the ones that did the most damage, Roman said.

The *Standards* were published by the Ministry of Trade, which throughout the Soviet era issued dozens of other Communist Party cookbooks with staid titles like *Russian, Bulgarian, and Hungarian Cuisine* and *Ice Cream Sundaes and Other Creams*.[36] But none would have the impact of the *Standards*, particularly *Standards for Warm Meals*, a heavy, seven-hundred-page encyclopedic tome leaden with impenetrable tables. In nine hundred recipes, this excruciatingly pedantic cookbook dictated what people could eat in restaurants for much of the communist era.[37]

The *Standards* drew heavily from an earlier socialist cookbook, *The Book of Tasty and Healthy Food*, written in the 1930s by Joseph Stalin's commissar of food, Anastas Mikoyan. At the time, Stalin was hell-bent on creating a single Soviet identity. The Soviets understood the cultural and political power of food and sought to recode Russian identity by reworking food through party-approved recipes.

Mikoyan's book was filled with happiness and abundance at a

time when most of the Soviet Union was suffering food shortages and even famine. Taking a page from Mikoyan's cookbook, the KSČ's *Standards* focused heavily on nutrition. Alongside cooking instructions, recipes contained charts with calorie counts and detailed vitamin lists as well as stern instructions about hygiene. The *Standards* were also more realistic than Mikoyan's book, focusing on cooking economically with available ingredients rather than relying on exotic imports.

"Because of collectivization, everyone everywhere in Czechoslovakia was literally growing the same thing. They were buying the same thing and eating the same thing," Roman said. "What was grown on [collectivized] farms dictated the regime's standards; it dictated what we cooked in kitchens and put in our mouths."

Like its authoritarian publishers, the *Standards* were incredibly pedantic, specifying serving styles for everything from sauces to side dishes to garnishes and levying inexplicable injunctions like the "prohibition of mayonnaise, salad with mayonnaise and mayonnaise toppings for fried foods."[38] Many restaurants still reflexively follow some of these rules. Roman laughed and said, "Anyone born after 1989 won't know why we always place three leaves of parsley on the edge of the plate. But it's because of *normićky*."

Standards for Warm Meals was certainly the most consequential of the communist-era cookbooks. But dozens of others published at the time also had roles in regulating Czechoslovak life. Reaching for a small stack of cookbooks on his kitchen table, some with recipes for Alaskan cod, Cuban cocktails, pomegranate pastries, and even sushi, Roman explained that most were just propaganda containing what he colorfully called "mythical bullshit recipes" to gaslight Czechoslovaks into thinking that those who were loyal to the Communist Party could eat exotically.

But "almost no one, not even senior party leaders, had access to ingredients necessary to make these recipes," Roman explained. "Maybe one or two [listed in a recipe], but not at the same time." The irony of this hardly went unnoticed. "Pomegranate! Alaskan cod! We never had those things here then. These recipes were lies," Roman recalled, incredulously flipping through a small red-and-white communist-era cookbook. "They had to lie to us. It was the only way to explain why every store sold the same few things. It was only to explain away the scarcity."

Roman paused for a moment. Then he turned to me with a smirk and asked: "How do you know you're in a bad communist restaurant?"

"I don't know," I said.

"The waiter has more food on his uniform than on your plate."

Before I could laugh, he was out with the next one: "Why do communist restaurants have such long menus?" Answering himself: "So customers have something to read before they realize there are only dumplings and cabbage."

Then came "What do you get when you combine Soviet technology and Czechoslovak food policy? The most modern empty shelves in the world."

Through a laugh, Roman said: "We may have had shit food, but we still had a good sense of humor."

•   •   •

A few miles from Roman's home, I met an old friend, Vašek Pecha, at U Matěje, a restaurant in the hills overlooking Prague. On a small porcelain plate, we were served a fish from a lake in southern Bohemia sliced into thick, finger-sized strips, battered in breadcrumbs, and fried to a brown crisp. It was accompanied by a few lemon slices, a pale green dill dipping sauce, and a fresh pilsner beer. The young blond server said the fish, a carp, had been marinated briefly in white wine vinegar before it was cooked. He didn't say that with any real conviction, so I reached for a bite to investigate.

U Matěje is a relatively new restaurant, having opened in 2019, right before the world shut down. In that short time, it became a beloved favorite among the people of Prague for its strict focus on cooking Czech dishes with Czech ingredients. The food at U Matěje is satisfying and familiar. Each meal is like a mini Thanksgiving meal, but tailored to the ingredients and big flavors of each new season. It's comfort food that allows you to walk away full without being weighed down.

A twenty-minute drive from the center of town, U Matěje feels like it's in a Bohemian forest. A wide stone path leads from the street through a great lawn up to the restaurant, a large, cream-colored country house with a roof that rises with waves of red tiles. The lawn is immense, almost pasture-like, and dotted with a dozen chestnut trees, each sixty feet tall. In the summertime, these giants form an emerald canopy. In a way, U Matěje's menu was written by those trees: "When I was planning a new restaurant and looking for spots, I had a few cuisines in mind. But when I saw this place, I knew I could only cook Czech food here," Jan Punčochář, U Matěje's head chef and owner, said when he came by our table, looking over the lawn with a childlike grin.

Between bites Vašek and I debated the marinade on the fish. The lemon juice and dill sauce, or maybe it was the hint of vinegar, did something magical, transforming it from a simple fried fish stick into sensorial delight.

. . .

Vašek's hometown is Český Krumlov, a small Renaissance and baroque castle town in Bohemia, south of the capital. Sitting at two bends of the Vltava River, surrounded by alpine forest, Český Krumlov looks like a living fairy tale. The pastel-hued village is a maze of narrow, winding cobblestone streets sitting in the shadow of an imposing spired castle built on a hulking and rugged granite slab.

As we snacked on our plate of fried fish, Vašek reminisced about his childhood, how as a small boy he fished the rivers and lakes around Český Krumlov in the summertime, occasionally hooking a carp for dinner. "Most Czechs only eat carp on Christmas Eve—in the winter," he said, looking up at the fully leaved chestnut trees to emphasize that we were eating in eighty-degree weather in late July. Eating carp at Christmas is a legacy of the country's conversion to Catholicism in the ninth century, Vašek explained. Catholics abstain from eating meat on the eves of certain holy days, but fish is allowed.

"A few days before Christmas, we'd bring one home and let it swim around in the bathtub," Vašek said amusedly while holding his hands two feet apart, approximating the size of a carp. The idea being, he explained, that the bathwater would both refrigerate and cleanse the fish of impurities before it was breaded, fried, and eaten. Kids, Vašek said while trying to contain his laughter, grew attached to their carp, even naming their new pets. Nowadays, he noted, most Czechs just buy cleaned fillets from their local fish shop to avoid Christmas dinner becoming a hostage negotiation with their children.

As he reached across the wooden table for another piece of fish, he said: "You know, for almost half of my life, Czechs were told we couldn't enjoy food like this." Vašek, like a lot of Czechs of his generation, has walked in two very different worlds. He was born in 1974 at the height of the Soviet occupation of Czechoslovakia but came of age after the Velvet Revolution in 1989 that ended communism in Czechoslovakia.

The thing about Vašek's family is that they have constantly been a thorn in the side of the Communist Party. In the 1950s, during collectivization, Vašek's grandfather chose a life in a labor camp after refusing to farm the communist way. In 1968, when Vašek's parents, Drs. Václav and Michaela Pecha, were young and talented medical students at Charles University in Prague, the Soviet tanks rolled in. For months, they were hunted by an insecure state. The freedom-loving, free-thinking couple made it to West Germany, but the secret police eventually found them and blackmailed them to return. They were allowed to finish school before being sent home to Český Krumlov to work in state-run clinics. "If we hadn't come back, there's no question our families would have been punished for our escape. They would have lost their jobs or probably gone to jail," Dr. Pecha told me before he passed away in March 2023.

The Communist Party harassed the Pechas endlessly for their nonconformism. For six months, the party refused to issue a birth certificate for Barbara, Vašek's younger sister, over her name. In Czech, "Barbara" is spelled "Barbora," an o replacing the second a. But Dr. Pecha loved Barbra Streisand (whose name at birth was "Barbara") and insisted on the American spelling.[39] As a young kid in Český Krumlov, Vašek was suspended from school for refusing to sing communist propaganda songs. When his teacher chided him to sing like a good comrade, he instead hummed a song by Karel Kryl, a Czech Bob Dylan–type musician who was banned in the country for singing about the hypocrisy and inhumanity of the communist regime. Even under pressure, Vašek never let slip that it was his parents who played Kryl's music at home. It was a minor offense, but it signaled to Václav and Michaela that their children might have inherited the dominant family traits: a strong individual identity, a love of Czech culture, and a healthy distrust of authority—the very things the KSČ was cleansing from the country.

This is why the Pecha family, like many Czechoslovaks, decided to leave. The communist rot had not only left their beloved Český Krumlov in crumbling cultural disrepair but also ruined the economy, making it impossible for Vašek's parents to sustain anything resembling a livelihood, let alone raise their two young children without risking their becoming apparatchiks. Vašek's father, Václav, had secured a job working as a doctor in Algeria; Czechoslovaks could travel only to other socialist countries, which Algeria was at the time. From there, away from the prying eyes of the KSČ, the Pechas planned to secretly emigrate to Canada. In early 1988, Václav and Michaela discreetly packed up their home and left their fairy-tale town on the banks of the Vltava River forever, or so the family thought. Vašek's family never went to Canada. They didn't have to: A year after they arrived in Algeria, on November 17, 1989, student protesters filled the streets of Prague, echoing the same call for freedom that had brought down the Berlin Wall eight days earlier. By late December, the Velvet Revolution, as the protests are known today, had peacefully brought down the communist regime in Czechoslovakia, pushing the Soviets back to Moscow.

Roughly twenty years ago, on my first or second trip to Český Krumlov, Vašek introduced me to Lojza Slepánek. A hard-drinking, gregarious man with a biting sense of humor, Lojza was also a constant thorn in the side of the local Communist Party during the normalization era; his "nonconformism," he said, sent him to prison for ten months for punching out the local party chief after he hurled lewd remarks toward several women in the town. Lojza was a cook in a Český Krumlov restaurant during the occupation; he possesses a wealth of local history that is rarely recorded. Part of what made him resent the regime, he gruffly explained, were the

Standards: "*Normićky* was a terrible and prescriptive system. You couldn't really change anything about a recipe," Lojza told me. "Everything had to be followed; they even had rules for how a restaurant should look, how tables were arranged and the plates stacked."

Lojza is in his late seventies, wears a long gray handlebar mustache, and has an immense belly that he carries proudly, like a billboard advertising his arrival. When I first met him, he told me: "I'd rather have a belly on my front from drinking and eating than a hump on my back from working in a factory." He's mostly cut out booze on his doctor's orders but retains his deep, raspy voice from years of smoking Marlboro Reds. Over plates of cold vanilla-laced *věneček* pastries and glasses of Jägermeister, Lojza explained how cooks in the 1970s and 1980s had to receive permission from the KSČ to deviate from the *Standards:* "No one did it; the less contact we had with them, the better. Plus, it was a waste of time, a complete fool's errand, because everyone knew the regime would never approve it. This is why the menus were all the same—everywhere."

Typical of this era of culinary monotony, Lojza said, was a tasteless, highly processed brown gravy. The gravy was called *univerzální hnědá omáčka* (universal brown sauce), which the Czechs mockingly shortened to the acronym UHO. The *Standards,* Lojza said half jokingly, required that the sauce be slathered on almost everything in restaurants or canteens. Lojza and other chefs, like Roman, point out that UHO is actually based on an old and difficult recipe. Done right, it is like a demi-glace, made by simmering roots, vegetables, and beef or pork bones together in stock for hours, reducing it to a thick, dark, intensely flavored soft gravy.

But daring to make UHO the traditional way—daring to defy the cookbook—could land you in jail or a labor camp, Lojza said. "They came and checked if you were following the rules. Every single restaurant had to have the same goddamn food because of *normićky*," Lojza said. "If you wanted to do something different, you couldn't, because no one had any money!"

Looking back, Lojza said, he thinks part of the recipe for the Velvet Revolution may have been written in the communist cookbook. My curiosity was piqued, and I asked him what he meant. "The *Standards* changed our food for the worse, but it also showed us how stupid the regime was," he explained.

"How so?" I asked.

"They made it easy for everyone in the food business to steal from the regime. Waiters, butchers, cooks, anyone who sold vegetables and ingredients supplied by the government, had an opportunity to make extra money selling stolen food on the side. If you weren't stealing, you were stealing from your family."

Taking a deep drag from his worked-over Marlboro, Lojza described how this informal "racket of resistance" operated: "Every day, cooks would make dishes smaller or use fewer ingredients than what the *Standards* dictated. Every day, the waiter was pouring smaller amounts of beer so there would be leftover beer in the end." He continued: "In the evening, when the restaurant was closed, the butcher who worked in a state-run meat market down the road would show up at the restaurant after his shift." Then, Lojza explained, "the restaurant guys would give him extra beer or extra ingredients in exchange for meat that the butcher had stolen from the government!" He stopped, took another drag, and then said: "Everybody was stealing, but nothing went missing. That's how it worked."

The government never really figured it out, Lojza said, and even if they did, they couldn't prevent it. "Even sending people to jail didn't stop people from stealing, since everyone was in on it," he said. It worked because no individual was harmed. "Everything was, you know, owned by the government. So you were not stealing from your friend; you were ripping off the regime."

In Lojza's experience, robbing the regime was commonplace. "The only people not stealing then were the sanitation workers, because the only thing they could steal was shit. As long as you didn't steal too much and didn't steal more than your neighbor, no one said a thing."

"Did it affect the quality of the food?" I asked.

"Of course," he answered in a drawn-out bellow. "So the *Standards* would say, 'You must make schnitzel with butter.' But instead of butter, which was much better, they'd make it with sunflower oil, which was cheaper, and take the butter home or sell it." He continued, "Obviously, the quality dropped like a rock in a river. The only thing of any quality left in these places was the beer. Meals became an afterthought in restaurants. You ate only when you were really hungry."

Taking a few seconds to reflect, he added, "The *Standards* only really affected restaurants. You could more or less do what you wanted at home if you had the ingredients. And that's a big 'if.' Shops were always short on things."

Lojza paused again to consider the past. "In the end," he said, "the *Standards* just created the kind of problems it tried to solve. The socialist utopia was a fool's errand. Everyone knew even if you worked twice as hard, you'd never get paid more. So why wouldn't you steal to get a leg up?"

In his highly influential essay from 1978, "The Power of the Powerless," Václav Havel, the playwright who would become the president of a post-Soviet Czechoslovakia, wrote: "If the suppression of the aims of life is a complex process, and if it is based on the multifaceted manipulation of all expressions of life, then, by the same token, every free expression of life indirectly threatens the post-totalitarian system politically, including forms of expression to which, in other social systems, no one would attribute any potential political significance, not to mention explosive power."[40]

When it came to restaurant cooking, Lojza proudly said: "The *Standards* killed the creativity in the kitchen, but it didn't kill our creativity in finding ways to fuck with the regime. That's why we stole from them."

. . .

At the time of the Velvet Revolution, Roman was working at the Czech News Agency, the national public service news agency, as a junior photographer. He turned his government-issued camera on the regime itself, capturing images of police beating demonstrators and sharing them with protest organizers to prevent the regime from covering up its crimes. "Who knows?" Roman told me. "Maybe it was my destiny to help others bring down the regime."

After the Velvet Revolution, Roman and a dozen other journalism students started *Studentské listy* (*Student Papers*), a wildly popular literary and photography magazine that covered the political and cultural aspirations of a people reemerging from decades of suffocating totalitarianism. Among the iconic moments Roman photographed then was an intimate moment between Václav Havel and Mick Jagger in August 1990. Havel, a poet and political prisoner, had just become the first president of a free Czechoslovakia, and the Rolling Stones had come to perform in Prague. Havel, a few steps in front of Jagger, is pulling the much-taller rock star forward by the hand in childlike excitement across the high, empty balcony of Prague Castle to be welcomed by an excited crowd on the street below. With the ornate, blackened

Gothic flying buttresses of St. Vitus Cathedral in the background, both men look like they're magically floating atop the castle city.

Havel and Jagger hadn't met until that day, but it was a highly emotional and consequential event for most Czechs to have a Western rock band like the Rolling Stones in Prague. For some, Roman's photograph of Václav Havel taking Mick Jagger by the hand captured the moment when Czechs and Slovaks reemerged from behind the Iron Curtain to reclaim their rightful place in the West.

Not long after taking that photograph, Roman had another encounter with the new Czech president. He recalled that during a *Student Papers* editorial meeting, a colleague half-heartedly joked they should start having their meetings in the catacombs under Prague. His colleague had just walked through them, their medieval beauty fresh in his mind. Another colleague agreed, offering that it would be even better if they brought a few kegs of beer and a few friends. Roman described the idea snowballing—others pointed out the catacombs had lights, toilets, and even a small kitchen. Next, Roman remembered someone joking that "hunger might just be thirst in disguise. But the only way to know for sure is if we had food."

Someone blurted out, "Pork goulash," Roman recalled. "Then everyone looked at me, since I was the cook of the group. Just like that we were having a party," he said, snapping his fingers. "And I had to cook!"

He continued: "While I was at home in my tiny kitchen on Letná Street, cutting thirty-five kilos of onions for the goulash for our editorial party in the catacombs, two *Student Papers* colleagues went to the castle and invited President Havel." They reasoned, Roman explained, that Havel was a fan of the paper; that Prague Castle, the presidential residence, was close to the catacombs; and that "we all knew he liked goulash and beer too." To the surprise of most of them, "the president actually came!" Havel's guards were ravenous, Roman recalled, and ate his goulash cold right from the pot. "But I was able to heat Havel's goulash." Havel loved it, Roman said. "For days afterward, I strutted around telling everyone I was the president's cook. In reality I was a shitty cook. I was only twenty years old, but I loved cooking." He continued, "Little did I know that a decade later, the world of food would swallow me whole."

Roman's activism lies in helping Czechs excavate culinary traditions buried under decades of communist conformity. In 2007, he founded the Prague Culinary Institute, or Prakul, a cooking academy for amateurs and professionals alike that focuses on recovering the creativity and quality that defined the cuisine of Vilém Vrabec and the First Republic. Prakul is also a publishing house through which Roman and his wife, Jana, have co-authored dozens of bestselling cookbooks.

Roman considers it his mission to spread knowledge about good Czech cooking. He created and hosted the popular online television series *Peklo na talíři* (*Hell on a Plate*), which has helped expose how the food industry shortchanges consumers, including an EU dual-foods scandal in the 2010s where inferior versions of identically branded foods were being intentionally sold in former Eastern Bloc countries. Roman famously summed up the public's justifiable indignation at the time when he said the Czech Republic was being treated like Western Europe's "garbage can."

He can be a stubborn traditionalist, but in a way that reflects his view of cooking as an art rather than a science. His peers say that's what separates him from other chefs and makes him approachable to amateurs, even children: Roman volunteers at summer camps teaching kids how to cook, including both Vašek's and his sister Barbara's children. Paging through stacks of old cookbooks on his kitchen table, Roman said, "I learned a long time ago, during the revolution, that if I had to change something, I had to do it from the bottom up. Not the top down. I used my camera then. Now I use food."

After the Velvet Revolution in 1989, many Czechs opened new restaurants. Lojza and his family opened U Dobráka (The Good Man), a small restaurant in Český Krumlov. Lojza closed U Dobráka in 2016 after nearly three decades in business, but it was a spectacular place, nestled deep in a sunken stone courtyard shared by several ancient buildings. One lingering online review affectionately described eating in U Dobráka as like "eating in a medieval garage." A poster of Karl Marx and a statue of Mao Zedong ironically watched over the restaurant and the bathroom, respectively, so Lojza could "forever rub his freedom [to cook] in their face." Open only in the summer, U Dobráka was known for intentionally charging more for its beer than other places in town, so as "to keep the drunks out," as well as for its obsession with serving the freshest meat and local fish like pike perch, a freshwater fish found in Bohemia, which Lojza grilled on a large open fire in the middle of his restaurant, a cooking technique characteristic of restaurants in the precommunist era.

The point behind U Dobráka, Lojza told me, was to revitalize the town's food traditions after a half century of communism. "Even now, most of the [Czech] restaurants in town are still serving some version of what we ate during normalization," he said. During the First Republic, Lojza explained, restaurant menus were shorter, but "there was more variety in the food you could eat throughout town. Why? Because each restaurant specialized in its own dishes, like tripe soup, local fish, meats and sausages, and sauces. The communists destroyed that creativity with their standards."

Vašek Pecha's family, too, entered the food business. After returning home from Algeria, the family devoted their time and savings to restoring what they could of Český Krumlov's physical and cultural heritage, which had decayed under the communists. In 1992, the tiny pastel-colored medieval town was designated a UNESCO World Heritage Site.

Bringing back quality Czech food was part of reviving the culture too. In 2002, the Pechas opened Hospoda 99, a small restaurant, café, and guesthouse built into the town's thick medieval wall. It is run by Barbara Pechová, Vašek's sister, who has turned it into one of Český Krumlov's most beloved places to gather. Barbara's menu is eclectic, reflecting the tastes of both locals and tourists. Czech classics like *svíčková,* a tender sirloin steak blanketed in a silky sauce made from root vegetables, stock, and cream, and *kulajda,* a tangy mushroom and potato soup, sit comfortably alongside contemporary smoked meat and sausage dishes that are best described as Tex-Czech barbecue.

"It's not that all of Hospoda 99's dishes are unique; they are all, in a way, traditionally Czech. But the ingredients we use in some ways are . . . ingredients like asparagus, fennel, legumes, and thyme that nearly disappeared under the communist way of cooking," Barbara explained to me. "Cooking with these ingredients, cooking Czech dishes the old way, is not something we advertise but something we are intentional about."

From celebrity chef–run restaurants like U Matěje in Prague to small-town taverns like the Pechas' Hospoda 99, this style of cooking is regularly described as a "modern take on Czech cuisine." In most cases, modernizing a cuisine would mean moving it in a direction that reflects a society's changing tastes, aesthetics, or mores, like the carp fries Vašek and I ate at U Matěje in Prague. By putting a winter dish on its summer menu, U Matěje is not only bucking Czech culinary traditions but also reflecting a modern Czech reality: Survey after survey shows the Czech Republic to be among the least religious countries on earth.[41]

Modernizing a cuisine can also mean the incorporation of new ingredients, modern cooking techniques, or the influences of immigration patterns. But "modern Czech food" can also be a euphemism for a style of cooking that purposely reflects the past, in which chefs as well as home cooks turn back to ways of eating that were forced out of favor under communism. Innovation is now about excavating a forgotten culinary heritage, bucking the conformity of the past, and cooking dishes that might once have landed chefs in a labor camp, all as an act of national pride. The anthropologist and food scholar Iveta Hajdáková describes this process as "restoration as a form of innovation."[42] For some cooks and chefs, it's called "decommunization."

Thirty-five years since the fall of communism, this back-to-the-future cooking has made Prague and other parts of Bohemia and Moravia, the historical Czech lands, among the most interesting places to eat and drink in Europe.[43] Even so, Czech chefs don't take this success for granted; they continue to point to the bleak years of communist conformity as a motivating force to keep them cooking good food: Polls show that young people don't understand what happened. Older generations, too, are suffering from a cultural amnesia about the communists.

The transition to democracy and capitalism has not been easy for everyone either, and insecurity has created nostalgia for the predictability of the authoritarian era, a smoldering notion that autocratic Russia is stoking in post–Eastern Bloc EU states like the Czech Republic. For some Czech cooks and chefs, Russia's invasion of Ukraine has added new importance to decommunizing Czech cuisine. "Czech gastronomy tells us a story about war and peace, about lost time, about the importance of protecting the things you love," Roman told me. "All of us should be reminded of that from time to time. And right now is one of those times."

Roman's Goulash

Makes 4 to 6 servings

This is the goulash Roman Vaněk made for President Václav Havel in the first days after the Velvet Revolution. He uses an equal amount of onions to meat, and he cooks the onions over low heat so they caramelize without burning. The onions act as a thickener, but if you wish to thicken the goulash further, you can add bread crusts or a roux. Roman made the goulash with pork shoulder for Havel, but you can use beef instead. Make it ahead if you'd like; it tastes better the next day. You can serve this goulash with potato dumplings or a rustic, hearty bread.

2 pounds boneless pork shoulder or beef chuck or shank, cut into 3-inch cubes
Kosher salt and freshly ground black pepper
½ cup lard
2 pounds yellow onions, finely chopped
2 garlic cloves
1 teaspoon crushed caraway seeds
2 tablespoons tomato paste

2 tablespoons sweet paprika
½ teaspoon hot paprika, plus more as needed (optional)
4 bay leaves
About 6 cups beef stock, heated
1 tablespoon dried marjoram
Bramborové Knedlíky (page 36) or rustic, hearty bread for serving, such as Timur's Halfghan Sourdough (page xxxiv)

1. Season the meat all over with 2 teaspoons salt and ½ teaspoon pepper.

2. In a large, heavy pot, melt the lard over medium heat. Add the onions and garlic and cook, stirring occasionally, until most are golden brown and some are the color of walnuts, 30 to 40 minutes. If a fond (caramelized bits) forms on the bottom of the pot as you cook the onions, remove the pot from the heat, add 3 to 4 tablespoons water, and scrape the bottom with a wooden spoon to dissolve the fond, then continue cooking until the onions are caramelized.

3. Add the seasoned meat and caraway seeds, stir well, and cook, stirring frequently, until all of the juices released by the meat evaporate and the meat starts to brown in the remaining fat, about 10 minutes.

4. Turn down the heat to low, stir in the tomato paste, and cook, stirring constantly, for 1 minute, again using a wooden spoon to scrape up any caramelized bits and work them back into the sauce to add depth of flavor. Add the sweet paprika, hot paprika (if using), and bay leaves and continue stirring for 1 minute.

5. Pour in enough hot stock to come three-fourths of the way up the sides of the meat and increase the heat to medium-high. Once again scrape the bottom of the pot to dissolve the fond into the liquid. Bring the liquid to a boil, turn down the heat to low, cover, and simmer until the meat is tender, 2 to 2½ hours. Uncover, stir occasionally, and taste for flavor; adjust the seasoning and add more stock if needed to keep the meat three-fourths immersed.

6. When the meat is tender, uncover the pot and add the marjoram, crumbling it between your fingers as you drop it into the pot. Stir well and then cook, uncovered, for 5 minutes. Taste and adjust the seasoning with salt, pepper, and hot paprika (if using) as needed. Remove from the heat, cover, and let rest for 15 minutes before serving.

7. To serve, spoon the hot goulash over potato dumplings or accompany the goulash with crusty bread for soaking up every last bit of the tasty stew. And in case you're wondering, yes, Timur's Halfghan Sourdough goes really well with this.

Roman and Jana's Šišky s Mákem

*(Potato Dumplings with Poppy Seeds
and Powdered Sugar)*

Makes 6 servings

This is a wonderful Czech dish typical of First Republic cooking. The recipe comes from Roman Vaněk and Jana Vaňková's bestselling cookbook, *Velká kuchařka Čech a Moravy* (*The Great Cookbook of Bohemia and Moravia*). It can be eaten as a meal or a dessert, depending on your mood. In some versions of this dish, the chef mixes vanilla beans from the pod with the poppy seeds before combining the seeds with the sugar. But if you'd like your dumplings on the savory side, there is a recipe from Roman and Jana for that too (see page 38).

1 recipe Bramborové Knedlíky
    (recipe follows), shaped as
    bramborové šišky and warmed
2 tablespoons lard, melted, for
    coating

1 cup poppy seeds
1 cup powdered sugar
2 tablespoons unsalted butter,
    melted

1.   Make and cook the bramborové as directed.
2.   Using a slotted spoon, transfer the warm dumplings to a large bowl. Add the lard and toss gently to coat evenly.
3.   In a deep bowl, stir together the poppy seeds and sugar. Working with one dumpling at a time, drop the dumpling in the bowl to coat one side. Transfer to a serving plate and drizzle with the butter. Sprinkle with more of the poppy seed–sugar mixture, if desired. Serve immediately.

Bramborové Knedlíky

(Potato Dumplings)

Makes about 30 dumplings

This is a classic potato dumpling recipe from Roman and Jana's cookbook. You can make any shape of dumpling you wish out of this recipe, but in Czech, the dumpling's name is dependent on its shape, similar to the specific names for various pasta shapes. For the Šišky s Mákem, you technically need to shape the dumplings as bramborové šišky, which are 2- to 3-inch cylindrical dumplings with *blunt* ends. The savory dumpling dish that follows calls for knedlíky shaped as bramborové šulánky, which are 3- to 4-inch cylindrical dumplings with *tapered* ends. But feel free to experiment with shapes. Keep in mind that the thicker you make them, the longer you'll need to boil them.

This recipe makes almost 3 dozen dumplings, which is a lot for just one or two people. You can freeze leftover cooked dumplings in an airtight container and reheat them in a microwave-safe container on high for 1½ minutes.

2 pounds medium russet
    potatoes, scrubbed
Table salt
1⅓ cups semolina flour, plus
    more for dusting

1 tablespoon potato
    starch
2 eggs, lightly beaten

1. In a large saucepan, combine the potatoes with water to cover by about 1 inch. Add ¼ tablespoon of salt for every 2 cups of water in the pot. Bring to a boil over medium-high heat, turn down the heat to maintain a gentle boil, and cook until the potatoes are fork-tender, start checking after 15 minutes. Drain the potatoes and let cool.

2. Once the potatoes are cool, peel them and cut them in half. Press the potato pieces through a fine-mesh sieve or pass them through a ricer held over a large bowl. Alternatively, put them into the bowl and mash them with a fork or potato masher. No need to be gentle, you don't want any clumps of potato.
3. In a medium bowl, whisk together the semolina flour, potato starch, and 1 teaspoon salt. Add the mashed potatoes and eggs to the flour mixture and mix with a wooden spoon until all of the ingredients come together in a ragged dough, then quickly knead with your hands until you have a smooth, homogenous dough that feels fluffy and light to the touch.
4. In a large pot, bring 6 cups of water to a boil and add ¾ tablespoon salt to the pot.
5. While the water heats, lightly dust a clean work surface with flour. Using your hands, shape the dough into small balls about the size of a golf ball. To shape the dough into bramborové šišky, roll each ball on the lightly dusted work surface into a cylinder 2 to 3 inches long with blunt ends. To shape the dough into bramborové šulánky, roll each ball into a cylinder 3 to 4 inches long and then apply pressure to taper each end.
6. When the water is boiling, working in batches, add the dumplings and cook until they float to the surface, about 3 minutes. Cook for 1 minute longer and then remove the dumplings from the water to a clean dry plate. Repeat with the remaining uncooked dumplings.

Roman and Jana's Bramborové Šulánky se Zelím a Slaninou

(Potato Dumplings with Sauerkraut and Bacon)

Makes 6 servings

This is a variation on the iconic Czech dish of roast pork, sauerkraut, and fluffy bread dumplings called *Karlovarský knedlik*. In my experience, this recipe, which calls for *bramborové šulánky*, a cone-shaped version of *bramborové knedlíky* (potato dumplings) with tapered ends, is not commonly found in restaurants, but it is an ideal comfort food and pairs perfectly with a Czech pilsner, like Pilsner Urquell. If you're in New York City, Threes Brewery in Brooklyn makes a few great Czech-style pilsners too.

This is a pretty flexible recipe, so feel free to dial up or down the amount of bacon, onion, and sauerkraut. If you use more bacon, dial back the lard, and you may have to drain some fat from the pan before adding the onion.

1 recipe Bramborové
    Knedlíky (page 36),
    shaped as bramborové
    šulánky
4 tablespoons lard or butter
10 ounces smoked bacon, cut
    crosswise into ¼-inch-wide
    strips

1 small red or yellow onion, finely
    chopped
1 pound store-bought sauerkraut,
    well drained and squeezed
Kosher salt and freshly ground
    black pepper (optional)
Chopped fresh flat-leaf parsley
    for garnish

1. Make and cook the bramborové šulánky as directed.
2. Line a large platter with paper towels and place it near the stovetop. In a large skillet, melt 3 tablespoons of the lard over medium-high heat. When the lard is hot, add the dumplings in a single layer and fry, turning once, until golden brown on both sides, about 10 minutes. Using a slotted spoon, transfer them to the towel-lined platter to drain briefly. Then transfer them to a large bowl, cover, and set the bowl in a warm place.
3. Wipe out the skillet, return it to medium-high heat, and add the remaining 1 tablespoon lard. When the lard melts and is hot, add the bacon and cook, stirring occasionally, until browned, about 10 minutes. Add the onion to the bacon and continue to cook, stirring occasionally, until the onion is golden brown, about 10 minutes. Add the sauerkraut and cook, stirring often, until light golden brown, about 5 minutes. Season with salt and pepper if needed.
4. Transfer the contents of the skillet to the bowl with the dumplings and stir gently to mix well. Sprinkle with the parsley and serve immediately.

2

Sri Lanka and
the Tamil Diaspora

Call It What It Is: Eelam Tamil Cuisine

IDON'T KNOW HOW, but my conversation with Rajiva that morning found its way to food, and we discovered each other's love for cooking. Rajiva was in her late fifties then, but the way she slung her braid of silver and jet-black hair around her neck, she could have been decades younger. She told me about her beloved Eelam Tamil crab curry, something I told her I had never tried. Unable to hide her irritation at my reply, she pointed sternly with her eyes at the notebook in my lap. Then in a maternal tone, she admonished me to write down her recipe for *nandu kari*.

I had met Rajiva in Chennai, India, in the autumn of 2010 outside the home of Jayaram Jayalalithaa, the powerful Indian-Tamil politician and actress, who was expected to be elected the next chief minister of Tamil Nadu at the time. Sri Lanka, which is only thirty-five miles from Tamil Nadu's shores as the crow flies, had just come out of a brutal twenty-six-year civil war between the government and Tamil separatists. From the beginning, Tamil Nadu politicians have been deeply enmeshed in the Sri Lankan war, providing shelter and support for their ethnic brethren, rebels and civilians alike. I was there to meet Jayalalithaa to report on how Indian politicians like her might influence Sri Lanka's postwar politics.

After I presented every possible form of identification, the guard at Jayalalithaa's home instructed me to wait, pointing with his wiry arm to an immense rain tree across the road. After a few moments of impatiently shuffling back and forth, I struck up a conversation with other people gathered around the trunk of the informal waiting room. I learned that several were Tamil refugees from Sri Lanka. They were living in different camps around Chennai and had come to ask Jayalalithaa for help.

Soon I was introduced to Rajiva, who seemed to hold prominence in the group. I learned it was because she had survived the shelling of Mullivaikkal. At the beginning of 2009, Sri Lanka's army had the opposition Tamil Tigers on the run in the Vanni, a forested and sparsely populated area in the northern tip of their raindrop-shaped nation. The fighting moved fast from west to east across the island. The army had compressed the battlefield between itself and the Indian Ocean, trapping thousands of panicked civilians, like Rajiva and her family, in the middle.

The Tigers' obituary had been written many times before in their thirty-year fight for a separate Tamil state, seemingly the only solution to decades of relentless discrimination by the Sinhalese-dominated Sri Lankan government against the island's Tamil minority. But the Tigers always managed to survive, regroup, and emerge stronger. No one could have guessed that the rebels, who at one point controlled a third of the country, would implode.

As the war raced eastward toward the sea, the government created "no-fire zones," safe areas where civilians could supposedly escape the cross fire. By May, the army had forced the front line, the Tigers, and three hundred thousand civilians into one of these zones on a beach not much bigger than Manhattan's Central Park. Pinned between the army and the ocean, farmers and fighters alike were shelled from air, land, and sea in an all-out effort by government forces to extinguish the Tigers.

For ten days that May, the "no-fire zone" on the Mullivaikkal beach was probably the most dangerous place on earth. Both sides were guilty of atrocities during the thirty-year conflict, but those committed by the government in the final months of fighting were for the record books. The UN, which initially downplayed the killings, later estimated that at least seventy thousand people were killed on that beach, a massacre that was clearly a war crime. In retrospect, it was also genocidal.

For Tamils like Rajiva who outlasted the bombs, the war didn't end with the demise of the Tigers. Devoid of magnanimity in its total victory, the government "liberated" the civilian survivors of Mullivaikkal by treating them as POWs and locking them in internment camps for two years. Through a combination of luck, bribery, and an act of extraordinary kindness by a naval officer, Rajiva had escaped the camps. She hid in the jungle for two days before leaving Sri Lanka at night on a fishing boat across the Palk Strait, over a ribbon of sandy limestone shoals arcing north toward the state of Tamil Nadu in India.

Sitting under that rain tree in Chennai, Rajiva explained to me that she had been traveling the city for days trying to meet with influential Tamil Nadu politicians, like Jayalalithaa. She wanted to convey to them what she and many others experienced on Mullivaikkal beach, in the hope of the politicians persuading the government to offer more support to Sri Lankan Tamil refugees in India. But that would have to wait. From across the street, the guard coldly barked to return tomorrow; the politician might have time for us then.

The next day when I returned, I found Rajiva again under the old rain tree. Despite all she had experienced, there was a natural ease about her that made her approachable. Rajiva was soft-spoken yet open about her life. Through a translator, we talked for what felt like hours. She told me more about Mullivaikkal beach, how she endured the shelling by eating *kanji*. A staple dish of Tamil homes, *kanji* is a simple and comforting porridge of rice and coconut milk. But on Mullivaikkal, Rajiva said, civilians were forced to make *kanji* from seawater to survive.

Then in a frank yet emotional tone, Rajiva told me about the family she had left behind, some of whom never made it off the beach at Mullivaikkal. She told me how she and other survivors of Mullivaikkal quietly commemorate their loved ones by making *kanji* with salt water instead of coconut milk. Today, this simple rice dish has become a symbol of resistance. Every May 18, the day the war ended in 2008, Eelam Tamils around the world mark the Mullivaikkal massacre by making saltwater *kanji*.[1]

At some point, our conversation turned to other parts of Rajiva's cherished Eelam cuisine, like *nandu kari,* an astonishingly beautiful dish made with blue swimmer crabs, a red chili, and fennel-heavy curry powder all mellowed with the sweetness of coconut milk and the distinctive citrusy smokiness of curry leaves. I recall looking up at Rajiva occasionally from my notebook and seeing joy in her eyes as she watched intently while I wrote down her recipe.

That late autumn day in Chennai in 2010 was the last time I saw Rajiva. But as we gently shook hands before parting ways, she told me: "I don't have many people left in this life to cook for." Then, tapping on my notebook, she said: "These things about us Eelam Tamils must not be lost."

. . .

Eelam Tamils like Rajiva are from the North and East of Sri Lanka, and the vast majority are Hindus. Today, there are roughly 2.5 million Tamils in Sri Lanka, most living in Sri Lanka's Northern and Eastern provinces, though many Tamils also live in Colombo, the capital. Colombo and the South of Sri Lanka are dominated by Buddhist Sinhalese, who constitute more than three quarters of the country's population of twenty-two million. For generations, Tamils in Sri Lanka have maintained strong commercial, cultural, religious, and linguistic connections with Tamils across the Palk Strait in southern India. Nevertheless, they have long endeavored to maintain a distinct identity from their Tamil Nadu cousins, referring to their Tamil lands in Sri Lanka as "Eelam" and themselves as "Eelam Tamils."

The recipe Rajiva gave me, *nandu kari,* is the jewel in the crown of Eelam Tamil cuisine, one of the most delicious, fascinating, and underappreciated cuisines of South Asia. The term "curry" actually comes from the Tamil word *kari,* meaning "sauce." The essence of any good Tamil crab curry, like any South Asian curry, really, is its *thool,* or masala powder, the blend of dried spices that gives the dish much of its flavor and color. The blue swimmer crab, fresh coconut, and handfuls of aromatic curry leaves all imbue the gravy with their luscious essence. But it is the brick-red *thool* that gives a Tamil crab curry its power to penetrate your senses.

To make *thool,* an eye-popping amount of chilies are dry roasted in proportion to piles of fresh curry leaves and whole spices like coriander seeds, cumin seeds, black peppercorns, and turmeric, as well as fennel and fenugreek seeds, both of which add hints of sweetness. Once cool, all the ingredients are thoroughly mixed together and ground into a powder so fine that, when added to coconut milk, it creates a rich crimson sauce that lacquers the crab in what is the epitome of *arusuvai*, the delicate balance of six tastes—sweet, sour, bitter, spicy, salty, and astringent—that Tamils look for in every meal.[2]

Still etched in my memory is the taste of my first Eelam Tamil crab curry. In late 2010, a month or so after I had met Rajiva, a friend of mine in Colombo had invited me for dinner. His family was from Jaffna, one of the northernmost cities of the teardrop-shaped country and the cultural capital of Eelam Tamils. The curry was one of several dishes served. I got vertigo after my first bite trying to catalog all the new tastes. Each bite uncovered a new dimension. The curry leaves, pandan leaves, and fennel seeds combined to create a single buttery, smoky, sweet taste, almost like a new element. The heat from toasted chilies in the *thool* built gradually—it was insistent but not overpowering. And the crabmeat was succulent and sweet, infusing a briny savoriness into the crimson coconut gravy.

Traditionally, the *thool* for a Tamil crab curry begins with ingredients grown in home gardens, which flourish in the arid climate of northern Sri Lanka. Padmini, a Tamil woman in her late thirties, lives on the outskirts of Jaffna. A few years ago, I trailed her through her generations-old garden filled with edible plants, herbs, and fruits, all of which find a way into her cooking. "This is *ponnankani*. We use it for stomachaches," she said as she bent over to pinch off a cluster of long, flat oval leaves. "Over there, that big one is *pappāli* [papaya]," she said, pointing through a thicket of low, heavy green tree branches. A few steps farther along she stopped again to kneel. "Oh, this low plant here is *rampe* [pandan or screw pine]. We use it in many curries," she said tenderly as she gently moved her hand through its thick fronds before we arrived at the next specimen. "*Kariveppilai* [curry tree], you must know this, of course."

Home gardens like Padmini's have traditionally been a source of culinary diversity for Tamil cuisine as well as a source of income for Tamil families. Not only were the heirloom varieties of herbs and vegetables grown in these gardens used to create unique family meals, but they were also sold in markets around the northern parts of the island. This sort of garden was once common, but as I learned, many were lost to the war. "Padmini's knowledge is rare," her niece Nalini told me as she translated for Padmini. "The thing is," Nalini continued, "it didn't use to be this way. It was common knowledge Tamil women possessed before the war."

Before Sri Lanka's civil war, it was uncommon for any two *thools* to be exactly alike; almost every family made its spice blend from scratch. Often passed between generations, the proportions of spices would be personalized, emphasizing the flavors dear to a family's history and place. In fact, the only major difference in the *thool* recipes was the quantity, not the variety, of spices used. Nowadays, Nalini explained, Tamil families are turning to store-bought convenience foods. "Before the war, Tamil families ground their own rice flour from rice they grew or traded for. Now families are buying packaged ground flour." The same goes for *thools* or curry powders, she said. Instead of making their own, many Tamil families are buying premade curry-powder mixes. "Not only are people forgetting our food and recipes from before the war," Padmini lamented, "but also the flavors, how our food tasted before the war."

• • •

To this day, I place Mrs. Chandran and Mrs. Krishnan among the most formative teachers in my life. They are sisters and Tamils from Sri Lanka who were both my preschool teachers in Ohio. Not only were Mrs. Chandran and Mrs. Krishnan patient with my childhood exuberance, but they also instilled in me pride in my South Asian heritage. They often made sure I understood that Sri Lanka and Pakistan, where my father was born, are part of the same colorful subcontinental family. What I remember most is that Mrs. Chandran, the elder sister, wore these exquisite silken Tamil saris every day, no matter the occasion. No one could resist complimenting her elegance. In hindsight, there was certainly exotification in that praise. But I also remember those compliments being like Mrs. Chandran winning an award every day just for being herself. As best I can remember, I have never seen her in Western clothes.

Like many Tamils, Mrs. Chandran's and Mrs. Krishan's families emigrated to escape the anti-Tamil discrimination that proliferated across the island after independence from the British in 1948. During colonialism, British administrators often placed English-language schools in Tamil areas, providing the island's minority Tamil community with more civil-service and professional opportunities than their Sinhalese counterparts.[3] After independence, the island's Sinhalese leaders saw this imbalance as an existential problem that needed solving and pushed through laws giving the Sinhalese majority a leg up in society.

In 1956, the Sinhalese-dominated legislature passed the Sinhala Only Act, making Sinhala the only language that could be used for official purposes in Sri Lanka. The law cut off millions of Tamils from government services and public jobs. In 1958, Tamils' protests were answered with anti-Tamil pogroms that killed 1,500 people. In 1971, the government ushered in "standardization," limiting

Tamils' access to universities. The government justified the plan as a way to create a fairer school system.[4] But all it did was force Tamil families like Mrs. Chandran's and Mrs. Krishnan's to seek a better life off the island.

Throughout the 1970s and early '80s, Tamils formed armed resistance groups in response to growing state repression. In 1979, the government introduced the Prevention of Terrorism Act, which resulted in the detention, torture, and forced disappearance of dozens of Tamil youth. In July 1983, as state violence ramped up, militarizing much of the Tamil region, one group, the Liberation Tigers of Tamil Eelam (LTTE), ambushed and killed thirteen soldiers in Jaffna. In response, the state used the deaths to organize anti-Tamil pogroms, which spread through Colombo and other areas in the South of the country with significant Tamil populations.

That July, Sinhalese mobs carrying voter lists with names and addresses of Tamil homes and shops, and armed with knives and gasoline, descended on Tamil families to drive them off the island. The wave of violence in the capital then washed over the country. It lasted for a week before then-president J. R. Jayewardene deigned to utter a word. When he did, he offered no sympathy to the country's besieged Tamil citizens. The death toll was clearly in the thousands, but no one knows for sure exactly how many were killed. Countless Tamils fled Sri Lanka, many forever. Black July, as it is now called, is often considered the start of the civil war between the Sri Lankan state and the LTTE.[5]

. . .

For most of the war, Tamil cultural life was severely constrained. Sanathanan Thamotharampillai, who goes by "Sanaa" for short, is another Tamil teacher I know who was forced to flee the island.

Sanaa was born in Jaffna but went south to Colombo to escape the fighting and finish school. Sanaa spoke Tamil and English then, but not Sinhala. Because the Tamil language was banned, Sanaa was forced to study in English. But then the schools switched to Sinhala only. In 1991, in a last-ditch effort to continue his education, Sanaa went to Chennai in Tamil Nadu, India, where Tamil is the official language. A week after he arrived, though, Indian and Sri Lankan politics collided: The Tamil Tigers assassinated Rajiv Gandhi, the Indian prime minister. In turn, Indian schools banned Sri Lankan Tamils from their classrooms.

The reasons for the assassination were complex, and there are different interpretations and theories about the motivations behind it, but the simplest version of the story is that the Tigers wanted revenge. In the early 1980s, India sided with the Tamils in the war, establishing training camps for Tamil militants in Tamil Nadu, giving them easy maritime access to northern Sri Lanka to fight the Sinhalese. By the late 1980s, things had changed. In 1987, Rajiv Gandhi sent Indian peacekeepers to disarm the LTTE, but Indian troops ended up fighting the very group their country had once armed and trained. The mission was a disaster; India abandoned the Tigers politically, and the peacekeepers carried out atrocities against Tamil civilians. A few years later, a Tiger suicide bomber killed Gandhi at an election rally in Tamil Nadu. Acts like these eventually led various countries to ban the Tigers as a terrorist organization.

The LTTE bans that were instituted in India, North America, and Europe were a blow to the Tigers, curtailing their ability to fundraise among diaspora communities and eventually weakening their ability to fight. But the bans did little to undermine support for the LTTE both on and off the island. Despite their heinous tactics, the Tigers were mostly seen as the only group able to defend the lives of Tamils. Their objective, Eelam—an independent country where Tamil culture could thrive, a home to which refugees could return to be reunited with their families—was, and still is, for many Tamils, the only way out of their political and human rights crisis.

Rajiv Gandhi's killing forced Sanaa back to Sri Lanka from India, but when the political climate cooled, he returned to finish his education at the College of Art in New Delhi. Now in his forties, Sanaa teaches art history at the University of Jaffna, a short drive from Padmini's garden. A slight man with a shaved head, sharp eyes, and a chic sense of style that contrasts with his drab campus office, Sanaa is also one of Sri Lanka's most accomplished contemporary artists and most astute observers of Tamil culture, including its culinary treasures. Since the end of the war, Sanaa's work has focused on cataloging the ways Tamils survive and resist violence.

Sanaa told me that during the fighting, farmers couldn't work and the flow of imports from the South became less frequent. Almost right away, Tamil food began to change. "Local potatoes were hard to come by [during the war]," Sanaa explained, since most potatoes are grown outside the Vanni. "Sometimes there were no potatoes at all for curries," he said. Potatoes play important roles in Tamil dishes like *kalyana urulaikizhangu kari,* a warm combination of tender pan-roasted potatoes, spices, red chili, and curry leaves. It is a dish often served at weddings. "For some time, they [potatoes] went from being an ordinary food to an extraordinary one." Potato shortages, Sanaa explained, sent wedding cooks searching for a substitute. Eventually they settled on a new recipe of elephant foot yams (yams that do indeed look like their namesake) and chickpeas. Postwar, potato curries are back, but it's not uncommon to see wartime substitutes at weddings.

Across the street from Sanaa's office, lining the roads around the university's main campus, is a string of small cafés. At first glance, there's nothing special about them. Like almost every other café in Sri Lanka, they serve chai, coffee, and a dizzying array of fried and baked goods called "short eats." Eaten in only a couple of bites, short eats, as their name suggests, are small, easy-to-carry snacks for any time of day. They are perhaps the most democratic thing in Sri Lanka right now, found in every corner of the country and sold and eaten everywhere from train stations to trendy cafés and from lively public beaches to exclusive luxury hotels.

These little delicacies come in all forms, including fish patties that resemble an empanada, doughnut-shaped lentil *vada,* and fried rolls and balls like fish cutlets filled with mashed potatoes and tuna spiced with chili, black pepper, and cardamom. A relatively recent addition to Sri Lankan cooking, short eats reflect not only the country's colonial past but also its culinary present: Each short eat is filled with flavors of the region in which it is eaten.

Setting apart short eats in Tamil areas from those found in the rest of the island is the *mithivedi.* During the war, as one version of the story goes, LTTE cooks in the Vanni reportedly created a new short eat to inject calories cheaply and quickly into the war-ravaged society. A base of sautéed garlic, onion, ginger, and green chili is mixed with tuna fish, beef, and potatoes and spiced with a *thool* and salt and pepper. The mixture is then topped with sliced hard-boiled eggs, wrapped in rice paper, breaded, and deep-fried until it looks like a golden-brown brick.

The name *mithivedi* is a bit of dark war humor. *Mithivedi* means "land mine" in Tamil, and the short eat is named as such since it roughly resembles the war crime of a weapon ubiquitously deployed by both sides during the conflict. More than twenty thousand people may have been killed or injured by land mines and other explosives during Sri Lanka's civil war. At the end of the war, in 2009, an estimated 1.6 million land mines were left in the ground, unmarked and mostly unrecorded. Many have been cleared, but even fifteen years on from the end of the fighting, many families cannot return home because their land is still mined.[6]

The history of the *mithivedi* is disputed. It was probably created between 1993 and 1996, according to Kunjanayan, the no-nonsense, down-to-business owner of the Mathy Hotel, a small but bustling blue roadside café in Puthukkudiyiruppu, a few minutes' drive from the Mullivaikkal beach where Rajiva spent her last days in Sri Lanka. Kunjanayan started selling *mithivedi* short eats in his shop in the late 1990s after he first tried one at an LTTE-run restaurant down the road in Kilinochchi, the town where the LTTE was head-quartered at the time. They were so popular at one point that the Mathy Hotel was making between five hundred and a thousand a day. The café has since become associated with the *mithivedi*'s ori-gin story, but Kunjanayan insisted he didn't invent it. "I just made it better," he said with a quick smile.

Unlike other short eats, the *mithivedi* is big and really can't be eaten in a couple of bites. "It actually used to be bigger because the meat was cheaper. The original size was two hundred fifty grams. Now it is down to one hundred fifty to two hundred grams," Kun-janayan said, mimicking a tipping scale with his hands. The ratio of ingredients has changed as well. When the *mithivedi* was created in the 1990s, the ratio of beef to potatoes was roughly two to one.

In the late 1990s, LTTE military victories brought extensive areas of the Northern and Eastern provinces under the Tigers' control. Not only did this create a certain military parity with the government, but it also allowed the Tigers to build a de facto state, complete with a national bank, TV and radio stations, a police force and judiciary, and a variety of other public-service depart-ments. For a time, Tamil Eelam (the name of the independent state the Tamils hoped to secure in the war) flew its flag, a crimson ground emblazoned with a roaring tiger, across much of the island's Northeast. Tamils traveling from government-controlled to LTTE-controlled areas said it was like crossing an international border, complete with border guards, where they were required to show identity cards and declare goods. I heard from people living there at the time that the LTTE also allotted land for cows, so beef for *mithivedi* was plentiful; however, the two-to-one ratio of meat to potatoes has flipped. Sri Lanka's astronomical postpandemic inflation has made beef and fish more expensive than ever, so Tamil cooks are using mostly potatoes in the filling.[7]

"On the one hand, things we ate before 1983 [the year the civil war began] are very hard to find now. Families collapsed. Knowledge was lost. Tastes changed. It's very likely specific dishes have been lost or forgotten to history," Sanaa told me on an uncomfortably humid day in his campus office. "On the other, new foods were created out of necessity during that war." He paused before adding, "People relied on their creativity to survive."

. . .

The civil war lasted just under three decades and ended in May 2009, when the Sri Lankan government announced that it had killed the LTTE leader, Velupillai Prabhakaran. The military took control of the Northern and Eastern provinces, including the Vanni, the Tigers' heartland. Since then, Colombo has returned some land to its original owners, but the military still occupies huge tracts of it. Today, the Tamil-majority areas of Sri Lanka are arguably among the most militarized places on the planet. Fourteen of the Sri Lankan army's twenty-one divisions are stationed there. Until recently, in Mullaitivu District alone—the site of Mullivaikkal, the beach where Rajiva was shelled—sixty thousand soldiers patrolled an area with a population of only ninety thousand people.[8] That was two soldiers for every three civilians. For context, military analysts say the ratio for a successful occupation is about two soldiers for every one hundred civilians.[9]

Fifteen years after the LTTE's demise, the Sri Lankan government still routinely invokes the potential for an LTTE resurgence to justify the heavy militarization and surveillance of the Tamil population living in the former war zone. To help pay for the occupation, the army has established a vast array of food-related businesses in the Tamil areas, including a handful of farms across the Northern and Eastern provinces. The farms not only are on appropriated land but also grow *everything* local Tamils have traditionally grown. As I drove across northern Sri Lanka in 2019, locals pointed out farms where the army raised livestock for meat and dairy products, an army-operated tea shop where motorists could take a break, and even an army tourist resort.

I heard about how the militarization of the Tamil homeland had penetrated even the most intimate details of Tamil life. Many Tamil women who lost husbands, fathers, brothers, and sons— the traditional breadwinners in conservative Tamil society—were pushed into exploitative and dangerous jobs. According to a study of the roles of women in postwar Tamil society, "Tamil women are often left to fill positions such as cleaning toilets in military camps where they are often subjected to sexual harassment and abuse."[10] It's not only women: Dozens of Tamil men have also come forward alleging sexual abuse at the hands of Sri Lanka's security forces.[11]

Sri Lanka is supposed to be a country at peace. But the horror stories Tamils were recounting over meals and cups of tea forced me to confront an uncomfortable truth about my own human rights work in the country. For years, during the war, some Western diplomatic missions, including parts of the UN, as well as Western human rights organizations—some of which I worked for—were suspicious of Tamil activists. Because many were sympathetic to the LTTE, their reporting was perceived as contrived to justify the Tigers' brutal tactics and a separate Tamil state, which some argued was the only way to guarantee their safety and future as a people. We thought more Tamil autonomy on a unified island was the solution.

From what I've gathered traveling over the years to postwar Sri Lanka, the Tamil activists we dismissed were mostly right all along. They were right when they warned that life for Tamils in a postwar Sinhalese-dominated state would be oppressive. They were right when they claimed something genocidal was under way in the Vanni in 2009. They were right about a victorious Sri Lankan army taking Tamil women and lands as spoils of war. And they were right about an extremist Sinhalese Buddhist clergy using craven politicians to finish the decades-long project of erasing non-Sinhalese *and* non-Buddhist cultures from the island.

In hindsight, many governments and human rights groups failed to adequately distinguish between the LTTE's separatism and its terrorism. The LTTE's brutality and its targeting of civilians made that incredibly easy to do; understandably, few wanted to be associated with the Tigers' tactics and political platform. That blinded us to the fact that the idea of Tamil Eelam had long predated the LTTE and that calls for a Tamil state were often steeped in liberal values, reflecting a belief that the fundamental human rights of the minority Tamil community could not be adequately protected in a state run by chauvinist Sinhalese nationalists. We failed to see that Tamil Eelam and the LTTE were not the same. We were so shit-scared of establishing a precedent for other places that we automatically dismissed a two-state solution as a viable settlement to end the war; to save Tamil, Sinhalese, and Muslim lives; and to keep the island's cultures intact.

One consequence of this failure is the industrial-scale militarization of northern Sri Lanka today, a fact that is increasingly top of mind for most Tamils, particularly fishing communities along the coast. Seafood, like the crab needed to make Rajiva's *nandu kari,* has long been a mainstay of the local economy and cuisine. Saravanan is a stocky, bright-eyed, well-built man in his forties from Velanai, a small island floating in the Palk Strait and populated by Eelam Tamil fishing families. Saravanan had fought for Tamil Eelam and had been a refugee in India twice. But fishing was what defined him.

For as long as anyone could remember, Saravanan's relatives had been fishing the Palk Strait and the lagoons around Jaffna. Like many of them, he had learned to fish the old *karavalai* way: by dragging huge nets from the shore in a massive loop and hauling them by hand back onto the beach. But today Saravanan fishes from a skiff painted in bright pastel blue and marigold yellow.

We were standing outside the Kakkaitivu fish market, looking across the lagoon. It was an early morning, and the sky and sea were both silver, making it impossible to locate the horizon. It was beautiful, like being inside a ball of mercury. Saravanan recalled a childhood memory then: "There were so many crabs here, we threw them back in the water. . . . They were like flies; we used sticks to beat them out of our nets." He said the fishermen always kept watch for the biggest and best crabs to bring home to be cooked into coconut-thickened crimson curries. But Black July in 1983 changed that. Saravanan and dozens of other Tamils told me that Sri Lanka's navy then banned Tamil fishermen from going out to sea for nearly a generation, and that in turn seafood, like blue swimmer crabs, the star ingredient in *nandu kari,* became hard to find in markets or too expensive for most Tamils to eat.

During the war, Saravanan told me, the Tigers relied heavily on fishing boats to smuggle in weapons and supplies. In turn, the Sri Lankan navy considered every fishing boat in the Palk Strait a potential threat. The navy barely made any effort to distinguish between Tamil fishermen from Sri Lanka and those from India; both were assaulted during operations to intercept weapons. Hundreds of innocent fishermen were killed with impunity, while many more had their boats sunk or confiscated. Still harboring rage from that time, Saravanan bluntly said: "Tamil fishermen were not collateral damage [of the blockades]. They were the target."

The violence forced scores of fishermen like Saravanan to fight or leave Sri Lanka as refugees. During lulls in the fighting or during ceasefires, the government did allow fishing in some areas along the coast, but only during limited hours, often from 6:00 a.m. to 6:00 p.m., and only with tiny engines, to ensure that fishing boats went no faster than a crawl. But the best fishing was to be had at night, so the curfew killed off the fishing economy. Seafood dishes like crab curry became almost impossible to make, forcing Tamils to turn inland for food to replace the fish in their diets.

Some Tamils say the naval blockades are why *koli kari*, Eelam Tamil chicken curry, is more popular today than its crab counterpart. Chicken curry has been around forever, they say, but wasn't as popular before the war as it is now. A former LTTE fighter, now cooking in a Vanni restaurant, told me the Tigers smuggled in chickens to help people make up for the lost fish protein in their diet. Over time, he said, habits and tastes changed. Another, albeit more recent, factor is the skyrocketing international demand for large blue swimmer crabs from Sri Lanka, the kind necessary to make a good crab curry, which has inflated local prices and put them out of reach for most Tamils.

While they've returned to fishing, Tamil fishermen in the Northern and Eastern provinces appear to have permanently lost traditional fishing grounds to army-backed businesses like industrial trawling and massive sea-cucumber farms. The vast majority of Tamil fishermen still use traditional fishing techniques, a senior member of a Jaffna-area fishing *sangam,* a local collective that advocates for fishing rights, told me. Most don't have access to capital to buy modern equipment, so they can't compete with industrial fishing trawlers operated by Sinhalese coming up from the south and Indian ships operating in the Palk Strait.[12]

The army's appropriation of farmland and fishing grounds has changed both what northern Tamils eat and how they eat in other ways too. According to local government officials and human rights activists, the army is using its own labor to harvest and sell its products at below-market rates at military-run shops, undercutting the livelihoods of an already impoverished population. Unable to compete, the families of farmers, fishermen, and small business owners all report having trouble affording food.

At a roadside rest stop outside Kilinochchi, the town that served as the Tigers' headquarters during the war, I met Rathan and Seeraalan, two thin yet muscular farmers in their thirties. Almost every day, the men walk this road to access their fields. It's about thirty minutes each way. Occasionally, they'll break up their walk at the rest stop to share a cigarette and catch up with a friend or two. I asked them where their fields were. They smiled awkwardly and pointed directly across the street to an emerald-green rice field where there was an army sentry post with an armed soldier walking the perimeter. Rathan and Seeraalan said the army had occupied a large part of their land after the war, forcing them to walk every day to the far side to access the small part they could still farm. Rathan stretched out his right hand toward me, pinching his thumb to his forefinger as if holding a single grain of rice. Then he said, as if summing up his life, "No rice, no money, no food, no family."

Many Tamils in the Northeast experience "the occupation as an extension of the war and a form of collective punishment for sharing the same ethnicity as the LTTE," said Lalitha, a prominent human rights activist based in Jaffna. This is most acutely felt by women, she said, who have historically been at the forefront of both fighting for Tamil liberation and preserving Tamil culture.[13] "It's exhausting on every level for [Tamil] women," Lalitha explained. "They are expected to cook, bring up the children, and do things that hold the family together. But how can they do those traditional things when they can't afford to feed their families?"

In this moment, I recalled something I'd heard in Padmini's garden outside Jaffna. After she showed me her plants, she led me into her kitchen, a large, well-lit, open-air room with a brown polished cement floor, lined with heavy wooden shelves filled with spice jars, utensils, and bunches of fresh green herbs from her garden. We were talking over plates of fish curry and coconut sambal when Padmini registered a nervousness about the future of Tamil cooking. Looking at her daughter, Priya, who was sitting nearby on the floor sketching in her notebook, she said, "Because of the new pressures of life, mothers don't have time to teach children about how to cook. They don't have time to teach them about our spices and [traditional] medicines." She paused as she gazed at Priya before adding: "It's not their fault."

Padmini mentioned *kool*, a hearty, briny, bright seafood chowder popular in the coastal areas of the Northeast. "The problem is families don't make this dish at home much anymore because of the new pressures we face after the war." To me, *kool* is reminiscent of some of the seafood chowders of America's northeastern coastal regions. Any available fresh fish can be used to make *kool*, and as a New England clam chowder is thickened with milk or cream, *kool* is thickened with flour made from the roots of the palmyra tree to give it a velvetiness. "It is very nutritional, but it takes time and money," Padmini said. "Two things we don't have much of anymore."

All over northern Sri Lanka, I heard variations on this theme of connecting time, cooking, and memory: that because of a generation of war, "Tamils have forgotten how to cook." Not long ago, at a new hotel in Jaffna, I spoke with a young chef who worked in the restaurant there. In the first years after the war, he said, large numbers of Tamil refugees and their children who grew up in the West were returning to Jaffna to visit their ancestral homes and to reconnect with their relatives and culture. "It was magic to see that," he told me.

"One day," he said, "some Tamil people at the hotel didn't like my food [and sent it back]. They said something like, 'I don't want hotel food. Please make it the old way, the way our grandmothers made it.' I thought, *Who are these fuckers?* They were rude. Diaspora Tamils! Just looking down on me because they grew up in Canada!"

But it happened again and again, he said. He continued: "I kept hearing this thing about the cooking from diaspora people from Canada, from America, from London. I got mad, but then I stopped and started asking questions. I started asking my elders about our food. How was it cooked then [before the war]? How is it cooked differently today?"

"What did they say?" I asked.

Eventually, he said, "I learned some of the Canadians were right; I wasn't always cooking our curries; I wasn't making the *thools* [curry powders] traditionally or using local herbs. The way I was cooking was like more [northern] Indian and Punjabi food. That cooking method is good, but it is not local."

The chef paused for a moment. "So many of us were born after the war and don't know some of our history and traditional foods. It took a very long time to learn it all. . . . I had to search for people with old cooking knowledge," he said. "It was not easy. Many of them left. Many of them died. Many were killed. But I now know where a lot of old cooking knowledge lives on." He paused, then in a tone that sounded as if he was letting me in on a secret, said: "In the diaspora. It's with all those aunties and uncles in Canada."

•   •   •

Back in my kitchen in Brooklyn, I attempted to decode Rajiva's crab curry recipe. Her *thool* called for "fistfuls" of curry leaves and chilies and "spoonfuls" of coriander and "big pinches" of black pepper and fennel. I realized that I had an incomplete map and needed a more experienced guide. In the early days of the coronavirus pandemic, I came across a series of Instagram Stories where a tall man in his mid-thirties, with a jet-black beard and a build like that of a boxer, posted detailed recipes for traditional Tamil dishes, including *idiyappa,* also known as string hoppers, a cross between noodles and a pancake, and *watalappam,* a baked custard flavored with palm sugar and spices. Some recipes were so detailed they spanned dozens of slides. Among them was his recipe for Tamil crab curry, which is eighty-one slides long.

The account is called @KitchenGuerrilla, and it's run by Roshan Kanagarajah, a Tamil Canadian chef. When I met Roshan in Toronto a few months later, he told me that his family had followed the path of many Tamil families fleeing the war, first going to Europe before eventually settling in Canada. "I was literally born in the middle of a gun battle in Jaffna," he told me. "The Sri

Lankan and Indian armies were firing at the LTTE in the area around the hospital where my mom was giving birth. We almost didn't make it out alive."

Among the most profound consequences of Sri Lanka's civil war has been the upheaval of the island's Tamil population, both internally and through migration abroad.[14] Today, there are approximately one million Tamils from Sri Lanka, mostly refugees and their descendants, living in diaspora communities across the world. Many, like Rajiva, are in Tamil Nadu in India, but many more are in Toronto, Canada, which is now home to the largest community of Eelam Tamils in the world.

. . .

Like many other young Tamil men coming of age in Toronto in the 2000s, Roshan ran with a rough crowd, occasionally getting into trouble with the authorities. The experience was isolating, he said, and forced him to channel his energy and creativity into something that would stop him from wasting valuable time. Roshan said he always found joy in food, especially cooking, something he attributes to his mother. But turning his passion into a career presented another problem. "In our culture, a career in the kitchen is still not fully accepted. It's ironic given how much we love and respect our food," he told me. "I just put my head down and did the work I love."

After a few years of working in Toronto restaurants, he launched his own catering business, which served traditional Tamil dishes with a laser focus on quality, using only the best and freshest ingredients. Then, in 2014, Roshan experimented with making hot sauces in his kitchen from the chilies his wife, Dalscene Jebanendran, grew at home. Dalscene decided they should put the hot sauce on Instagram. "We just gave it away," Roshan said through a laugh. That created buzz and the confidence, in 2015, for the couple to launch Kitchen Guerrilla, which has since developed into a successful line of sauces and marinades sold around Toronto.

"The food and politics of Eelam are inseparable," Roshan told me. "That's how I have always approached my cooking." That's why, he told me, he put his recipe for crab curry online free of charge. "I didn't have to fight [for Eelam]. I thought to myself, *At least let these old recipes be a contribution. At least I did something for my community, for my culture.*" Since he started posting his recipes, several Tamil restaurants in the Toronto area have poached them for their menus. Indicative of the generosity he exudes, Roshan said, "Someone else might be fucking pissed about that. For me, it's an honor, in a way. I am just happy my people are eating good food."

Since then, Roshan has continued innovating with his cuisine, mixing Tamil flavors into dishes that are traditional to other cultures. In 2019, Roshan opened Ksira Gelato, a café serving Italian-style gelato incorporating Tamil and South Asian flavors. For example, Ksira's *watalappam* gelato, its most popular flavor, is sweetened using syrup made from the sap of the *kithul* palm tree, which is native to Sri Lanka and has an earthy, floral, and smoky taste. *Watalappam* itself, in taste and texture, is the tropical cousin of crème caramel or flan but made with coconut milk, jaggery, cardamom, cloves, nutmeg, and vanilla and topped with chopped cashews.

In 2020, with the pandemic summer approaching and seeing that outdoor grilling was likely to boom with everyone sick of being stuck indoors, Roshan launched a line of Tamil-flavored sausages—Jaffna mutton curry and Tamil fire—and partnered with local butchers to sell meats premarinated in Kitchen Guerrilla sauces. Since the 1980s, thousands of Tamils fleeing the war have gone through Germany and Switzerland to get to Canada or sought asylum and settled there. Largely because of their experience in these two sausage-loving countries, Roshan explained that diaspora Tamils incorporated pork and sausages into their cuisine. Adding *thools* and spices traditionally used in Tamil cooking was a "new take on something kind of new to our cuisine and palates."

Through Kitchen Guerrilla and Ksira, Roshan made himself one of Toronto's most respected chefs cooking Eelam Tamil food. He is planning a new restaurant to return to his roots, serving traditional Tamil dishes with the best ingredients possible. One of Roshan's suppliers is Nam Thayagam, a sparsely decorated, large two-room store in Scarborough with white walls and wooden shelves. It sources high-quality ingredients directly from Mullaitivu and communities around Mullivaikkal beach, like whole spices and premade *thools,* sea salt, rice flour, moringa, and cooking oils. In Tamil, *nam thayagam* means "our homeland," and all of the store's products are made by former fighters, war amputees, and war widows trying to rebuild their lives in northern Sri Lanka. Almost all the proceeds flow back to them from Toronto. Roshan says he occasionally uses Nam Thayagam's *thool* as the base for his curries but personalizes it with his own combination of spices. Using Tamil-made ingredients from Tamil-owned land, Roshan explained, "is a small but necessary act, pushing back every day against the army trying to undo the culture."

Siva, one of Nam Thayagam's owners, explained to me, "Our purpose is totally different from other stores'. We don't source anything from India even though it is easier to import ingredients from there. Everything comes from the Northern and Eastern provinces." Some of Nam Thayagam's customers want to buy exclusively Tamil products. "Some customers won't come to us if they know we sell Indian ingredients," Siva said. "Even though Indian products are cheaper, we want to keep money in Tamil hands. The situation in Sri Lanka can make imports from the Tamil areas shaky, so we run out of stock often. But thankfully it doesn't deter customers." Nevertheless, profit margins are slim, he says. "But it feels good to be helping people back home."

For several decades now, the Tamil diaspora has been among the most powerful forces, on or off the island, shaping the politics, society, and culture of Tamils in Sri Lanka. While dreams of an independent Tamil state have been diminished, Eelam Tamil culture is thriving in places like Toronto. "Our people are living under military occupation, where just being Tamil is a crime," Roshan said. "We have a responsibility to the people back home to keep our traditions alive and moving forward here."

Perhaps how diaspora Tamil chefs will have the biggest impact on protecting their cuisine is by just saying its name. Babu Takeout and Catering occupies the corner of a small redbrick strip mall in Scarborough. Babu's, as it is known locally, is an institution. So is its owner, Babu Rajakulasingam. A warm, charismatic man in his early sixties, Babu came to Canada as a refugee by way of Germany in the late 1980s. Since 1992, Babu has cooked what he calls "Eelam Tamil food."

"One reason why I call this 'Eelam food' is so I have to explain it to people," Babu said as he slapped the counter. He'll often pull out a map of Tamil Eelam, encompassing Tamil-speaking areas of Sri Lanka in the North and East, to explain the civil war and why he and other Eelam Tamils now call Toronto home.

As we walked the length of an immense counter surveying the multitude of curries simmering away, Babu explained that his food from northeastern Sri Lanka shares ingredients with Sinhalese and South Indian cooking traditions, yet it is its own cuisine and thus has its own name. "When someone comes in and says they want to try Sri Lankan food, I say to them, 'Madam, sir, I only have Eelam Tamil food.'"

The Eelam Tamil identity was mainstream long before the militancy of the Tigers. Yet "Eelam" is still synonymous with the LTTE and its terrorist label. What Babu is doing seems risky to other Tamil restaurant owners, inviting unwanted scrutiny. During the Sri Lankan civil war, the Canadian authorities investigated Tamil-run businesses for fundraising for the LTTE, which stigmatized the entire Tamil community.

Although the LTTE is long gone, and relations between the Canadian government and the Tamil community have improved, restaurant owners still remain wary of openly labeling their food "Eelam food" for other Canadians. What's more, they say, local food media still frames cuisines from countries it doesn't understand through generalizations. Roshan, who uses both the "Sri Lankan" and "Eelam" labels to describe his Tamil cooking, said, "From both a business and a political perspective, it can make sense to stick to the 'Sri Lankan' label. By being too specific, some believe you could lose customers. But I haven't experienced that."

As I was leaving his restaurant, Babu handed me a white paper bag with two freshly fried fish cutlets, thick with the aroma of black pepper and green cardamom, and said: "You give something power when you name it. And you must name it to celebrate it. We are not Sri Lankan. We are not Tamils from India. We are from Eelam and so is our beautiful Eelam food."

Rajiva's Eelam Nandu Kari

(Crab Curry)

Makes 4 servings

This is Rajiva's crab curry almost as she gave it to me. She recited the recipe in pinches, fistfuls, and spoonfuls. Since then, I've sought the help of Kitchen Guerrilla, plus a friend's mother and sister, and a few good cooks in Jaffna, to get the measurements right. The ingredient list is long, but this is not a difficult recipe, and you can break it into parts by making the curry powders in advance.

Any fresh or frozen crab can be used for this recipe. Fresh shrimp works well too. I have also routinely made this dish with a combination of shrimp and canned lump crabmeat. If you want to go this route, make the curry sauce, then slip in the shrimp and crabmeat and let simmer for a few minutes to heat through. This curry can also easily be made vegan by substituting roasted squash, like kabocha, for the shellfish. Slice the squash into half-moons, seed, and toss with olive oil and salt. Roast in the oven at 425°F for 30 to 35 minutes and then add the squash into the curry sauce. Whether using shellfish or squash, let this curry cool for a few minutes before serving; you want to enjoy this dish warm, not piping hot.

Rajiva's curry calls for several ingredients, like curry leaf sprigs, moringa leaves, pandan leaves, tamarind pulp, and fenugreek seeds, that will require an online purchase or a visit to your local South Asian or Southeast Asian market. The dried spices you'll need to make the *thool* are often more affordable and easier to find at these markets as well.

3 to 4 ounces fresh tamarind pulp

1 cup boiling water

4 pounds live blue crabs or thawed frozen crabmeat

4 tablespoons coconut oil

5 Asian shallots or 1 medium red onion, coarsely chopped

1 long fresh pandan leaf, torn into 5 or 6 pieces

1 teaspoon fennel seeds

1 teaspoon cumin seeds

1 teaspoon black mustard seeds

1 teaspoon fenugreek seeds

8 garlic cloves, roughly chopped

4 fresh green chilies, coarsely chopped, plus 4 halved lengthwise, plus more for serving

Thumb-size piece fresh ginger, peeled and coarsely chopped

Leaves from 4 curry leaf sprigs

Kosher salt

1 cup Jaffna Thool (page 70), plus more as needed

2 to 3 cups unsweetened coconut milk (see Note, page 70)

1 to 2 teaspoons red chili powder, such as Indian or cayenne (optional)

Leaves from 2 moringa sprigs (optional)

½ teaspoon Roshan's Vaasa Thool (page 72)

Cooked short-grain white rice for serving

Lime wedges for serving

1. Put the tamarind in a small heatproof bowl and pour in the boiling water. Using the back of a spoon, press down on the tamarind so it's covered with water and let sit for 1 hour. Remove the pulp from the water and squeeze it with your hands to soften it up. Transfer it to a fine-mesh sieve set over a small bowl and use the back of the spoon to press it through the sieve into the bowl. Discard the solids left behind in the sieve. Measure out ¼ cup of the strained pulp and set aside.

2. While the tamarind is soaking, prepare the crabs for cooking. Put the crabs on a bed of ice or in the freezer for 15 minutes to numb them. Working with one crab at a time, lift off and discard the top shell. Remove and discard the gills (feathery strips), liver (aka tomalley), and other organs. Some cooks prefer to leave the greenish yellow liver—"golden fat"—in place for a richer taste. Hold the crab under cold running water, rinsing it well, then place on a cutting board and, using a cleaver or a large chef's knife, cut it in half lengthwise. Repeat with the remaining crabs.

3. In a large, heavy pot, warm 3 tablespoons of the oil over medium heat. When the oil is shimmering, add the shallots and pandan leaf and cook, stirring, until fragrant, about 5 minutes. Add the fennel, cumin, mustard, and fenugreek seeds and cook, stirring, for 1 minute. Next, stir in half of the garlic, the chopped green chilies, and the ginger and cook, stirring, until fragrant, about 3 minutes. Toss in half of the curry leaves and stir until they just begin to wilt, 2 to 3 minutes.

4. Add the crabs and 1½ teaspoons salt and stir to coat the crabs with all of the seasonings. Cover and cook over medium heat for 5 minutes to allow the crabs to pick up heat. (Skip this if you are using shrimp and/or crab or roasted squash as mentioned in the headnote.)

5. Uncover, add the Jaffna thool, and stir well to coat the crabs thoroughly. Add 1 cup of the coconut milk, the reserved tamarind, and the chili powder to taste (if using) and stir to mix well. Add the remaining 1 to 2 cups coconut milk to your desired consistency. (For a thicker curry, only add a small amount; for a thinner curry, add more.) Don't worry if the crab is not submerged in the liquid. Re-cover and continue to cook for 10 minutes.

6. About 5 minutes before the curry is ready, heat the remaining 1 tablespoon of oil in a small skillet over medium heat. When the oil is shimmering, add the remaining garlic and the halved green chilies and cook, stirring occasionally, until fragrant, about 2 minutes. Add the remaining curry leaves—work carefully, as they will pop when they hit the hot oil—and cook for 30 seconds. Remove from the heat.

7. Uncover the curry and stir the garlic mixture into the pot. Turn down the heat to medium-low and continue to cook the curry, stirring occasionally, until the sauce thickens, 3 to 4 minutes. Taste and adjust the seasoning with Jaffna thool, salt, and chili powder (if using), then stir in the moringa leaves (if using).

8. Remove the pot from the heat and sprinkle the vaasa thool over the crabs to finish. Serve the curry warm with the rice, lime wedges, and whole green chilies for extra heat.

There is no shame in using high-quality canned or frozen coconut milk. But this curry is truly like no other when made with homemade coconut milk. To make fresh coconut milk, select a heavy coconut that contains plenty of liquid when you shake it. To open the coconut, I prefer to hold it in one hand over a large bowl and carefully whack at the equator with the back of a heavy chef's knife. It should crack in the middle after a few hits. Alternatively, you can use a hammer to drive in a pointed screwdriver. Once opened, drain the coconut water into the bowl, then strain it into a blender. I like to use a coconut scraper to grind out the flesh. If you don't have a scraper, just slip the tip of a paring knife, butter knife, or thin metal spoon between the shell and coconut meat and pry the meat from the shell. Use a vegetable peeler to peel away the thin brown skin from the larger pieces of meat. Cut the meat into small pieces. Add enough warm water to the blender to total 3 cups of liquid, then add the chopped coconut, and blend on the lowest speed. As the coconut meat breaks down, increase the speed to medium and then to high, stopping to scrape down the sides of the blender jar as needed, until you have a thick, milky-white pulpy mixture. Line a large fine-mesh sieve with cheesecloth, place it over a medium bowl, and strain. Squeeze the cheesecloth to release as much coconut milk as possible into the bowl. Discard the pulp in the cheesecloth. You should have about 3 cups of coconut milk.

Jaffna Thool

(Curry Powder)

Makes about 4 cups

This recipe is based on the version Rajiva gave me in Chennai as well as one given to me by Roshan Kanagarajah. This *thool* is the essence of many Eelam Tamil curries, and it might just become a pantry staple. You'll need to make (or buy) this curry powder before making Rajiva's crab curry and Roshan's goat curry (see page 74). You can also tailor this recipe to your liking. For example, I like the bite of black pepper and the sweetness of fennel, so I will often add a few extra tablespoons of each. And no need to restrict this *thool* to just Tamil curries. I often toss vegetables in a mixture of this *thool*, salt, and olive oil before roasting them.

That said, the key to a good curry is good spices. As Roshan puts it: "The fresher the spices, the better the curry." When purchasing spices, he advises choosing those with vibrant colors and strong aromas. Most manufacturers and grocery stores deal with spices in bulk, so the chance of old spices sitting on the shelf is high. Roshan ensures he's getting the freshest ingredients by purchasing spices from a South Asian market that has high turnover. This *thool* can be made up to 3 months in advance and stored in your pantry.

1 long fresh pandan leaf, torn into 5 or 6 pieces

2 cups coriander seeds

2 tablespoons black peppercorns

2 tablespoons cumin seeds

1½ tablespoons fennel seeds

1 tablespoon fenugreek seeds

3 cups loosely packed fresh curry leaves

2 tablespoons ground turmeric

½ teaspoon coconut oil

5 cups dried red chilies, such as árbol or Kashmiri or a mixture of both

1. Set a large bowl near the stove. Place a medium skillet over medium-low heat. When the pan is hot, add the pandan leaf and dry roast until the edges are dry, 3 to 4 minutes. Transfer to the bowl to cool.

2. Return the pan to medium-low heat. Add the coriander seeds and peppercorns and dry roast, stirring and tossing frequently, until the coriander is golden brown and fragrant, 3 to 4 minutes. Add to the bowl to cool.

3. Return the pan to medium-low heat. Add the cumin, fennel, and fenugreek seeds and dry roast, stirring and tossing frequently, until fragrant and the seeds have toasted, about 2 minutes. Add to the bowl to cool.

4. Return the pan to medium-low heat. Add the curry leaves and dry roast, stirring and tossing frequently, until the curry leaves are dry and slightly crispy but still green, 7 to 10 minutes. Add to the bowl to cool.

5. Return the pan to medium-low heat. Add the ground turmeric and swirl it around for 15 to 30 seconds to release the aroma. Add to the bowl to cool.

6. Set the pan to medium heat and add the oil. When the oil is hot, add the chilies and heat, stirring and tossing frequently, until they are deep reddish edging toward brown, 10 to 15 minutes (see Note). Watch the pan closely and adjust the heat if needed, as the chilies can go from perfect to burned in the blink of an eye. Add to the bowl to cool.

7. Let all of the spices cool to room temperature, then stir to mix well. Working in batches, grind the spices to a powder in a spice grinder or in a mortar with a pestle. Return the ground batches to a clean bowl and give the mixture a good stir to distribute all of the spices evenly before transferring it to a tightly capped glass jar for storage.

NOTE

Inhaling chili smoke and getting it into your eyes can be painful as well as upset people you live with. Don't forget to turn on your stove's hood fan or open up some windows for ventilation while you toast the chilies. Better yet, make this *thool* the old-fashioned way and roast the spices outside if you can.

Roshan's Vaasa Thool

(Finishing Curry Powder)

Makes about ¼ cup

This recipe comes from Roshan Kanagarajah. This spice mix is a close cousin of garam masala and is often used as a finishing spice, similar to a flaky sea salt that is sprinkled over finished dishes for one last burst of flavor. Like Jaffna *thool,* there's no reason to limit *vaasa thool*'s use to

Tamil crab curry or goat curry (see page 74.). This curry powder can be made up to 3 months in advance and stored in your pantry.

1-inch piece fresh pandan leaf	2 tablespoons fennel seeds
15 black peppercorns	1-inch piece Ceylon cinnamon
8 green cardamom pods	stick (see Notes)
(see Notes)	Small handful of fresh curry
8 whole cloves	leaves (20 to 30)

1. Set a medium bowl near the stove. Place a small skillet over medium heat. When the pan is hot, add the pandan leaf and dry roast until the edges begin to dry, 2 to 3 minutes. Transfer to the bowl to cool.
2. Return the pan to medium heat. Add the peppercorns, cardamom, cloves, fennel seeds, and cinnamon and dry roast, stirring and tossing frequently, until toasted and fragrant, about 5 minutes. Add to the bowl to cool.
3. Return the pan to medium heat. Add the curry leaves and dry roast, stirring frequently, until dry and crispy but not burnt, 5 to 10 minutes. Add to the bowl to cool.
4. Let all of the spices cool to room temperature, then stir to mix well. Working in batches, grind the spices to a powder in a spice grinder or in a mortar with a pestle. Return the ground batches to a clean bowl and give the mixture a good stir to distribute all of the spices evenly before transferring it to a tightly capped glass jar for storage.

NOTES

For cardamom, look for large and vibrant green pods when shopping. Smaller pale pods can lack fragrance and flavor.

Where cinnamon is called for, try to use only Sri Lankan cinnamon—which is often called Ceylon cinnamon. The only true cinnamon comes from Sri Lanka, which has an incomparably warm and sweet yet delicate flavor. Watch out for impostors like cassia; it tastes like cinnamon, but its flavor can be overpowering and will suffocate the flavors of the other spices.

Roshan's Aatu Erachi Kuzhambu

(Goat Curry)

Makes 6 to 8 servings

This is Roshan Kanagarajah's (aka Kitchen Guerrilla's) recipe for *aatu erachi kuzhambu,* or goat curry. Goat has a rich taste, and it has historically been the choice of red meat for Tamils in Sri Lanka, since cows are sacred for Hindu Tamils. In Sri Lanka, goat can be expensive for families and is reserved for special occasions. In fact, Roshan's parents recall eating goat curry only a few times in the years before they left Sri Lanka.

Roshan's goat curry is based on his mother's recipe. "When I was growing up as an impatient kid, my mom would make goat curry on the weekends. I would always sneak a few glorious pieces before getting shoved out of the kitchen," Roshan wrote when he sent me this recipe. "But I would sneak right back in, and I was always the first one waiting at the lunch table. I would always eat way too much and then collapse on the sofa until dinnertime."

When it comes to goat meat, Roshan recommends using a bone-in goat leg for this curry. "Cooking goat meat with bones," he notes, "adds a splendor that cannot be achieved with boneless meat alone." If you live near a Tamil butcher, Roshan advises asking for a *pangu,* which is an assortment of different cuts of goat. *Pangu* means "share" or "portion," which Roshan explains comes from a time when a goat would be slaughtered, and all of its parts divided equally among several families. A *pangu* will often include *nalli elumbu,* which are marrow bones prized among cooks for adding lusciousness to curries. "Personally," Roshan says, "I like to make my goat curry with a goat leg and a few added pieces of *nalli elumbu* and a little extra goat fat."

You'll notice this recipe calls for a neutral cooking oil like sunflower, grapeseed, or vegetable oil. Tamils traditionally cook with unrefined coconut oil, which has a noticeable coconut flavor and can sometimes overpower the tastes of delicate ingredients. Here, Roshan prefers using a neutral oil for his *aatu erachi kuzhambu* because it allows the flavors of the goat meat and spices to stand out.

MARINADE

1 medium yellow onion, diced

1 garlic clove, minced

1-inch piece fresh ginger, peeled and minced

1 teaspoon minced fresh green chilies, such as Thai

½ teaspoon ground turmeric

1½ tablespoons Jaffna Thool (page 70)

2 teaspoons kosher salt

¼ cup neutral oil

4 to 5 pounds bone-in goat meat, such as leg, shoulder, or ribs, cut into ½-inch to 1-inch cubes

3 to 4 ounces goat fat, cut into 1-inch cubes

CURRY

4 tablespoons neutral oil

1 teaspoon black mustard seeds

4 dried red chilies (such as árbol or Kashmiri), torn in half

½ teaspoon fennel seeds

¼ teaspoon fenugreek seeds

20 to 30 fresh curry leaves plus 10 to 15 torn leaves

Four 1-inch pieces fresh pandan leaf

4 medium red onions, diced

18 garlic cloves, smashed

Thumb-size piece fresh ginger, peeled and roughly chopped

5 fresh green chilies, such as Thai, stemmed and halved

Kosher salt

¾ cup unsweetened coconut milk

½ cup Jaffna Thool (page 70), plus more as needed

1 heaping teaspoon Vaasa Thool (page 72)

Lime wedges for squeezing

Cooked white rice for serving

1. Make the marinade: In a large bowl, combine the onion, garlic, ginger, green chilies, turmeric, Jaffna thool, salt, and oil and stir until thoroughly combined. Add the goat meat and fat and toss to coat. Cover the bowl tightly and refrigerate for at least 8 hours or up to overnight.

2. Make the curry: In a Dutch oven or other heavy-bottomed pot over medium-high heat, warm 2 tablespoons of the oil. Add the mustard seeds and cook until they start to pop, 1 to 2 minutes. Immediately add the dried chilies, fennel seeds, and fenugreek seeds and cook until fragrant, about 1 minute. Add the whole curry leaves and pandan leaves and cook until they turn a deep, glossy green, about 30 seconds. Add the onions, garlic, ginger, and green chilies and 1 teaspoon salt and cook, stirring frequently, until the onions turn translucent and the garlic and ginger turn golden brown. Transfer half the contents of the pan to a heatproof dish and set aside.

3. In the same heavy-bottomed pot, heat the remaining 2 tablespoons of oil over medium heat until shimmering. Add the marinated meat and 1 teaspoon salt, and stir to combine with the half of the onion-spice mixture still in the pot. Cover the pot and increase the heat to high. Cook until the goat is pale on the exterior, cooked through, and has released its juices, stirring every 5 minutes for 10 to 15 minutes. The liquid in the pot should just cover the meat; if there's not enough liquid, pour in a little water.

4. Turn down the heat to medium-low and cook until the meat is tender, 40 to 45 minutes, checking occasionally to see if the liquid level in the pot is too low. The liquid should have slightly reduced, revealing the top ½ inch of meat in the pot. Taste a piece of the goat; it should have the bite texture of a medium-rare steak. If it's still firm and chewy, cover and cook for another 20 to 30 minutes.

5. Increase the heat to medium-high and once bubbling, add the reserved half of the onion mixture to the pot, stirring until combined. Cook, uncovered, until the garlic cloves begin to soften, 7 to 8 minutes.

6. Add the coconut milk and Jaffna thool and stir until thoroughly combined. Increase the heat to high and let the curry pot boil aggressively, allowing the liquid to reduce and thicken slightly while

stirring to ensure the bottom of the pot doesn't burn, 7 to 10 minutes. After boiling, a quarter of the liquid should have reduced out. Taste and adjust the seasoning with Jaffna thool and salt if desired.

7. Turn off the heat and add the vaasa thool and stir until thoroughly combined. Add the torn curry leaves and mix well. Cook for 2 minutes and taste. The flavor should be balanced equally between the juicy meat and spices. (At this point, your mouth should be salivating at your creation.) Squeeze lime juice into the pot to taste.

8. Serve with the rice.

3

Myanmar and Bangladesh

Rohingya Cuisine, the Incredible Food You May Never Know

> *Once I was born, survived in different worlds*
> *One where I have lived for generations,*
> *Another where I am merely a refugee*
> *In both places, I have displaced*
>
> *Terrified eyes,*
> *emaciated bodies*
> *God only knows*
> *how many days they have not eaten*
>
> *They are afraid of eating what they find*
> *Because they will be hungry again when it's*
>   *finished*

—"No Place on Earth," Mayyu Ali

NOOR GENTLY RAN her hand over her cheeks, smoothing out the golden streaks of *thanaka*, a sunscreen made of sandalwood. A small, bright-eyed girl no more than five years old, Noor sat cross-legged in the kitchen doorway of her family's bamboo shelter, looking in from the outside. Sunshine flickered off her back. Her gaze was fixed on what was transpiring under her mother's bare feet.

Maryam, Noor's mother, a tall woman, had just made herself small. Squatting on her haunches, she reached under a low wooden shelf for the smooth-worn handle of a heavy three-foot *guwa dhaw,* a sharp knife with a curved blade resembling a parrot's beak. Maryam laid the knife flat on her kitchen floor, the hooked end away from her body. Still squatting, she then slid the knife's handle under her right foot, threading it between her big and index toes, and turned the blade upward. The parrot knife now on its back, its beak curving upward toward the ceiling, Maryam locked it in place with the weight of her body.

Maryam took a deep breath to focus. She then reached down with her left hand to uncover thick cuts of beef resting in an old steel pot on the floor beside her. She pulled a six-inch cut from the bowl, stretching it taut with both hands in front of her body. She extended the meat toward the parrot's beak, pushing it through the curve of the blade, slicing it into two pieces. She dropped the beef in her right hand into a clean bowl while catching the dangling edge of the meat still in her left. She pulled it taut and sliced again. She continued this rowing motion for several moments.

This type of knife work is common practice in the Rohingya Muslim community in Myanmar, where Maryam grew up. It resembles the style of cutting, common across the cultures of the Bay of Bengal, known as *boti,* which uses horizontal force rather than the vertical pushing force of a handheld kitchen knife. The uniqueness of the Rohingyas' knife is in the posture required to use it. One must sit on the floor or on one's haunches like Maryam.[1] "To those used to working with a knife," the food historian Chitrita Banerji writes, "the delicacy with which the rigidly-positioned blade cuts seems miraculous: it peels the tiniest potato, trims the tendrils from string beans, splits the fleshy stems of plants, chops greens into minute particles for stir-frying, and even scales the largest fish."[2]

Maryam paused to gather the bottom of her navy-and-silver skirt, tucking it back between her knees to keep it from catching the blade. Just then she caught a glimpse of her tiny audience in the doorway blowing a kiss her way. I watched Maryam play along, extending her hand to catch Noor's kiss and bring it close to her chest. Fortified by her daughter's affection, she returned to cooking lunch.

. . .

Maryam was pregnant with Noor when she fled from Myanmar to Bangladesh in August 2017. Under the government of Aung San Suu Kyi, the Myanmar military began a sweeping campaign of massacres, rape, and arson targeting Rohingya Muslim communities in northern Rakhine State. For decades, governments in Myanmar, which have mostly been military dictatorships, have denigrated and dehumanized the Rohingya, castigating them as illegal Bangladeshi immigrants and scapegoating them as criminals and Islamist terrorists. During the summer of 2017, security forces killed thousands of Rohingya and burned down nearly four hundred villages, including Maryam's, in an act of genocidal violence. Nearly eight hundred thousand Rohingya—more than half of Myanmar's entire Rohingya population—were forced into Bangladesh, joining hundreds of thousands of other refugees who had fled there during earlier waves of persecution. For nearly a decade now, Maryam, Noor, and the rest of their family have been living precariously in a dense, undulating city of bamboo-and-tarp shanties in a sprawling refugee camp outside the city of Cox's Bazar in southern Bangladesh.

Through Ro Yassin Abdumonab, a photojournalist and friend who was translating for us, Maryam told me that Noor was born into this claustrophobic camp city. She had never tasted her food in her own country, a mere fifty miles away. If there is a dish that typifies the Rohingyas' deep connection to their homeland, it would be the *goru ghuso* Maryam was making that day. A common but important curry, it is made with beef from cattle that grazed the open pastures of northern Rakhine State. Simmered for hours in a scarlet sauce of chili, onions, garlic, and tomatoes and seasoned with salt and a dozen spices, the beef becomes soft, almost butterlike. Often prepared for Eid al-Adha, the Islamic day of ritual sacrifice, *goru ghuso* occupies a special place in Rohingya culture. For Muslims, sacrificing a cow or a goat during Eid is also an opportunity for charity. Advancing social justice through the redistribution of wealth is a central tenet of Islam and something in which Rohingyas take deep pride. Families will often cook *goru ghuso* several times during Eid to distribute among the poor.

Goru ghuso is almost unknown outside Rohingya society, and like the people to whom it belongs, it faces an existential threat. For the past forty years, the Myanmar military has systematically confiscated Rohingya homes and farms to make way for new Buddhist settlements as part of a government project to ethnically cleanse Rakhine State of its Muslim minority. In the process of stealing the Rohingyas' land, the military also looted their livestock, pocketing the profits after selling the animals at a discount to traders who moved them out of state or into the hands of Buddhist settlers. This scam, coupled with cattle-butchering bans aimed at curtailing Islam in Rakhine State, has made beef increasingly hard to find.

Displacement has compounded this culinary destruction. Today, the majority of the Rohingya population is dependent on food aid in refugee camps in Bangladesh. Separated from their land and livestock, Rohingya refugees don't have easy access to quality beef. Instead, they must rely on informal butchers within the camps, often supplied with old and inferior meat. Bangladesh has banned the Rohingya from working in the country, which puts buying meat out of reach for most refugees. Even for those who can afford it, severe movement restrictions within the camps make holiday food distributions almost impossible.

Normally, distributing food like *goru ghuso* helps to reinforce family and political relationships that have traditionally steadied Rohingya society while also emphasizing the obligations the wealthy and the powerful have in caring for their community. But Rohingya elders explain that their inability to perform these food-based rituals in the camps is weakening the foundations of society they have long relied upon for governance and stability. In turn, elders say, this has created a dangerous power vacuum in the camps that is now being filled by violent armed gangs involved in trafficking drugs and people.

I have known Maryam's family for over a decade now. I first met them at their home in Rakhine State when I was working for the UN Office of the High Commissioner for Human Rights, investigating acts of violence targeting the Rohingya people by Myanmar's government. I had come to the home of Maryam's relative after Myanmar's security forces attacked Du Chee Yar Tan, a lush and lively village of farming families a few miles away.

In January 2014, the police and ethnic Rakhine Buddhist civilians joined forces to go from house to house, hunting Rohingya Muslims. Their aim, ostensibly, was to find a missing person; instead, they attacked the innocent and elderly with long knives, drove thousands from their homes, and burned down half the village.

The attack was so horrific—eyewitnesses said they found severed heads floating in a water tank—that even its remoteness couldn't keep the violence off the front page of *The New York Times*.[3] In hindsight, the attack was a dry run for the genocidal violence that Maryam and her family narrowly escaped in August 2017.

Among the many casualties of Myanmar's genocide, one is often forgotten: food. For over a decade, I worked alongside Rohingya activists in Myanmar and Bangladesh as well as diaspora communities in the United States and Malaysia to report on the human rights crisis facing their society. I saw up close how the Rohingya genocide is more than mass murder. I saw how it was also destroying their culture, including their cherished cuisine, not only in their homeland of Myanmar but also in exile in Bangladesh.

For half a century, Rohingya culinary traditions have been worn down by the destructive forces of genocide and displacement. Like a glacier grinding down a mountain, slow and insistent, these forces erode not just specific dishes but also the culture and people that make them possible. Without mass graves, the culinary aspects of genocide are easy to miss.

• • •

The Rohingya homeland is a stunning place. Rakhine State, or Arakan as it was called until 1974, is a narrow strip of land stretching from north to south along the eastern edge of the Bay of Bengal. Wedged between the Chittagong Hills in Bangladesh and the Irrawaddy delta of the Myanmar heartland, Rakhine State contains a staggering confluence of ecosystems. Its coastline is dotted with wide gray sandy beaches and indented with estuaries and river mouths leading inland to a system of intricate waterways.

Like veins and arteries, these waterways carry life through the land, feeding impenetrable mangrove forests and an expansive, fertile coastal plain abutting lush mountain rainforests.

Food binds the Rohingya to this well-watered landscape in almost every way. Before being pushed into Bangladesh, most families lived on small farms, often just a few acres in size. They were self-sufficient, growing chilies, onions, beans, and betel. They paid attention to the plants they grew, not just for their nutritional qualities and culinary applications but also for their medicinal properties. Food also bound the Rohingya to one another. They shared grazing fields, orchards, and ponds. Neighbors worked one another's rice fields, the staple of their cuisine, sharing the harvest. The flavors of Rohingya cooking were fresh and the food seasonal. Rohingya will say that it was in Arakan where Allah perfected the human ideal of eating well from the land.

Rakhine State is not an easy place to access. To get there from Yangon, Myanmar's largest city, you must cross the Arakan range, a strip of tall, rugged coastal mountains covered in thick tropical forests with very few roads or passes. Running north to south from Manipur in India to the Irrawaddy delta, the mountains are like a fortress wall, cutting off Rakhine State from central Myanmar to the east. Even today, these mountains make travel extremely difficult. For much of its history, then, this forbidding geography has naturally oriented the Rohingya homeland westward toward South Asia and the Bay of Bengal and away from the rest of Myanmar and Southeast Asia.[4]

Arakan's early rulers were Hindus, but Islam arrived in the seventh century via ocean trading links with South Asia and Arabia. The region remained multiconfessional, much like India, with Hindus, Buddhists, and Muslims sharing the land. In the ninth century, the Rakhine people, who share a Tibetan-Buddhist ancestry with the Burmese, penetrated the Arakan range and began to curtail the Rohingyas' influence in the region.[5] Over the next two and a half centuries, Rakhine kingdoms maintained a strong navy, which they used to raid Bengal in the north for slaves. The raids inflated Arakan's Muslim population, a point Buddhist chauvinists use today to justify their claims that Rohingyas and Muslims are not indigenous to Myanmar.

Even with Rakhine Buddhists in charge, Rohingya language, art, architecture, and music were heavily influenced by India and the Bay of Bengal. Their cuisine would eventually absorb dishes like biryani, popularized in Mughal India, and the unique cooking techniques of Chittagonian Bengalis. Today, this is reflected in the bedrock dishes of Rohingya cuisine, like *goru ghuso,* the beef curry Maryam was making, and *duras kura,* where a whole chicken is rubbed in a masala paste and set in hot oil fizzing with salt and turmeric until charred and crispy.

Yet what makes Rohingya cuisine so special is its power to cross geographic and religious divides. The way some Rohingya make biryani is an example of that. Biryani is a dish of spiced rice and meat, often marinated in yogurt, layered and slow-cooked in a sealed pot. Biryani dates back to Akbar, the sixteenth-century Mughal emperor who fostered religious tolerance in India through public dialogue among Hindus, Muslims, Christians, Parsis, Jains, Jews, and atheists. Akbar's syncretism extended into the subcontinent's kitchens, where biryani, the love child of Persian pilafs and Indian spices, was born.[6]

Rohingya biryani departs from South Asian biryanis by incorporating ingredients that reflect Buddhist Southeast Asian cuisine. I have eaten biryanis in Rakhine State made with a wonderfully obscene amount of fresh green chilies that are purposely mellowed by the fat of fresh coconut. In Maungdaw, in northern Rakhine

State, where Maryam is from, I have eaten versions where Rohingya cooks add lemongrass and lime along with slender green pandan leaf (also known as screw pine), giving the biryani rice a tropical, sweet butteriness. This syncretism extends across all of Rohingya cuisine. Vegetable dishes are often flavored with a little dried meat, fish, or shrimp, as is typical in other parts of Myanmar and China. Rohingya cooks will add dried fish to curries for savory depth, similar to how Southeast Asian cooks use fish sauce. *Dhuin feera,* a common Rohingya sweet, resembles an Indian chapati but tastes of Thai coconut sticky rice.

For centuries, mainly because of the mountains, Arakan and ancient mainland Myanmar were largely separate. But in 1785, the ethnic Bamar (or Burman) from the Irrawaddy delta conquered the region, cutting off its connection to the subcontinent[7] while also acquiring a border with British Bengal, today's Bangladesh. For the next hundred years, the Bamar and the British fought for control of Myanmar, which was called Burma at the time. Fighting ended in 1886 with the British annexing the entirety of Burma and ruling it as part of India until 1937, when they made it a separate colonial state. The British incorporated Arakan into the new state, decisively turning it away from the Bay of Bengal and reorienting it toward central Burma.

As in other parts of their empire, the British played Burma's ethnic groups off one another as part of their ruinous policy of divide and rule. In central Burma, the British relied heavily on non-Buddhists and Indian immigrants to staff the administrative service, infuriating both the ethnic Bamar majority and the Buddhist clergy, which in turn fueled Buddhist supremacist ideologies and resentment toward non-Buddhist minorities. Many Indians fled Burma after anti-Indian race riots in the 1930s, but their presence left an indelible imprint on Burmese cuisine. Today, samosas and parathas are sold in almost every tea shop, and in cities like Yangon, it's easy to find a Tamil- or Telugu-inspired meal at lunchtime.

During the Second World War, the Japanese occupied Burma and forced the British out of Arakan into Bengal. The Buddhist Rakhine sided with the Japanese, as did the broader Burmese anti-colonial independence movement, while the Rohingya, like many of Burma's other non-Buddhist minorities, went along with the British, believing the Allied forces would support their independence after the war.

During the occupation, Japanese forces, along with Rakhine mercenaries, massacred nearly one hundred thousand Rohingya for their disloyalty.[8] Armed Rohingya units fought back but ultimately failed when the British backed out of their promise to create a Rohingya homeland after the Japanese surrendered. This wartime violence eventually segregated Arakan into an informal but well-defined Muslim Rohingya Rakhine North and Buddhist Rakhine South, a division that persists today.[9]

At independence in 1948, Burma's leaders inherited a huge, multiethnic, multiconfessional, and multilingual society, pulling this new kite-shaped country the size of Texas in different directions. Communist and separatist insurgencies raged in the Northeast near China and the South in the Irrawaddy delta. Looking for a thread to sew the country together, its leaders turned to Buddhism to build a new national identity. This hardened in 1962 when General Ne Win took over in a coup, initiating his "Burmese Way to Socialism," a rigid authoritarianism that closed Burma to outsiders, shut down free expression, and placed absolute power in the military.

For Ne Win, Islam was anathema to Buddhism; Burma had to be for Burmese Buddhists. He privileged the most virulent elements of the clergy, using the monks to stoke fears over Muslims taking over the country. Those not fully on board with this bigotry were deemed traitors. In turn, Ne Win's junta and those that followed encouraged prejudice, if not outright violence, against Rohingyas (and Muslims more generally) to emphasize one's commitment to Buddhism and the country.

In the 1980s, the military renamed the country Myanmar. In 1982, the government enacted a law that stripped the Rohingya of their citizenship, making millions stateless in their own country. It also codified a lie, generations in the making, that the Rohingya were foreigners. To be stateless means no country recognizes you as a citizen. In a world where legal protections are often tied to citizenship, stateless people are generally denied basic rights, such as education, healthcare, employment, housing, marriage, freedom of movement, voting, and even the dignity of a death certificate when they die.

Today, the fallout from the 1982 citizenship law reverberates across Asia. By rendering generations of Rohingyas stateless, the Myanmar military believed it had given itself the green light to wage both a cultural and a physical war to drive them out of the country to Bangladesh, Malaysia, Thailand, Pakistan, and Indonesia. To do this, it has instituted a system of apartheid in Myanmar, segregating Rohingya society into enclaves across Rakhine State and restricting Rohingyas' movement so much that I have met Rohingya adults who have spent their entire lives within an area no larger than a couple of New York City blocks.

Inside these ghettos, the Rohingya language has been banned in schools. Mosques have been destroyed. Rohingya books have been burned. In the 1990s, the government started restricting schooling for Rohingyas, denying entire generations an education, resulting in widespread illiteracy and cultural amnesia. When I lived in Myanmar, I often spoke about this with a Rohingya elder and former schoolteacher named Suleiman. I asked him how this apartheid affected food culture. He told me: "There's no such thing as a Rohingya cookbook. How can there be if we are not permitted to read or write our own history?"

Repealing the Rohingyas' rights, making their lives ever more miserable, is probably one of only two things in Myanmar's fractious society that everyone can agree on, from the Buddhist clergy to the military to Aung San Suu Kyi, the country's most famous politician and a Nobel Peace Prize winner, who headed the government during the 2017 genocide. The other thing is never saying the name "Rohingya." Instead, they refer to these Myanmar people as "Bengalis" to falsely insinuate a foreign otherness and an illegal-invader status.

This racism infected the UN as well. Top UN officials in Myanmar while I was there between 2013 and 2014 actually instructed staff not to use "Rohingya" in memos or meetings. They even attempted to prevent me and another UN human rights officer from traveling to Rakhine State. The officer and I were of South Asian heritage, and they were concerned that our shade of brown was too close to the Rohingyas' and that the Myanmar government might perceive us as biased toward the besieged minority. Eventually their racism was called out by their bosses and we were allowed to travel to Rakhine State.[10]

Technically speaking, my UN job in Myanmar then was to document human rights abuses all over the country. But the crisis facing the Rohingya was so dire that my bosses directed me to work almost exclusively in Rakhine State. At the time, foreigners in Myanmar needed special permission to travel to Rakhine, which I had working with the UN, despite the bigotry I just described. It wasn't hard to get permission; it just meant dealing with head-lolling bureaucracy that put off most from trying. I was often asked what Rakhine State was like. I remember telling people that if they wanted to know what genocide felt like, Sittwe, the state capital, was a good place to start.

Sittwe is a sweaty and segregated town. In 2012, a tidal wave of organized anti-Rohingya violence washed through the city. Hundreds were killed, and most of the Rohingya community was then interned in squalid displacement camps just outside of town. City officials did their best to erase signs of Rohingya life from Sittwe. Though walking through town, I still caught glimpses of charred minarets of Rohingya mosques poking through tangles of overgrown palm trees and tropical vines. Not so obvious were the origins of the piles of moss-covered rocks I occasionally encountered. Those, I learned, were the foundations of Rohingya homes razed by Rakhine mobs.

Almost anyone the authorities and local Rakhine population suspected of helping the Rohingya faced hostility and even violence. When I was working there, the Rakhine Buddhist population violently expelled the UN and aid agencies that were helping the Rohingya in the camps. In February 2014, Rakhine groups fanned out across Sittwe ransacking and destroying our offices. My colleagues had to be evacuated. The police stood by, ignoring calls for help.

When I was cleaning up my UN office in Sittwe after the attack, a colleague came by to show me a photograph he had found of the destroyed World Food Programme (WFP) offices down the street. The WFP was particularly hated by elements of the Rakhine community for providing the Rohingya with their only source of food after the 2012 pogroms. They reasoned that if they could force the WFP out of Rakhine, the Rohingya would starve to death or leave Rakhine too. The picture was shocking, not because of the file cabinets and their contents strewn all over the courtyard but because sitting in the middle of the debris were two Sittwe police officers and an army soldier dressed in blue camouflage posing proudly with their assault rifles and satisfied smiles.

Yet in spite of this tremendous tension and violence, the food glimmers with hope in Rakhine State. It doesn't matter if it's coming out of a Muslim Rohingya or a Buddhist Rakhine kitchen; the cuisines of these two communities reflect the enduring, if often denied, positive influences they've had on each other. Soups and salads, particularly those featuring prawns, are among the glories. When I worked for the UN in Rakhine, I lived in the Royal Sittwe Hotel, an old, moldy edifice on the sea with a perpetually empty pool that was home to a family of very vocal bullfrogs. The hotel restaurant served a Rakhine prawn salad made with fresh herbs, red onions, and green chilies spiked with a few types of citrus and seasoned with black and white pepper. I ate plates of it in the evening after hours of taking harrowing testimony from victims of human rights abuses in the camps. Somehow that salad always seemed to reaffirm that humans were still capable of good.

. . .

The first time I went to Sittwe, in 2013, I asked a UN colleague to show me Narzi, a Rohingya neighborhood that was the epicenter of the 2012 pogroms. A few minutes after leaving downtown Sittwe, he stopped the car and pointed out the window toward an empty overgrown field and simply said "Narzi" in a haunted tone barely above a whisper. Perhaps it was the green of the field that prompted me to picture a chalkboard that had been indifferently erased.

In early 2012, Narzi began to feel like a war zone. At the time, the Buddhist clergy across Rakhine State (and Myanmar) were openly calling Muslim Rohingyas "terrorists" and claiming they were planning to overrun Rakhine State by diluting its ethnic Rakhine and Buddhist complexion through "uncontrollable" birth rates. They were distributing pamphlets that read "You need to wipe out these people, or they'll take your land."[11] Soon, ethnic Rakhine residents took to the streets with machetes and guns. They doused Rohingya homes, shops, and mosques with gasoline while state police shot at families trying to put out the fires. Narzi, home to about ten thousand Rohingyas, was wiped off the map. Homes and businesses were burned down, and countless fishing boats were looted and destroyed. A few days later, the Sittwe government bulldozed away any evidence of Rohingya life left standing.

Most of Sittwe's Rohingya population was interned in the camps outside Sittwe, with multiple families packed into a single room in long houses with a dozen other families. Rohingya men had been the backbone of Rakhine's fishing industry. But the centuries-old industry was decimated by the Sittwe violence, severing many Rohingya from an activity that had shaped their way of life for centuries. "Fishing defines the Rohingya people," a Rohingya elder and lifelong fisherman told me once. "It is a communal effort, keeping the bonds within our community strong. It is one of the most important ways we pass ideas between our generations."

When I was investigating human rights abuses in Rakhine State, I was often invited to eat in Rohingya homes, and I often hoped that I would be served *isamas salan*, a fragrant prawn curry.[12] Like *goru ghuso* (beef curry), *isamas salan* is a staple of Rohingya cuisine. A curry vaguely reminiscent of a Thai *tom yong*, this prawn dish is often made with lentils, long beans, and crescents of bitter gourd. Some versions call for bottle gourd and banana root, vegetables that give the curry a cucumber- and rhubarb-like freshness. It is always spiced with turmeric and fresh green chilies, but cooks will often add a squeeze of lime juice and a pinch of garam masala. And as it has with the beef curry, the genocide has also threated the life of this dish in the Rohingya homeland.

In the winter of 2014, I arrived at a tiny shanty in the Sittwe internment camp to see Salim, a fisherman from Narzi. A woman's voice called out from behind a closed door, ushering me and Kobir, my translator, inside. Yasmeen, Salim's wife, was sitting on the floor at the foot of her husband's bed on the far side of the room. Sitting cross-legged, crowded around him were five of Salim's crewmates. Holding her light pink veil over the bottom part of her face, she gestured for me to sit down. Salim lay still and shirtless on a woven mat along the wall. It was dark in their shanty, but I made out that Salim was a short man, maybe five feet tall. A few spears of bright, hot sunlight shot through the loose weave of the bamboo walls, highlighting his broad shoulders and formidable arms. I could also see that Salim's sleep was not peaceful; his face was twisted in a grimace, and his torso was covered in welts and bruises.

Despite its tininess, Salim and Yasmeen's shanty was a unique luxury. Theirs was a single room made of bamboo, but it was a stand-alone structure in the shade of a few giant coconut palms. It provided the young couple a modicum of privacy. And it was the only bit of solace they possessed after losing everything—their home, fishing boat, and expensive nets—in the government's operation to erase their people from Sittwe. For two years after the violence, Salim had been unable to fish. It was only recently that aid organizations had attempted to rehabilitate the Rohingya fishing community by providing survivors, like Salim and his crewmates, with new boats and nets.

I could hear the fronds of palm trees just outside softly scraping across one another in the wind. Yasmeen tugged her husband's big toe. No response. She tugged again with more force. On the third try, Salim's eyes popped open, and he rose up on his elbows to take all of us in. "Salam alaikum," he said, looking at me, in a strong voice that belied his battered body. Then each of his five crewmates, sitting on the floor only a few inches away, leaned in to touch him as a sign of respect and relief.

He indicated to Yasmeen with his eyes to place a pillow between his lower back and the wall so he could sit upright. A few nights earlier, he told me, he and his crew had been fishing in the Bay of Bengal when they saw a searchlight speeding across the black glass of the still water, prying open the midnight darkness. Shock waves of anxiety rippled through the crew as they fought to stay calm. They all had seen a navy patrol boat, the source of the light. Arif, the captain of Salim's boat, assured them it was just a routine document check and ordered them to leave their nets in the water.

Salim went on to describe how Captain Arif steered his boat toward the light a few hundred yards away, eventually bringing it along the port side of the hulking gray patrol vessel. Arif listened as his crew was ordered by the Myanmar naval officer to throw up bowlines and tie up to the patrol ship. Arif was startled by these unusual orders. His crew, including Salim, protested. They had left in the water not only their catch but also, far more important, their brand-new nets—the tools of their trade, the source of their livelihood. Those fishing nets were supposed to be a new start for Salim and his crew.

I noticed Salim wincing in pain each time he shifted to get comfortable. He brushed off my offer to stop the interview and return later. Captain Arif, he said, had managed to convince the Myanmar navy officers to let his crew collect their nets. But there was a condition: A crew member from the Rohingya fishing boat must stay behind to ensure that the rest would return. If they fled home to the Sittwe beaches, the navy officer said, he would hunt them down, tow their boat out to deep water, and sink it and its crew. Salim and his crewmates said they immediately understood they no longer needed their nets and livelihood. They needed to save their lives. Hearing this, Yasmeen interjected. In a strong, confident voice much like her husband's, she said, "Since Narzi, Rohingya in the Sittwe have only one choice now: survival." It was the only time she spoke that afternoon.

Described by his crewmates as a practical man, Salim also spoke fluent Burmese, the language of the navy officers. He volunteered to stay behind. Once Salim was aboard, a young naval officer pointed him to a deck chair at the rear of the boat. The officer disappeared below deck for a moment and, eyeing the twinkling lights of Sittwe on the horizon, Salim thought he could jump overboard and swim the mile back to shore. Just as Salim's muscles twitched to stand and jump, the young officer returned with a biscuit and a small cup of tea.

The ship's commanding officer watched this tiny act of humanity. He strode across the deck, hurling insults at the young officer, asking how *he*—a proud Burmese Buddhist—could show any kindness to a Rohingya Muslim like Salim, who was scum only to be treated like the animal he was. The young officer cowered under the weight of the tirade. The commander hissed, shoving his subordinate aside in disgust. Then he took a few steps toward Salim, hitting him across the face so hard he fell to the deck.

When the fishing boat returned, the navy officers again ordered it to tie up alongside and told the captain to come aboard. This time, the commanding office made it clear that the Rohingya would be taught their place. For the rest of the night, Salim and his captain were beaten savagely, he told me, pointing to his heavily bruised body. Recounting the horrors of that night, one of Salim's crewmates sitting with us added, "We tried to sleep but were kept awake by their screams." As the weight of the statement settled on us all, Rohim Ali, the youngest of the crew members at Salim's home, briefly lightened the mood, blurting out that while all this was happening, he was actually eating dinner. "I eat when I get nervous," he said shyly through a smile, causing his crewmates to giggle and roll their eyes.

Kobir's eyes widened. His curiosity piqued, he insisted Rohim Ali tell us all what he ate. "Rice and *fuwana mas*," the young fisherman whispered shyly. Often called *shukti* in Bangladesh and India, *fuwana mas* is a variety of intensely flavored sun-dried and salt-cured fish. Similar to anchovies or fish sauce, it is used by the Rohingya as a condiment or an ingredient to add flavor and depth to dishes and even nutrients to a simple plate of rice. "But it wasn't mine. It was his. I took it in the middle of the night," Rohim Ali said, embarrassed as he pointed to the older crewmate beside him. There was more quiet laughter and a few more eye rolls. Rohim Ali, I learned, had a habit of this.

At daybreak, Salim explained, the wind had picked up and there was chop in the water. A thunderstorm menaced the horizon. A few hungover navy officers staggered around the deck, shouting orders to other fishermen still on their boat. They were told to get in the water and scrub clean the hull of the navy patrol boat until it shined like the sun. Trembling with fear, believing they might be drowned somehow, maybe shot while swimming, the Rohingya refused. Incensed by the insubordination, the navy officers ordered all the Rohingya to climb up onto their ship. Once aboard, the fishermen were lined up and pushed forward to the bow, where they were ordered to strip and lie face down on the hot metal deck. For hours, their bodies burned as they were forced to roast in the tropical sun.

In what the fishermen had hoped would be an act of mercy, the commanding officer finally ordered the Rohingya to stand up and move to a shaded part of the ship. The shade, it turned out, was not for them but for the comfort of the officers, who beat the fishermen with wooden canes on their backsides while they held their ankles.

By midafternoon, the soldiers had exhausted themselves, and "by the grace of Allah," one crew member said, "we were allowed to leave." But the commanding officer issued a condition: If they were asked how they were hurt, the Rohingya were told to say it was a fishing accident, that it was *their* fault. The Rohingya captain, Salim said, was forced to thumbprint a document in Burmese, which he couldn't read but everyone knew detailed the lie that the navy had rescued them. Right before they were freed, the commanding officer issued a final order: "Bring us your nets and your prawn catch."

With so many Rohingya confined to internment camps in Rakhine and others afraid of being tortured at sea by the Myanmar navy, well-intended programs to support Rohingya fishermen with boats and nets never really amounted to much after the 2014 violence. Then in 2017, during Nobel laureate Aung San Suu Kyi's government, the miliary carried out the genocide in Rakhine State that pushed eight hundred thousand Rohingya into Bangladesh. Afterward, the Myanmar authorities issued an outright ban on Rohingya fishing across the state.

Today, a civil war rages in Rakhine between the Myanmar army and ethnic Rakhine insurgents. The Myanmar military, short on troops, is again presenting Rohingya fishermen in the Sittwe camps, like Salim and his crewmates, with an impossible choice: Fight for us or leave Myanmar.[13] The military has set up a blockade of Rohingya farms and fishing grounds, causing food shortages and a

200 percent spike in the price of food in markets.[14] Those who risk going to a market have to walk across battle lines and mined fields.[15] Rohingyas in northern Rakhine say they can scarcely pull together a meal of rice and lentils, let alone afford a prawn curry like *isamas salan*. A dish that was an everyday comfort is quickly becoming a costly extravagance. Given how much the Rakhine Buddhist community relied on Rohingya fishermen, it's hard to imagine that aspects of their incredible cuisine, like that hotel prawn salad, haven't suffered too.

. . .

Maryam gently submerged a small spoon into the *goru ghuso*, pulling a cube of beef from the curry simmering over a small fire in her tiny kitchen. Resting on her haunches, she raised the spoon to her mouth, cupping her hand underneath to keep the scarlet sauce from staining her skirt. She chewed it to assess whether it was done. Then she reached for another small spoon and dipped that into the curry.

She handed it to me. "What do you think?" she asked, testing me.

"It is wonderful," I responded. Then I nervously added: "But the meat needs more time, I think."

"I thought so too," she said, smiling. Test passed.

Cooking in the Rohingya refugee camps in Bangladesh is a complicated, even risky affair. It requires skills unlike any other cooking I've seen. Maryam's "home kitchen" is identical to thousands of others in the camps: dark and cramped, with a rough cement floor just big enough for a single adult. It is simply a sliver of space carved out for her family, in their four-hundred-square-foot bamboo-and-tarp shack.

There are no sinks or running water. No refrigerators or electricity. Maryam just has the basics, like knives, spoons, pots, and rolling pins, all provided at one point by aid agencies. In the middle of the floor is a small wood-burning clay stove, around which Maryam must carefully pirouette to avoid igniting a blaze that could burn down her bamboo shanty and hundreds more around hers.[16]

Maryam's ancestral home in Rakhine State was built in the traditional Rohingya style. It was a large, sturdy, single-floor teak structure with a thatched roof. It sat on stilts, roughly five feet off the ground. It had an open-air veranda overlooking a dirt courtyard shaded by coconut palms next to a rice field. Cooking was done outside in a devoted section of the courtyard. Maryam still cut and cooked on her haunches over an open fire, but there was space for multiple cooking fires—and multiple cooks.

Despite the camps' cramped confinement, life inside the cage can feel normal at times. There are dozens of neighborhoods with brick-lined streets, tiny restaurants, and tea stalls. There are fruit and vegetable markets and fishmongers and butchers. Food carts roll past, selling snacks like *fuwana moris,* breaded and deep-fried green chilies, samosas, and *sanabot,* a *pakora*-like deep-fried chickpea fritter spiced with chilies and garam masala. There are barbershops, bridal boutiques, and even a few jewelry stores.

The camps can be verdant spaces too. Tiny gardens grow wherever one can fit in this cramped world—on roofs, between shelters, and on walls. Gardening is a cherished pastime in the camps, particularly among Rohingya women, who take pride in providing their families respite from the monotony of rations with home-grown sources of fresh food.[17] Gardens are not only a way for the Rohingya to personalize their space but also to puncture their drab surroundings. "For many," as Hujjat Ullah, a photographer living in the camps, writes, "the sight of these green gardens offers joy and comfort, reminding them of the homes and the lands they left behind in Arakan."[18]

These morsels of normalcy, however, mask daily miseries. Malnutrition and diseases like dengue and scabies are rampant in the camps. Adults are diagnosed with diabetes and hypertension—conditions once rare among Rohingya—at alarming rates. Armed gangs operate with impunity. Traffickers steal young girls for sex work, while others force young boys to fight in Myanmar. Adding to the despondency, the world appears to have given up on solving the Rohingyas' statelessness, the source of their severe vulnerability.

Rohingyas routinely described the camps as an "outdoor prison" or even an "animal cage." They are disturbingly precise terms when you consider that the Rohingya are prevented from leaving. A few years ago, the Bangladeshi authorities began fortifying entrances and walls around the camps with heavy-duty fencing. At the time, an army soldier manning the gate told me it was for the Rohingyas' protection. I asked him, "Protection from what?" but he didn't answer. That was in 2019.

When I returned in 2023, what I saw was dystopian: miles of massive, fifteen-foot-high fences painted in UN blue, wrapped in reams of barbed wire, and fitted with mechanisms to prevent people from climbing over them. I recalled what the soldier had said in 2019, realizing only then what his silence meant. The cage isn't to protect vulnerable refugees from terrible things getting in but to prevent their problems from getting out.[19] Summing it up, a senior UN official told me then: "As long as what happens in the Rohingya camps stays in the camps, no one gives a shit about what happens in the camps."

Confinement in the camps had made *biddya* more important than ever. *Biddya* is the Rohingya concept of informal education or learning by doing. Through it, history and knowledge are passed between generations to regenerate and reify the Rohingya identity. *Biddya* takes place on a farm or in a garden when a parent teaches a child which plants are edible or medicinal. It happens out at sea among fishermen like Salim learning the seasonal cadence of the currents from their elders. *Biddya* was the background music to Maryam's childhood in her kitchen in Myanmar. It was how she learned to construct dishes like *goru ghuso* and *isamas salan* from her grandmother, mother, and half a dozen aunts.

"Rohingya women must learn how to cook; it's important for marriage and it's important for family," she said through her veil. "For me, it wasn't an obligation, though, but something I loved. That's why I cook when I can for everyone here." For many Rohingya women like Maryam, cooking inside the camps is foremost a process of rebellion against forgetting. "It's how we teach our children which plants to grow and how to cook them, things they will need to know if we ever go home." On another occasion, getting at that delicate feedback loop between farmers and fishermen and cooks and kitchens, Maryam explained that if something isn't grown, if something isn't caught, it isn't cooked. In other words, if something stops making sense, it dies.

It's hard to overstate how widely this sentiment is shared among families in the camps. As with their broader culture, there's tremendous diversity to Rohingya cuisine; the way the Rohingya eat is driven as much by Rakhine State's varied ecosystems, seasons, and regions as by their Islamic faith or a cook's ingenuity. Naturally, this means there's a vast spectrum of ingredients the Rohingya incorporate into their cuisine. For example, the Rohingya eat a wide variety of fish, like baril, hilsa carp, catfish, mackerel, and pomfret, as well as prawns. They use them not only fresh, for curries like *isamas salan,* but also dried, fried, and fermented.

The problem, Maryam explained, is that many of the ingredients the Rohingya had access to in Myanmar are difficult to find in the camps or most likely impossible to afford in the makeshift markets there. Bangladesh doesn't allow Rohingya refugees to work, believing they would take scarce local jobs outside the camps, and the informal jobs that do exist in the camps don't pay much. This means everyone relies on humanitarian food aid to survive. Geared toward meeting their basic nutrition and calorie needs, food aid, while lifesaving, is often out of step with how the Rohingya typically eat.

To an outsider, this can sound like a frivolous critique, like biting the hand that feeds you, but take the case of *fuwana maas,* the sun-dried and salt-cured fish condiment that the Rohingya use to flavor rice or add depth to curry. The World Food Programme (WFP), the primary source of food aid for the camps, provides Rohingya families with an abundance of *fuwana maas.*

Ro Yassin Abdumonab, my translator, is also a photojournalist living in the camps. In 2021, he helped establish Rohingyatographer, a collective of dozens of photographers, writers, and artists who publish a print and digital magazine about Rohingya refugee culture. When we met, Ro Yassin and Rohingyatographer were working on a new issue, "Food for Thought," documenting Rohingya food culture in the camps. He told me *fuwana maas* is not something the Rohingya eat every day, and especially not in the quantities supplied by the WFP.

"Every family gets *fuwana maas* in their rations," Ro Yassin explained. "We eat *fuwana maas* much more often than usual in the camps to keep hunger away. Because we can't work, we can't afford to eat much else." I also heard from Rohingyas throughout the camps that the dried fish supplied by the WFP is not always fresh and has made people sick. Taken together, Ro Yassin said, these quantity and quality issues have led to *fuwana maas* losing its cultural value. Many families in the camp, including his own, Ro Yassin said, would eat less *fuwana maas* if they could afford to. "Eating it now doesn't mean the same thing to Rohingya people as it did back home."

· · ·

The *goru ghuso* simmered away on the stove. Maryam, still on her haunches, reached for a plate of *dhuin feera* wrapped in a tea towel beside her. Earlier I mentioned that *dhuin feera* are sweet flatbreads that taste like a cross between Indian chapati and Thai coconut sticky rice. Maryam had made them from a dough of rice flour and salt, which she divided evenly and rolled into five-inch disks. Before steaming them over a fire, she topped each with freshly chopped coconut and a pinch of jaggery that melted into the dough. Maryam had made them earlier for dessert but offered them as snacks while we waited for the curry.

It was truly out of the ordinary for Maryam and her family to be eating like this, but I was their guest. Food and hospitality form an essential nexus for the Rohingya; it is core to their Islamic identity, where providing for a guest is akin to providing for Allah. Families derive great pride from lavishing guests with food as a way of showing respect. Rohingya children are taught these customs early; cooking for guests is often how special recipes are passed between generations. The genocide, however, has weakened this cherished aspect of Rohingya culture. In the refugee camps, where a lack of livelihoods means money is always overstretched, hosting guests, even with a simple cup of tea, may not make much sense for a family's finances.

The story of genocide changing Rohingya cuisine is also the story of Rohingya women and girls. Rohingya women retain the most culinary knowledge from the homeland, but they also bear the brunt of the genocide's trauma. Violent conflicts magnify gender inequalities while destroying social networks, which increases women's vulnerability to sexual violence and exploitation; intergenerational statelessness heightens these dangers by orders of magnitude.[20]

For Rohingya women and girls, who are traditionally discouraged from working outside the home, marriage is the primary means of obtaining social, economic, and physical security. Marriages are often arranged and based on dowries (usually a monetary gift from the bride's family to the groom's), and they're increasingly happening at earlier ages in the camps, in part to protect girls from being stolen by human traffickers and sold abroad for marriage and/or prostitution.

Forced to leave everything behind in Myanmar, and barred from working in Bangladesh, refugee families have almost no wealth to draw on to pay a dowry. A few years ago, I met Sayedah and Mushtaq, a middle-aged couple both from fishing families near Sittwe. They were in a good mood then—their daughter, Ishrat, had just been married. However, the weeks and months before the wedding were tense and uneasy. Sayedah and Mushtaq worried the marriage might fall through since their family couldn't afford a large dowry for their daughter. However, cooking, they said, literally saved the day.

"Before the *nikah* [marriage under Islamic law], they [the groom's family] wanted to make sure our daughter understood two things: the Quran and how to cook traditional Rohingya foods," Sayedah said. "Cooking was very important to them. They asked me to confirm if she could, and I said, 'Yes! Of course, I taught her! She is better than me!'" Because of the increased significance of marriage among refugees, more than a few Rohingya families appear willing to accept a prospective bride's cooking skills as compensation for a smaller dowry. Sayedah, a few moments later, added through a soft laugh, "Admitting my daughter is a better cook than me was very difficult!"

Sayedah and Mushtaq, as well as other Rohingya families in Myanmar and across the diaspora, emphasized that cooking skills have always been an important attribute for brides but said that they have indeed taken on added importance in the camps—not just because Rohingya elders see cooking as a means for younger generations to maintain a connection to their culture but also because it helps with marriage, which creates extended family networks that can offer protection to female children from the gangs and traffickers slithering through the camps.

. . .

Once, on a trip to Cox's Bazar, I sat with Maryam and her family in their shelter as monsoon rain pelted the tarp roof with a deafening roar. We were sitting a few feet from each other, but yelling was the only way to communicate. It was like God had soaked up the entire Bay of Bengal into a cloth and was wringing out every last drop.

Maryam's shack stands at the base of a ravine; it was among the first built after she fled to the camps in 2017. Dozens of others had been constructed precariously above, stripping away the hillside vegetation and leaving almost nothing to hold the wet soil together. Before the rain started, Maryam had been teaching her daughters how to cook *danpauk,* a Rohingya version of biryani. The rice, *danpauk*'s essential component, had just begun to boil when Maryam leaned forward and switched off the small gas stove.

Through the open door of her shanty, we watched a dozen drenched children stream past, then a few more I thought were playing in the rain. But the speed at which they moved said something else. Maryam ordered her children outside and uphill into a clearing overlooking the sprawling refugee camp. The rain had made it too dangerous to cook. A landslide on top of a lit gas stove could be explosive. "They didn't survive the Myanmar army to die in a landslide," she told me.

Landslides are not the only hazard. The camps are an apocalypse of combustible bamboo shanties that a cooking fire can instantaneously transform into a forest fire–sized blaze. Every year thousands of shelters burn down this way, injuring and killing hundreds. Why? Because the donor governments and UN agencies like the International Organization for Migration (IOM), which manages the camps for the Bangladeshi government, are unwilling to push back on Bangladesh's refusal to construct shelters out of safer and more durable materials.

Here's the reason a UN official gave me in March 2023 for this cowardice: "The Bangladesh government doesn't want to give Rohingya culture a permanent foothold here. They're uninvited guests. IOM defers to this." And here's the reason a Bangladeshi government official gave me a few days later: "We don't want them [the Rohingya] to be too comfortable here. And IOM understands that."[21] The irony that a government in Myanmar headed by a Noble Peace Prize laureate, Aung San Suu Kyi, inflamed this misery, and that the government in Bangladesh now led by another Noble Peace Prize laureate, Muhammad Yunus, is compounding it, is not at all lost on the Rohingya.

In the face of this abandonment, Maryam said, cooking has become a mode of both solace and resistance. That was the reason behind the *goru ghuso* she was cooking. It was a dish that, when family finances allowed, she prioritized teaching to her daughters. For Maryam, *goru ghuso* was a repository not only of her family traditions but also of her people's culture. "The fragrance of the masala paste is the fragrance of our home [in Myanmar]. Those smells and that taste are too important for our children to forget them or never know them," she said, sitting on her kitchen floor with Noor still looking in from the doorway. "Everything we endure in the camp that is working against Rohingya culture—the fires, the gangs, the illness—makes a simple thing like cooking even more important."

For a Rohingya family, their tiny shelter is more than just bamboo and tarp. It's their home. A home, even in a refugee camp, is like any other. It is where births, deaths, and marriages happen. It is a place of respite and intimacy, a repository of memories. A home's destruction, whether intentional or accidental, can deny a person dignity and humanity.

Food and home are truly connected and indivisible. You can't think about them separately. They are simply part of the same equation. For outsiders trying to help peoples with primarily oral cultures, like the Rohingya, understanding this is critical. Without cookbooks, *biddya* in a camp kitchen is the primary way their cuisine lives on. In other words, donors, UN, Bangladesh government, it's time to afford the Rohingya the dignity these people and their culture deserve: Build them better homes. Better yet: End their statelessness. Close the camps and put them on a path to citizenship.

. . .

After a few more minutes, Maryam tested the curry again and then turned to the small group of us crowding the doorway of her tiny kitchen. "*Oiye* [done]," she said with a satisfied smile, and then shooed us into the room next door, where we'd eat. I watched as Noor led a conveyor belt of children, some Maryam's, some her neighbor's, in and out of the kitchen, each carrying a part of the meal: bowls of curry; platters of steamed rice; plates of fresh cucumber; a salad of green chilies, onions, and limes; baskets of warm handmade *loori feera,* a dusty white flatbread made from rice flour. In less than a minute, every square inch of the patterned dining mat spread out on the floor was filled with Maryam's homemade feast.

"What do you think now?" Maryam asked me about the curry as we ate.

"It's exceptional," I replied. The beef was tender and buttery. The punch of cardamom, ginger, and garlic hit with the right force. And the heat from the chilies, both fresh and dried, made my head sweat in the way only a good curry can do.

But I was curious what Maryam thought about what she had made. I find good cooks often overly critical of their own cooking but almost unfailingly honest when they think they got a recipe right. So I asked Maryam, "What do you think?"

"It's good for *here.*"

"For *here*? What do you mean?"

"It's good for Bangladesh. It's good for how we can cook in the camps." She reflected for a moment and continued: "The ingredients aren't fresh. They're grown with pesticides here. At home we had fresh food—food we'd collect fresh from our land each day. We can all taste the difference; the quality is not the same." Waving her hand over the dozen bowls spread out in front of us, she added: "This food, it's like a picture. It looks the same, but it's not true Rohingya food."

• • •

The Rohingya people of Myanmar have a saying, *Fet shaanti, duniyai shaanti.* It means, "When your belly is peaceful, the world is peaceful."

Maryam's Goru Ghuso

(Beef Curry)

Makes 6 servings

There are two ways to make this curry. One method is known as *gaita*-style, in which you mix most of the raw ingredients together at the start and cook them all at once. It's the way very experienced cooks like Maryam make this dish, and it yields a tremendously luscious curry. But it requires constant vigilance and repeatedly fine-tuning the cooking heat; it is hard to get right without a lot of practice.

This recipe uses Maryam's ingredients but follows the second method of preparation—an easier step-by-step process that should be familiar to most cooks. For this second method, I consulted with Maryam as well as a few Rohingya friends here in the United States, including Sharifah Shakirah, whose organization, the Rohingya Women's Development Network, has been documenting recipes throughout the Rohingya diaspora. It's a recipe that works pretty well.

To make this curry, you'll need Indian bay leaves, which are olive green, longer and narrower than the laurel bay leaf, and have a slight cinnamon flavor. You'll also need pandan leaf, a long, slender tropical leaf prized for its grassy, buttery, and subtly sweet flavor. Indian bay leaves and pandan leaves can be found in South Asian and Southeast Asian markets or online. Garam masala, an aromatic and pungent blend of warm spices that varies from region to region and household to household, is available in well-stocked supermarkets. If you like to make yours from scratch, Ro Yassin's family garam masala recipe follows.

Finally, this dish is meant to be fiery. I have included a range for the chilies and you can adjust the heat depending on the type you're using and your own tolerance for heat. I recommend making the chili mixture first and adding it a spoonful at a time to the curry. Always taste before adding more to see if the heat is to your liking. Also, keep in mind that the chili heat will mellow when it cools, so serve this dish warm, not steaming hot.

5 to 10 small dried red chilies, such as árbol or Kashmiri

5 to 10 small fresh green chilies, such as Thai or serrano

Kosher salt

1 to 1½ pounds red or Yukon Gold potatoes, peeled and quartered

1 teaspoon red chili powder, such as Indian or cayenne (optional)

1 tablespoon ground turmeric

1 tablespoon garam masala

5 green cardamom pods, lightly crushed

1 teaspoon black peppercorns

5 whole cloves

4 or 5 dried Indian bay leaves

1 fresh pandan leaf, torn into thirds

1 tablespoon peanut oil, plus more as needed

2 pounds boneless beef short ribs or 3 to 4 pounds bone-in beef short ribs, cut into 1-inch cubes

2 medium red onions, finely chopped

2-inch piece fresh ginger, peeled and finely minced

5 to 7 garlic cloves, finely minced

Lime wedges for squeezing (optional)

FOR SERVING

Fresh cilantro leaves

Cooked short-grain white rice

Lime wedges

Fresh green chilies, such as Thai or serrano

1. Put the dried chilies into a small bowl and add warm water to cover. Let soak for 10 minutes to soften, then drain, setting aside the soaking liquid. Stem the softened dried and fresh green chilies and transfer to a mortar or a food processor. Add 1 tablespoon of the reserved soaking liquid and a pinch of salt and grind with a pestle or process until reduced to a chunky paste. Discard the remaining soaking liquid and set the chili paste aside.

2. In a large saucepan, combine the potatoes with water to cover by 1 to 2 inches. Add a big pinch of salt and the chili powder, if using, and stir to dissolve. Bring to a boil over high heat, turn down the heat to a simmer, and boil gently until the potatoes are tender when pierced with a knife but still hold their shape; start checking after 10 minutes. Drain and set aside.

3. In a small bowl, stir together the turmeric, garam masala, cardamom pods, peppercorns, cloves, 1 teaspoon salt, the bay leaves, and the pandan leaf. Set the leaf-spice mixture aside.

4. In a large, heavy pot, heat the oil over medium heat until it shimmers. Working in batches to avoid crowding, add the beef and sear, turning as needed to color evenly, until browned on all sides. As each batch is ready, use a slotted spoon to transfer it to a plate. Set the browned beef aside.

5. Add oil to the pot as needed to equal ¼ cup fat. Skip the oil or reduce the amount if there is enough rendered beef fat to continue cooking. Heat the oil/fat over medium heat until it shimmers. Add the onions and cook, stirring occasionally, until lightly browned, about 10 minutes. Add the ginger and garlic and cook, stirring occasionally, until fragrant, about 3 minutes.

6. Return the meat to the pot, then add the reserved chili paste and leaf-spice mixture, stir to mix well, and cook, stirring occasionally, for 2 to 3 minutes. Add water just to cover the meat and bring the mixture to a gentle boil. Turn down the heat to low, cover, and simmer gently, stirring occasionally and adjusting the seasoning with salt and a few squeezes of lime if needed, until the meat is fork-tender, 1 to 2 hours, but start checking after 45 minutes.

7. Add the reserved cooked potatoes to the pot and stir gently to mix them into the curry. Using the back of a spoon, break one or two potatoes against the side of the pot to release their starch and help thicken the curry. Cover and cook over low heat for a few minutes to rewarm the potatoes.

8. Remove the curry from the heat, uncover, and let cool for about 10 minutes before serving. Serve the curry from the pot or in a serving bowl. Top with the cilantro and serve with the rice, lime wedges, and whole chilies to nibble on for extra heat.

Ro Yassin's Family Garam Masala

Makes ⅓ to ½ cup

Ro Yassin Abdumonab's family uses this garam masala almost every day, both when they cooked at home in Myanmar, and now in the refugee camps in Bangladesh. What is interesting about this recipe is that it calls for long pepper, also known as *pippali,* which is a little sweeter and less pungent than black pepper; it is a spice, like Rohingya cuisine, that deliciously straddles the South Asian and Southeast Asian culinary worlds. It will hold its flavor for a few months when stored in a lidded glass jar in the pantry.

2 star anise pods	1 tablespoon black peppercorns
2 mace blades	1 tablespoon whole cloves
1 large cinnamon stick	1 tablespoon green cardamom
1 tablespoon ground long pepper	pods (5 to 6 pods)

1. Set a medium bowl near the stove. Place a small skillet over medium heat. When the pan is hot, add all the ingredients and dry roast until fragrant, 2 to 3 minutes. Add to the bowl to cool.
2. Once cool, use a mortar and pestle or a spice grinder to grind all the ingredients together into a fine powder and mix thoroughly. Transfer to a tightly capped glass jar for storage.

4

China and the Uyghurs

The Genocide of a Cuisine

WAS TWENTY-SIX WHEN I first went to the Uyghur homeland for a teaching job. Depending on whom you asked, I was in either 伊宁 (Yining) or غۇلجا (Ghulja), a small city with a split personality in Xinjiang, a sprawling, troubled territory in far northwestern China about twice the size of Texas, on the Kazakhstan border. As far as the Chinese government was concerned, I was officially in Yining. But if you asked a local Uyghur or Kazakh, one of the original Turkic-speaking inhabitants of the city, I was in Ghulja.

Early in my time in Ghulja, I found my way to a restaurant at the end of town run by a Uyghur man in his seventies named Mehmet. His eatery was housed in a wooden shack with a single window, doing its damnedest to stay upright in the winter wind. It was loosely attached to a derelict auto shop whose open gate revealed heaps of scrap metal and a rusted-out maroon taxi. Outside were two newly paved streets in front of a sprawling field cleared for yet another superblock of drab concrete apartments to house Han migrants from the East. The only giveaway that Mehmet served food was the lingering scent of *zire,* a magical mixture of cumin, chili, white pepper, and salt, from the empty kebab grill smoldering out front. If not for the freezing rain, I might have passed it by.

Inside, Mehmet's restaurant was warm and colorful, with a low ceiling adorned with Christmas-like ornaments. The seating was eclectic: wooden chairs with red velveteen cushions, folding fluorescent and red plastic stools. Several old writing desks stood in for dining tables. The restaurant was empty except for Mehmet, a bearded, ancient, and lanky man sitting crossed-legged on what appeared to be a turquoise throne. Wearing a white shirt, an amulet, and a black-and-silver embroidered *doppa,* a traditional square skullcap worn across Central Asia, on his gray hair, he barely moved when I walked in, like he was expecting me. Pointing to an old writing desk, he creaked as he stood up to hand me a single-page menu written in the Uyghur language.

Uyghur employs an Arabic-derived script. I studied Arabic in grad school and I could roughly sound out the menu. Just above a whisper, I sounded out *polo,* which is often called the "king of the Uyghur table," a rich and deeply satisfying fusion of spiced mutton and buttery rice. Mehmet made his by frying piles of sliced white onions, native to Central Asia, and hefty lamb shanks together in an enormous blackened pot over charcoal. He then added a mountain of shredded carrots, another Central Asian native vegetable, followed by spoonfuls of cumin, salt, and brown sugar and a pinch of dried mint, and cooked the mixture until it caramelized.[1]

Next Mehmet spooned soaked short-grain rice over the mixture, sprinkling it with handfuls of green and gold raisins and a few slivered almonds. He then covered the pot until the rice was cooked through. When the *polo* was done, Mehmet gently mixed the ingredients together from the bottom of the pot, making sure each grain of cumin-scented rice was coated in the fragrant, velvety lamb fat and that each bite would contain the perfect amount of silky, savory lamb, sweet carrots, and raisins and the delicate crunch of almonds.

Mehmet also served *leghmen*, the most recognizable example of Uyghur cuisine outside China. Foremost in *leghmen* are the noodles. The best *leghmen* has hand-pulled noodles made from a wheat-flour dough that is stretched, rolled into long ropes, then oiled, coiled, and boiled. Cooks like Mehmet will spool the ropes of *leghmen* dough around both hands and then stretch it by opening and closing their arms as if playing an accordion. Next they'll raise the ropes above their head and, in a swift but controlled motion, slap them against the table again and again. With each slap, the noodles become longer, thinner, and more uniform. With each slap, a little more gluten inside the dough develops. With each slap, the noodles become softer, springier, chewier.

Some cooks chop their noodles into bite-size pieces after they're boiled, but Mehmet serves them as they were meant to be—as long as the table they were slapped against. "The longer the noodle, the longer one's life," he said, invoking a playful superstition some Uyghurs have inherited from the Han. Once at home in a bowl, they're covered in a savory scarlet stew of fat-tailed lamb, peppers, onions, and tomatoes spiced with chili, cumin, black pepper, and the delightfully fermented funkiness of white pepper. Done right, it has you thinking about a second bowl after your first bite.

Mehmet's version of *leghmen* was a tragedy, unfortunately. The few times I suffered through it, the noodles were mostly warm and pliant, but they were inevitably submerged in a greasy broth with sharp lamb-bone shards, edible only if I was willing to risk stitches. *Leghmen*, I learned, just wasn't his forte.

Like Uyghur homes and restaurants across the world, Mehmet's restaurant had a poster of the Tängri Tagh, a stunning and jagged mountain range that bisects Xinjiang, hanging on the wall. The Tängri Tagh, or Heavenly Mountains, also called the Tian Shan, are always on the horizon of Uyghur cultural life. For many Uyghurs, especially cooks like Mehmet, those peaks are integral to their cuisine.[2]

The Tängri Tagh, which run east to west through the middle of the province, are the spine of the Uyghur lands. This topography creates two distinct climatic and culinary regions on either side of the range. On the northern side is the Dzungarian Basin, with a formidable desert in its center. Uyghurs rely on the vast, grassy steppes on the basin's edge as grazing lands for fat-tailed sheep, which are a source of milk, meat, and cooking fat.[3] The Ili River Valley, where Ghulja is located, lies below a western spur of the Tängri Tagh near China's border with Kazakhstan. Fed by Tängri Tagh snowmelt, the Ili River irrigates farms around Ghulja that grow staple crops like barley, hops, rice, wheat, carrots, onions, apples, cherries, and pomegranates.

On the southern side of the Tängri Tagh is the Tarim Basin, home to the majority of Uyghurs. Most live in the Altishahr, or Six Cities, the half dozen or so major oasis towns lining the edge of the massive Taklamakan Desert. Uyghur cuisine arguably would not have developed in the same way if not for the Altishahri oases and their engineers, who built the *karez,* an ancient system of underground wells, to channel snowmelt down from the Tängri Tagh and bring the Taklamakan to life. In the eighteenth century, the *karez* stretched thousands of miles, putting this engineering feat on par with the Great Wall. Today, the *karez* continues to water Altishahri orchards and vineyards. That cool mountain water, combined with low altitude and desert heat, creates nearly perfect growing conditions for the fruits and nuts central to Uyghur cuisine.

For Mehmet and most other Uyghurs, mutton dishes like *polo* and *leghmen* are bedrocks of their cuisine, drawing on the best ingredients from all parts of the Uyghur homeland. Rice for *polo*, wheat for *leghmen* noodles, and the vegetables required for both dishes are all grown in the Ili River Valley. The spices, dried fruits, and nuts that give these dishes their distinct flavors, fragrances, and textures come from Altishahri towns in the South. And the fat-tailed sheep, the source of mutton, *leghmen*'s and *polo*'s star ingredient, are raised on the steep pastures of the Tängri Tagh.

But recently, the government appropriated sizable areas of grassland for industrial cattle ranches run by Han settlers from the East, China's dominant ethnic group. Compared to fat-tailed sheep, cattle eat five times as much grass. This has shrunk not only the grasslands available to Uyghur and Kazakh sheep herds but also the herds themselves. Consequently, mutton prices have soared. Today, it is often cheaper for Uyghurs to use beef in *leghmen* and *polo*.[4] James Millward, an expert on the Chinese Communist Party's policies in Xinjiang, described the situation to me this way: "It's pricing Uyghurs and Kazakhs out of their own food culture." Uyghurs, I know, go further. Pressuring their people to abandon mutton for beef, they say, is just another part of China's project to erase their people and their culture.

. . .

In China, the Uyghur region is officially Xinjiang, which means "new frontier" in Mandarin, but Uyghurs don't call it that. They call their homeland *Sharqi Turkestan* (East Turkestan). Their lands were initially conquered by the Qing Empire in 1759. After the Qing Empire collapsed in 1912, the Uyghurs twice formed an independent Turkic state, once in 1933 and then again in the 1940s, before the region was annexed by Mao Zedong and the People's

Republic of China in 1949. Six years later, the Chinese Communist Party officially renamed the territory the Xinjiang Uyghur Autonomous Region, as something of a compromise. Uyghurs reject that name too, not only because of its clear colonial overtones but also because there's nothing autonomous about their lives there.

The party is deeply insecure about Xinjiang. The region is geographically and culturally so far west that areas of it are closer to Istanbul than to Beijing. For millennia, the region has been dominated by Uyghurs, Kazakhs, Mongols, and other peoples who have more in common with Central Asians than with the Han Chinese. The same can be said for Uyghur cuisine, which is as much a function of eons of Central Asian exchange as it is of indigenous Uyghur creativity.

The party has long grappled with how to remake Xinjiang in its image. For millennia, the region was a stage for Central Asian geopolitical struggles and a major trade route for people, products, and ideas like *polo* and *leghmen*. *Polo* almost certainly came to the Uyghur land from the West with the spread of Islam, while during the Qing dynasty, Hui and Han traders and farmers from eastern China likely brought *la mian*, the hand-pulled noodles the Uyghurs eventually indigenized into *leghmen*.

During Mehmet's lifetime, the party has changed Uyghur life enormously. Over his seven decades, he watched how Uyghurs, Kazakhs, and other Turkic-Muslim communities became minorities in their own land, a fact he would state only in hushed tones and in the company of trusted Uyghurs. In 1949, the year Mao and the Communist Party established the People's Republic of China, Han Chinese were only a small percentage of Xinjiang's population; today they are the majority.

Since 1949, the party has careened between periods of allowing ethnic pluralism and prosecuting Uyghur identity as a kind of mistake—asserting that Uyghurs were really just Chinese yet to be integrated. In the 1950s, eighty thousand former troops were relocated to Xinjiang, along with thousands of women from the East to encourage marriages and families. These families formed the core of the Xinjiang Production and Construction Corps, or Bingtuan, a paramilitary force that Mao Zedong, the head of the Communist Party, used not only as a buffer against potential foreign incursions but also as the state's primary tool to resettle millions of Han to build cities and farms on Xinjiang's best land.[5]

The Cultural Revolution was a nightmare for millions of Chinese, and particularly hellish for people the party saw as separatists, like Tibetans and Uyghurs. In Xinjiang, during Mao's brutal campaign from 1966 to 1976 to eliminate political rivals and enforce communist orthodoxy in China, the party designated Uyghur Islamic customs as counterrevolutionary. Mehmet recalled a visit to his house by members of the Communist Party, who forced his uncles to toss aside their colorful *doppas* and dress in the drab suits favored by Mao.

Mehmet once described to me how the government banned the call to prayer and ordered the destruction of mosques, *mazars,* and madrassas in the area. Party cadres also burned and banned books and savagely beat clerics.[6] Some mosques were draped in portraits of Mao, while red party flags flew from minarets like victory flags over a battlefield. Another time, Mehmet recalled a period during the Cultural Revolution when some Uyghur families were forced not only to rear pigs but also to turn their local mosques into pork slaughterhouses.

I later learned that communist revolutionaries went so far as to force Uyghurs and other Muslims to eat pork as a way to debase them physically and psychologically. They also coerced Uyghur families "to sleep in the same pen as the pigs" and even made them "refer to pigs as 'political animals' that would teach them how to be 'red.' "[7] Over the years, I have talked with dozens of older Uyghur men and women who, like Mehmet, experienced the Cultural Revolution. No other attack on their identity was more degrading to this generation than those on their Islamic culinary culture.[8]

．　．　．

When I was living in Ghulja, the party faced a crisis in Xinjiang. For nearly seven decades, the party had diluted the province's Uyghur and Turkic majority by resettling millions of Han from the East. As it did in Tibet, the party tried to assimilate the Uyghurs into its vision of the future, which only fueled ethnic tensions, occasionally exploding into protests or deadly violence.[9] Uyghurs were able to resist aspects of this cultural assimilation, retaining much of their language, faith, and food.

But all that changed in 2001 after the 9/11 attacks and President George W. Bush's declaration of a so-called war on terror, which almost immediately unleashed governments worldwide to recharacterize existing enemies—especially Muslims—as "terrorists."[10] In China, the government quickly seized on this dynamic to recast its repression of minorities, formerly labeled "separatists," as part of a new global war on terrorism and Islamic extremism. In Xinjiang, this new counterterrorism battlefield became Uyghur culture, and among its major fronts was Uyghur cuisine.

After my time in Ghulja, I lost touch with Mehmet. Through friends, I heard he had moved away after he was evicted and his tiny eatery bulldozed to make room for more housing blocks. What I remember most clearly about Mehmet was that for the time I knew him, he did what he loved, and mostly on his terms. "Cooking Uyghur food for as long as Allah and my hands will let me" was his fate, Mehmet once told me in a mix of Uyghur and English. But Mehmet wasn't naïve. Deep down, he knew neither Allah nor his hands were truly in control. Rather, the party and its fear of Uyghurs would determine his destiny.

Darren Byler, an anthropologist who has extensively documented China's assimilation policy in Xinjiang, points out that until recently, food was perhaps the one area where Uyghurs could still set the rules of their relationship with the Chinese authorities.[11] A Uyghur's food choices could even have been a low-risk form of political resistance against Han resettlement in the Uyghur homeland. But now, just abstaining from pork or alcohol, among the basic tenets of Islam and Uyghur culture, is enough to justify sending a Uyghur to prison for years. Undoing Uyghur cuisine is not just a by-product of what many now call China's genocide of Uyghur culture in Xinjiang. It is a central feature of it.

. . .

In Uyghur cities and towns, the air is often thick with the smell of naan, a braided fragrance of warm sesame, salt, and yeast. Like other leavened breads in South and Central Asia, Uyghur naan is baked in the intense heat of a *tonur,* or tandoor oven. It's almost always baked outdoors on sidewalks, and so its scent forever meanders like a wanderlusting friend through every Uyghur neighborhood. In some Uyghur villages I've visited, naan is not just a smell in the air; it is the air.

Naways, Uyghur bread bakers, start with a simple dough of flour, water, salt, and yeast, which they knead and leave to rise. Next they shape it into flat disks with a thicker rim and thinner center. Typically, *naways* will decorate their naan using a *durtlik,* a wooden, floral-patterned bread stamp with long, needle-like fingers that make holes, allowing steam to escape the dough so that the center remains flat while the naan rises. I have seen *naways* sprinkle any combination of salt, sesame, nigella, and even cumin seeds on the dough before slapping it inside the *tonur*. Uyghur naan bakes quickly, and a good one will have a crackly golden exterior and be warm, tender, and tangy within.

Tahir Hamut Izgil is perhaps the greatest living Uyghur poet. In his memoir, *Waiting to Be Arrested at Night,* he writes: "For Uyghurs, this flatbread is not merely food; it has rich symbolic meaning. Newlyweds take bites out of naan dipped in salt water. People sometimes invoke naan when taking an oath. Naan must not be laid upside down, nor may it be stepped on. When visiting someone, naan is a valued gift. Elders say that 'on a journey naan is a companion' and advise taking naan wherever one travels."[12]

At his home in Virginia, over a dinner of *polo* that his wife, Marhaba, had made, Tahir told me that naan reminds him of how Uyghurs approach poetry. It isn't something reserved for quiet moments or special occasions but is woven into the fabric of everyday Uyghur language and life. Naan is the great equalizer of Uyghur society. Every Uyghur, from rich to poor, has naan as a part of almost every meal. At some point in the day, someone from nearly every household ends up at their local *naway,* which serves as the hub of every Uyghur neighborhood. Their *tonurs* are often a source of warmth for cold and weary travelers, those needing a cheap meal or a good night's rest on a winter night.

The *naways* see life in Xinjiang in a way most others never do. Awake and baking before dawn, they see who is coming and going, who is up for morning prayers, who is running from trouble. The *naways* carry forward an ancient tradition of Uyghur village life, but they are also the connective tissue of Uyghur communities in modern cities. The *naway* is where neighbors cross paths to share the day's gossip and news. A Uyghur friend once told me, "The *naways* know who's who. The *naways* know what's up."

Out for a walk one brisk evening in 2017 in Dawan, his neighborhood in Urumchi, the capital of Xinjiang, Tahir, the poet, sensed something was off.[13] Gone were the warm zephyrs of sesame, salt, and yeast from freshly baked naan that always seemed to gently blow through the streets. He said he looked around, but the *naways* were nowhere to be found. Nor were their *tonurs*—only patches of charred sidewalk where they usually stood. In the days that followed, the *kawapchilar*, the men who meticulously twirled their lamb kebabs over smoldering coals, disappeared too. Then he noticed the butchers were gone. Then the fruit and nut sellers.

One day on his way to work, Tahir stopped his car at a red light. At the intersection was an apartment complex, and through his car window Tahir could see into its courtyard. Standing silently were hundreds of Uyghurs slowly being pressed into buses by the Chinese police. A few forlorn souls looked in Tahir's direction. Tahir said he froze, gripping the steering wheel tightly as if it might crumble between his fingers. Panic and clarity hit him at once. That's when he knew what had happened to the *naways*, because something similar had already happened to him.[14]

. . .

The son of dairy farmers, Tahir was born in 1969, during the Cultural Revolution, and raised outside Kashgar in a village he described as a "poor, unattractive little settlement on the northwestern edge of the Taklamakan Desert."[15] Food was scarce, and what he ate was mostly made of corn flour provided by the local

Communist Party. "Meat, oil, rice, vegetables, and wheat flour were precious," he wrote in his memoir. "Sometimes we would go months without sugar."[16] A tragedy for a culture with a colossal sweet tooth.

He came of age during the 1980s, a heady era of cultural, political, and economic openness in China, a time that feels like a mirage now. Tahir was a brilliant student, publishing his first poem in high school. At college in Beijing, he quickly mastered Mandarin. As a sophomore, he organized hunger strikes and marches during the 1989 Tiananmen Square protests. As it did for others who survived the tanks on Tiananmen, the experience deepened Tahir's desire for democracy. After college, he worked in Beijing before returning to Xinjiang to teach Mandarin, a remarkable feat for someone from the Uyghur-speaking world.

The 1990s were altogether different for Tahir. Uyghurs were mostly left out of China's economic miracle. The Communist Party had been incentivizing ethnic Han to colonize Xinjiang, cutting Uyghurs and Kazakhs out of the local economy. Gambling and alcohol and drug misuse took root among jobless Uyghurs. To address the problem, Uyghurs revived the ancient practice of *meshrep*. Traditionally a male affair, a *meshrep* is a community gathering that is part song, dance, food, and poetry and part informal court to coax "young people to take the right path."[17] The authorities, however, badly misinterpreted the point of *meshreps* and banned them as a form of religious extremism. In 1997 in Ghulja, the town where Mehmet's restaurant was located, Uyghurs protested curbs on their culture, like the *meshrep* ban. Police opened fire on the protesters and declared martial law for weeks. In 2010, UNESCO declared *meshreps* a form of cultural heritage in need of "urgent safeguarding."

In the run-up to the Ghulja violence, the government had been deeply anxious about unauthorized expressions of Uyghur identity. It banned and burned Uyghur books and arbitrarily arrested anyone suspected of extremism. In 1996, Tahir tried to leave China to study in the relative openness of Istanbul, where there was a large Uyghur exile community, but he was arrested at the border. Under torture he confessed to the fabricated charge of "attempting to take illegal and confidential materials out of the country." He was sentenced to three years of "reform" through hard labor in Kashgar. The conditions were inhumane, and Tahir was overworked and underfed. "In prison I only ate *omach* and *mantou*," he told me, referring to a gruel of white corn flour and water and steamed buns. "It was never enough to make me full," he said over dinner on another occasion, at Eerkin's, a Uyghur restaurant in Virginia. "At night I dreamt of eating fatty lamb," he said, lifting a few tangles of *leghmen* into the air with his chopsticks. "I dreamt of stealing one to make *leghmen*." When Tahir left prison, he was twenty-nine years old and weighed less than one hundred pounds.[18]

Tahir returned to Urumchi after prison and rekindled an old relationship with Marhaba. They married in 2001 and had two girls, Aséna and Almila. Tahir kept up his poetry, but his police record made work hard to find. He was eventually hired as a film director, later founding his own production company.[19] And by the early 2000s, his colleagues and friends say, Tahir had established himself as among the most creative in the industry. Tahir's film work took him across the Uyghur region and in retrospect, he says, exposed him relatively early to the sprawling system of internment camps the Communist Party was quietly building to dismantle his culture.

In one instance, on a business trip to Turpan in central Xinjiang in May 2015, Tahir was invited to dinner by a poet friend. His friend made the unusual request to meet near the entrance of a new government complex just outside the city. When Tahir arrived, his friend asked him to wait in the car. From the window, he saw his friend hand the police inside the guardhouse a large plastic sack. Tahir overheard him explain to the police that the contents were clothes and personal-hygiene items for his elder brother inside. Driving to dinner, Tahir's friend told him the complex was a reeducation center for Uyghurs whom the state determined were too religious. "The elder brother of my friend was a gentle farmer," he wrote. He was put inside for taking a religious class long ago as a child.

Later that year, on a filming assignment in Kashgar, Tahir coincidentally drove past his former labor camp. He surveyed the gravelly yard where he had once been brutalized but didn't see any prisoners outside. A few moments later, however, he noticed through a cluster of trees a newly built complex of gray buildings fitted with barbed wire and surveillance cameras. "It was silent and cold with not a soul in sight," he wrote later. And it had "a massive black gate."[20] In the following weeks and months, Tahir, like other Uyghurs, began hearing stories of entire villages in the countryside being swallowed up by these "black gates." Uyghurs from his native Kashgar were terrified, some fleeing to Turkey.

By 2016, alarm had spread across the Uyghur region. Some Uyghurs speculated that Urumchi, where Tahir and his family lived, would be spared the party's internment campaign. Its status as the provincial capital would "prevent such things happening there."[21] That's when Tahir and his wife, Marhaba, observed a change in their eldest daughter. Aséna, who was "usually quite lively," had been coming home from school in "low spirits and heading straight to her room where she would stay silently for long stretches," Tahir wrote. "When we asked Aséna what was wrong, she told us that over the past week, each day a few of her classmates had quietly disappeared."[22]

In the fall of that year, Tahir's wife asked him to fetch some mutton from the nearby Uyghur butcher shop. Inside, he saw the butcher carving a new lamb hanging from a meat hook. But something was off; the butcher was moving clumsily, making a mess of the meat. Tahir leaned forward over the counter and saw a three-foot-long heavy chain hanging from the butcher's knife. The chain was fixed to a post, tugging on the butcher. The butcher's small meat axe and other cleavers were also chained down.

Across Xinjiang at this time, the authorities were obsessed with discovering "Three Illegals and One Item" objects.[23] The "three illegals" were religious publications, audiovisual media, and activities like praying. The "one item" referred to everyday objects, like knives, that were potentially used for "terrorism."[24] Uyghur assailants had used knives in attacks on civilians, like one in Kunming in 2014 that killed 29 people and injured 143 more. As a result, all Uyghurs and Turkic Muslims were required to chain and padlock all their large kitchen knives, wood axes, and other bladed tools to a fixed object—a butcher's block, a table leg, a nearby pipe, even window bars, anything bolted down and difficult to move.

What's more, each knife had to be taken to a special facility and engraved with a QR code containing the owner's biometric data and a list of the other knives they owned. If a knife was used in a suspected crime, the QR code would identify its owner. Cutlery shops and hardware stores were also required to install specialized equipment to turn ID cards into QR codes that were laser-etched into every knife sold to Uyghurs.[25] Cooks were fined nearly three hundred dollars for not having knives chained and secured with a QR code.[26] Some were detained for weeks. "The government," Tahir told me, "saw Uyghur butchers and cooks as a menace hiding in plain sight."

This is also when Tahir noticed that the scent of naan had vanished too.

President Xi Jinping, who came to power in 2013, embarked on a campaign of authoritarian oppression against the Uyghurs of Xinjiang in response to a series of attacks by suspected Uyghur separatists both in and outside Xinjiang. In 2014, Xi ordered a new "People's War" on terrorism to finally bring the Uyghurs under near-total control through a combination of mass surveillance, indoctrination, internment, and large-scale forcible transfers of people out of Xinjiang.[27] As far as Xi is concerned, any organic and uncensored expression of Uyghur cultural life is an indication of violent separatism and Islamist terrorism.

That is why Xi and his party have interned more than a million adult Uyghurs and other Turkic natives of the region in what Darren Byler describes as an "archipelago of nearly three hundred camps" designed to reengineer their culture.[28] What's more, Xi's party has also removed nearly half a million Uyghur children from their families, placing them in Han-run boarding schools, treating them as "orphans," and forcing them to adopt Han language and food customs.[29] Erasing Uyghur cuisine does not appear to be collateral damage of China's social-engineering program in Xinjiang but rather an intentional target.[30]

Through 2016 and 2017, reports of intensive surveillance, mass arrests, and internment camps began streaming out of Xinjiang. Government documents were leaked, including one in which the Xinjiang authorities outlined seventy-five behaviors supposedly indicative of religious extremism among Uyghurs that could justify reeducation and internment. Members of the public were encouraged to spy on their neighbors and report any Uyghurs or Kazakhs engaged in so-called suspicious activities as mundane as quitting smoking, purchasing exercise weights, or even wearing pants that were a bit too short.[31]

They were told to watch the *naways* too. Among the absurd list of seventy-five things that could ruin a Uyghur's or Kazakh's life was buying or storing large amounts of food. The *naways* were unwittingly enlisted in China's war against their own people. Tahir and other Uyghurs described to me how the police and the Han public kept a close eye on the *naways*, monitoring the amount of bread they sold and to whom. The police figured that anyone buying large amounts of naan could be hiding and feeding someone wanted by the state.

Inevitably, many of the *naways*, like the ones who disappeared from Tahir's neighborhood, were arrested and interned themselves, but for different, more insidious reasons. The anthropologist Darren Byler told me the authorities eventually came to see any Uyghur independently engaged in their native cultural trades and their traditional products, like the *naways* and their naan, as symbols of religious extremism and separatist pride.[32] Attacking them weakened the foundation of Uyghur culture, making it easier to manipulate to serve the party's goals. For the party, the Uyghurs' and Kazakhs' forced abandonment of their food culture might be the ultimate sign of submission. As Tahir told me, "The Communist Party really thought about destroying the family. They learned our food. They learned our stories. They learned our poetry. The party put themselves between our hands and our mouths."

Around the same time as the knife ban, the party rolled out a new program called Becoming Family. It was a massive expansion of the state's surveillance of everyday Uyghur and Kazakh life. Becoming Family sent more than a million people, mostly Han party members, across Xinjiang every month to impose weeklong homestays on Uyghur and Kazakh families and, in a few cases, on Han families that were deemed too close with their Muslim neighbors.

With pen, paper, and smartphone in hand, officials tailed Uyghur families throughout their homes, investigating every detail of their daily lives for signs of extremism. They documented eating habits and routine errands, reporting to their superiors behaviors they deemed suspicious, like praying five times a day or having large amounts of food. Homestay officials also noted whether Uyghurs and Kazakhs adhered to Islamic halal standards, particularly with regard to abstaining from pork and alcohol. Why should Turkic Muslims and Han have separate foods when, as Xi Jinping proclaimed, all of Xinjiang's communities "should be tight as seeds in a pomegranate"?[33]

During the homestays, party cadres would teach Uyghurs how to cook Han dishes like *jiaozi* (a type of dumpling). Pinched by hand into half-moons, *jiaozi* are filled with finely chopped vegetables, like spring onions or cabbage, and ground meat, usually pork. In these instances, Han cadres supplied the meat. Darren Byler, who has interviewed homestay investigators, told me they would hide the origins of the *jiaozi* meat to probe a family's piety. He said if Turkic Muslims asked about the meat, investigators would see that as a sign of extremism and report them.

Alcohol was another tactic homestay investigators used to uncover potential terrorists. Uyghurs told me that investigators would bring *baijiu,* a strong, clear grain spirit, and urge Uyghur people to drink it with them. Uyghurs were also pushed into public drinking contests to demonstrate their loyalty to China. In a YouTube clip, reportedly filmed during Ramadan, two Uyghur men, with clear looks of despair on their faces, were forced to chug beer as Han crowds cheered. Another shows four Uyghur women lined up on a public stage chugging large bottles of beer. Even the elderly were made to drink. Another video shows two older women pressured by their Han homestay minder to drink shots of *baijiu*. Muslims were so shaken by the homestays that some said they "started to be afraid of [being seen] *not* drinking alcohol or eating pork."[34]

As for the Han investigators, they didn't see the homestays as sinister intrusions into Uyghur life. Rather, Darren Byler explained, they saw the Becoming Family campaign as a "rescue mission." Homestay officials described Uyghurs to Darren as being uneducated and easily duped by foreign extremists. "At least for some of them," Darren said, "it wasn't so much a campaign of violence as it was an operation of saving Uyghurs from themselves, from their infection, which was Islam." He continued, "They [homestay cadres] saw pork like a gift of medicine. Teaching them [Uyghurs and Kazakhs] that pork and alcohol are good—and not the bad things they've been brainwashed to believe all their life—was a way to demonstrate the kindness and compassion of the Chinese people and the state. In other words, it was a complex form of tough love to justify the violence."

· · ·

By the summer of 2017, Xinjiang was a gigantic prison, pushing Tahir toward panic. His friends were being taken to internment camps in the middle of the night, and at his apartment complex police were coming to seal the apartment doors of disappeared neighbors. Nothing was clear to Tahir except that he and Marhaba could be taken at any time. It quickly dawned on them that they had to do something drastic; they would be risking their family's future if they stayed in Xinjiang.

Tahir and his family still held valid U.S. tourist visas from an earlier trip. But with the crackdown under way, the government banned overseas travel for most Uyghurs. Through a well-connected friend, Tahir learned there were rare medical exemptions. He and Marhaba invented an illness for their daughter Aséna that required special treatment abroad. They spent ten thousand dollars on fake medical records to support the claim. It was a fortune for their family, but Tahir and Marhaba knew that leaving was the only way to keep their family together.

In August, Marhaba received a call from the police saying they had been approved to travel. Tahir jumped out of bed and rushed down to the station to get the necessary stamps in their passports. Two days later, he and his family trembled with fear of being caught as they boarded their plane in Beijing for Boston.

Today, Tahir lives in Virginia. His family's escape is rare. Few, if any, Uyghurs have left China since 2018. The heartbreak of leaving his beloved home is ever present on Tahir's face. But so is the relief that Marhaba and their children are within arm's reach of an embrace. Tahir told me that the last thing his family ate before leaving China was naan, because of what the food means to his people.

After Tahir and his family left, the party proclaimed southern Xinjiang a "pig-raising hub." Every year, forty thousand pigs would be slaughtered on a new farm in Kashgar, a city that for Uyghurs is a close second to Mecca in its sacredness. Billed as an antipoverty scheme, the farm would ostensibly help "poor households" become "rich and well-off," as well as "ensure the supply of pork" for a city where Muslims comprise 90 percent of the population. Muslim farmers would also generously be given pig manure from the facility to fertilize their fruit farms. The party clearly intended to offend: The farm was formalized on April 23, 2020, the first day of Ramadan.

It's hard to exaggerate how much Uyghurs are repulsed by pigs. For Uyghurs, abstaining from pork is among the most important expressions of their identity, and a dividing line between their values and Han lifestyles.[35] "Eating the halal way is not simply one aspect of our food culture. It defines our food culture," a

Uyghur chef in California once told me. "For me, and many, many Uyghurs, not cooking pork, not eating pork, *is* Uyghur." He continued, "I know Uyghur families who are not very religious, many who drink, but who *still* avoid pork out of respect for the culture."

Forcing Uyghurs to consume pork goes beyond cultural contempt. It's also outright theft. In Xinjiang, the government's anti-halal campaign served as a cover to steal the Uyghur economy. In cities like Urumchi, the authorities shut restaurants, like the popular Miraj chain, known for its heritage Uyghur cooking and dazzling bazaar-like atmosphere. It told myriad small grocers to remove HALAL signs from their storefronts and food packaging. Removing a HALAL sign on a window is simple, but repackaging food could bankrupt a business.

Darren Byler explained that shutting down Muslim businesses gives Han Chinese companies opportunities to appropriate new parts of the economy, including the production and sale of halal foods. "Instead of a native Uyghur commercial structure, like a bazaar or bakery, that is tied to the broader market, business is now controlled by Chinese managers," he said. "Instead of going to the bazaar to buy halal items, you should go to the Han shopping mall. Instead of going to a Uyghur bakery for naan, you go to a Han grocery store."

Inside the internment camps, the party has taken Becoming Family's anti-halal tactics to a sadistic extreme. According to former detainees, they were forced to starve while staring at rules posted on the walls of their cells against saying the word "halal" or its Mandarin equivalent, *qingzhen*.[36] Then, on Fridays, the Islamic holy day, camp authorities turned their desperation and hunger against them and fed them pork.

"They have intentionally chosen a day that is holy for the

Muslims," recounted Sayragul Sauytbay, who was among the first victims to publicly detail life inside Xinjiang's secretive internment system. A Kazakh Muslim doctor, author, and activist from Xinjiang, Sauytbay was tortured for a year in a camp before escaping to Kazakhstan in 2018. She explained that if you refused to eat pork, you "would be punished more severely with harsher treatments or longer detention. . . . Everyone was scared and forced to eat pork."[37] Recalling her torture, Sauytbay said: "When you sit in a concentration camp, you do not decide whether to eat, or not to eat. To be alive, we had to eat the meat served to us."[38]

Today the Bingtuan, the paramilitary organization Mao Zedong used in the 1950s to colonize Xinjiang with Han, is one of the main administrators of the cultural genocide under way in Xinjiang, operating hundreds of prisons, reeducation and labor camps, and boarding schools where Turkic Muslims like Sayragul Sauytbay are denuded of their language, faith, and culinary traditions.[39] To keep the prison guards comfortable, as scholars like Timothy Grose have documented, the government has built Han restaurants inside prisons.[40] In Aksu Prefecture in western Xinjiang, authorities opened a Chongqing-style cafeteria in one prison. The guards were so pleased that one, named Lü, proclaimed that to eat "delicious" Chongqing cuisine in faraway Xinjiang made him better at his job.[41]

The West is not guilt-free here either. The Chinese government's war on Uyghurs relies on weaponizing an array of artificial intelligence and high-tech surveillance technology, much of it developed in the West. The fires of Islamophobia lit in the United States after 9/11 and now stoked in Europe have also been central to China's efforts to justify the genocide in Xinjiang. That said, Western countries have taken steps to hold themselves and others accountable. In 2019, Congress passed the Uyghur Human Rights Policy

Act, sanctioning Chinese officials involved in the Xinjiang crackdown, and in 2021 it enacted the Uyghur Forced Labor Prevention Act, banning most imports of products from Xinjiang, seizing shipments at the border, and releasing a public blacklist of the companies operating in Xinjiang.

Still, Western corporations and their supply chains continue to be implicated in Uyghur forced labor. Recent investigations by journalists at the Outlaw Ocean Project found that factories using Uyghur forced labor have exported to importers that supply federal agencies like the U.S. Department of Agriculture with fish for the National School Lunch Program.[42] Another investigation by *The Guardian* in 2025 uncovered how Australia continues to allow thousands of imports from blacklisted Chinese companies implicated in Uyghur human rights abuses.[43]

. . .

Today, the party is working overtime to offer a sunnier narrative of Xinjiang. Hundreds of Uyghur villages have been renamed to names that translate to "Happiness," "Unity," and "Harmony."[44] Tourist boards promote Xinjiang as a tourist destination that is so exotic it "can give you the feeling that you have never visited China before."[45] In promotional videos, smiling Uyghur women wearing bright etles dresses in traditional zigzagging print dance and pick grapes as Han tourists excitedly proclaim how "Xinjiang has changed a lot."[46] And in a dystopian twist, the state media even promote it as a place where tourists can experience village life through "homestays," where they can "dine with the locals and help graze their livestock."[47]

While the party breaks the Uyghur spirit, it promotes Han tourism as a patriotic duty to "culturally replenish Xinjiang" by "passing on the genes of Chinese culture."[48] In 2023 alone, more than seven million tourists visited Xinjiang to experience a party-approved version of the Uyghur homeland. Explaining this surge in interest, a senior official at the Xinjiang Department of Culture and Tourism matter-of-factly states that it was because of the "well-protected cultural traditions of all ethnic groups and famous local cuisine."[49] The party is also getting help from Western travel bloggers whose posts feel like Chinese propaganda.[50] In 2024, a British tourist, claiming to debunk Western media reporting about Xinjiang, declared in his popular vlog that "the Uyghur people, everyone seemed fine," after what appeared to be his first day in Xinjiang.[51]

Social media is peppered with images of Han and foreign tourists with smiling eyes and open mouths in Urumchi, leaning in to take pretend bites out of a giant sculpture of a Uyghur naan, golden brown, with pinched edges and stamped with a *durtlik*.[52] The sculpture sits outside the city's Grand Bazaar, next to a six-foot-tall plastic lamb kebab with alternating cubes of skewered meat and sizzled fat grilled to perfection. Today, the government promotes naan as belonging to "all ethnicities" in Xinjiang, making it hard to find fresh naan made by a Uyghur outside of tourist areas like the Grand Bazaar.[53] With native tradesmen like the *naways* pushed out of sight, much of it is now produced in industrial bakeries and sold in modern grocery stores.

"The Uyghur people in East Turkestan are now living in a dystopian Disneyland, where we are just cheap labor and entertainment for the Chinese people," Adil, a human rights lawyer from Xinjiang living in Turkey, told me. Today, in what some describe as the museumification of Uyghur culture, shrines that were once important sites of pilgrimage have been transformed into tourist attractions "full of Han Chinese tourists, souvenir sellers, and guides."[54] Outside, Uyghur dancers wearing traditional costumes and fake long beards twist and twirl for tourists—the bleak irony here being that long beards remain an illegal symbol of extremism.[55] By Adil's account, almost every activity that made the "Uyghur culture a living breathing thing" has been banned or is now tightly controlled by the state. In their place, he says, are sanitized and secular versions ready for sale in gift shops around the Grand Bazaar.[56]

In the past few years, mosques have reportedly been converted to cafés, and Uyghur restaurants cater mostly to tourists.[57] "Han tourists really want to try the food. That's a large part of the reason why they're coming to Xinjiang," Darren Byler told me. "The government wants to make [Uyghur] restaurants available to tourists, but they don't want them controlled by the Uyghurs. And they certainly don't want them to reflect a Muslim identity either." As far as the party is concerned, Darren said, "a Uyghur restaurant and its food should be a subordinate element of the bigger culture. In other words, a regional variation on Chinese cuisine. Not the cuisine of a distinct and autonomous people and culture."

With few exceptions, Uyghurs appear to accept, even celebrate, the fact that their culinary traditions are not static, that they change, particularly when living alongside other vibrant cultures like the Han Chinese. They frequently point to dishes like *leghmen* as being a product of creative exchange with people from eastern China. The deep concern among Uyghurs, however, is that Han tastes and desires, which already determine the Xinjiang economy, will now be an immutable determining factor in the direction of Uyghur food culture in China. In short, as a Uyghur chef who recently left China told me: "The problem is not change. It's stupid to think our food will always be the same. The problem is Uyghurs are being forced to satisfy someone else's desires."

. . .

As the party uproots Uyghur culture in Xinjiang, that culture is being replanted in exile communities outside of China. As you walk through Zeytinburnu, a neighborhood in Istanbul, Turkey, you almost feel like you're in a Uyghur neighborhood in Urumchi. Dozens of Uyghur restaurants line the streets, serving staples like *leghmen* and *polo,* while others specialize in rare dishes like *öpke-hésip,* braised sheep lung served with lamb sausages stuffed with rice. Uyghur bookstores and bakeries are on every block, a welcome sign of cultural life, given that both have been targeted in Xinjiang. In between Uyghur fashion shops and fruit stands, there are Uyghur banks and real estate agents helping families find their financial and physical footing in exile. A Uyghur woman living in Japan but on vacation in Turkey told me, "Istanbul is the closest we can get to home now."

Down a tiny side street, situated above a bakery, is a small women's collective that helps Uyghur refugees ease in to their new lives in Istanbul. Tall and charismatic, Mihrigul is in her mid-twenties and is a social worker at the collective. She told me about the unique role the women's collective plays in the city. "In the past, Uyghur refugees came to Turkey as a family," Mihrigul explained. "What's different today is that many young children are here [in Turkey] without their parents." Gesturing toward two young girls standing off to the side, huddled closely together over a mobile phone, she continued, "Most of them don't have family here or have lost contact with their family at home. Our job is to help them get settled and grow."

We were talking in a large communal room on the second floor of the collective, sitting on the edge of a *supa,* a raised platform typical of Uyghur homes, where people lounge, eat, and sleep, when the door below burst open with the sound of laughter.[58] "Here we go," Mihrigul said, smiling and rolling her eyes as a dozen teenage girls cheerfully bounded up the steps. The happy chatter, however, ended almost as quickly as it began as the girls caught sight of their teachers emerging imposingly from the kitchen doorway. The women, in jet-black chadors and bright red, pink, and white etles-print aprons, motioned to their students to take seats at the large table set with cherry-red place mats. "They're learning how to make *narin* today," Mihrigul said in a hushed tone, leaning in to me.

Narin is to Uyghurs what chicken noodle soup is to many Americans: a brothy bowl of warm, savory vegetables, small cubes of meat, and silky, thin, handmade egg noodles with magical powers to heal a cold or a broken heart. After the girls listened for a few moments to their teachers explaining the mechanics of making *narin,* the room suddenly boomed again with chatter as they stood to help one another cinch their etles-print aprons. The contrast of a dozen people in black chadors and fluorescent pink and white aprons lent the room a Technicolor electricity.

The students laughed and took selfies as their teachers brought out small bags of flour, glass pitchers of cool water, and stacks of mixing bowls, setting them on the long table. The elder teacher said something stern in Uyghur to the group, the laughter immediately ceased, and cellphones disappeared. A few moments later, the momentary quiet had given way to the soothing, thumping syncopation of dozens of hands simultaneously kneading dough.

Since the 1930s, Turkey has been an important place of refuge for Uyghurs fleeing different periods of Chinese repression. Ethnic cousins, Uyghurs and Turks share deep and tangled cultural, linguistic, and religious roots. Today, as many as fifty thousand Uyghurs live in Turkey. While there are many more Uyghurs in the Central Asian states, Turkey has played an outsize role among exiled Uyghurs, providing Uyghur activists and intellectuals a safe haven to shape their resistance to the conflict in their home-land.

Uyghurs, however, worry the country is losing its safe haven status as economics and politics pull China and Turkey closer together.[59] As it dangles billions of dollars of investment in front of Turkey's leaders, China is pressuring Turkish politicians to ratify a new extradition treaty between the countries.[60] Even if Turkey is able to resist Beijing's pressure, Uyghurs believe they will remain at risk. "Uyghurs here [in Turkey] are pressured to work with the Chinese to inform on each other," Adil, the human rights lawyer, explained. "The Chinese police track Uyghurs here in Turkey. They call Uyghurs on their phones and tell them if they don't cooperate, the police will punish our relatives at home."

In China, the party transformed Xinjiang into what Darren Byler calls a "high-tech penal colony" for Uyghur and other Muslim communities. In the past several years, cameras have grown like "barnacles on every surface" in every city in Xinjiang. Uyghurs are digitally tracked coming and going from their homes.[61] Everyone's internet activity is quietly scrutinized—from what someone types on WeChat to which news articles they share. The authorities have built AI systems to distill the Uyghur language into lines of code that have learned to read Uyghur speech en masse for signs of extremism.[62]

China has long financed a network of informants who monitor and silence Uyghur activism in cities like Istanbul.[63] But now Beijing appears to be using the same surveillance technology used in Xinjiang to track Uyghurs in Turkey. For example, Mihrigul explained that the Chinese restrict the number of children Uyghur families can have. Urban couples are allowed to have two children and rural couples three. It is a crime to have more, but many did; families who had more children brought them to Turkey to stay with friends or relatives. It was a way for parents to keep both themselves and their children from being taken to a camp or a state boarding school.[64] But it didn't always work. Mihrigul suspects that some of these parents were digitally tracked during travel, arrested at home, and disappeared into camps.

This is something Mihrigul shares in common with her students. She came to Istanbul from Urumchi with her husband and three children in 2014. Like many other Uyghurs, she came to Turkey for higher education, which is increasingly closed off to Turkic Muslims in China. In 2017, Mihrigul's mother came to Istanbul to help her daughter after the birth of her new baby. Shortly after returning to Urumchi, Mihrigul's mother was called to a police station and interrogated about her travel to Turkey. Mihrigul said her mother disappeared for a year and a half.

In August 2022, the UN indicated that China's pattern of separating families "may amount to enforced disappearances," and in the context of depriving Uyghurs and Kazakhs of human rights more generally, it "may constitute international crimes, in particular crimes against humanity."[65] Without their parents, many Uyghur children in Turkey now live with other Uyghur families or distant relatives, who struggle to support them. Mihrigul said that many of her students lack confidence and have difficulty communicating. "These are typical life skills they would have naturally learned if they were together with their family," she says.

That's where the women's collective for Uyghur refugees steps in. Cooking classes, like the one Mihrigul and I were watching, help children build their identity outside their homeland, she explained. "A lot of them were very young when they got here," she said. "They don't know much about our food, about how it's tied to our religion, or about our eating customs and hospitality, which Uyghur children learn when they're young."

Mihrigul motioned toward students still kneading dough at the table. "They show clear signs of depression from being separated from their families and homeland," she said. "Learning about our food helps them. It continuously builds a connection among us here and to our land back home." Mihrigul paused before emphasizing that most of the young women at the table were born in East Turkestan. "The food is real and something connected to home they can touch."

While their dough rested on the table, the students crammed themselves into the kitchen with their teachers to learn about *narin* broth. A *narin* broth takes hours to simmer, so the teachers deconstructed one made earlier that day. As one teacher explained the recipe, a dozen cellphones shot up into the air, jockeying for a clear shot of the other instructor straining a huge pot of steaming golden broth. Cubes of lamb, carrot, and onion—the quintessential base of *narin*—plopped into a bowl.

A few moments later, the students returned to the table to roll out dough. The lesson turned into a master class on making the perfect noodle. Again phones shot up overhead to catch the hypnotic rhythm of both teachers in sync as their hands glided effortlessly from the center to the edge of their three-foot rolling pins and back again. I stood captivated as the teachers transformed a ball of dough the size of a small orange into a tissue paper–thin disk as large as a coffee table.

That's when Mihrigul gently nudged me and said: "Inshallah, one day if we go back to China, we can replant all this to revive our culture." She paused to look at her students, some crouching now to be eye level with the rolling while others stood on chairs filming it. "The way I see it, these young women are like yeast starters." I glanced at her curiously. "Not for naan, of course," she said with a quick giggle, "but for the future of Uyghur culture."

Marhaba's Uyghur Polo

Makes 4 to 6 servings

This is Marhaba Izgil's *polo*. It is the dish she made for me when Tahir, her husband, first recounted their family's daring escape from Xinjiang, China. Marhaba is coincidentally from Ghulja in Xinjiang, the town where Mehmet's little eatery once stood, and her *polo* is as good as Mehmet's. Mehmet, however, added pinches of black and white pepper as well as a little dried mint to his *polo*, which is unusual. I love white pepper, and it's perhaps why his *polo* still sticks out to me.

2 cups short-grain white rice

½ cup olive oil or rendered
   lamb fat

1 to 1½ pounds boneless lamb
   shoulder, preferably with
   some fat, cut into 1-inch cubes

1 large red or white onion,
   chopped

1 teaspoon ground cumin, plus
   more as needed

1 teaspoon kosher salt, plus more
   as needed

1 teaspoon sugar, plus more as
   needed

Pinch of freshly ground black
   pepper (optional)

Pinch of white pepper (optional)

Pinch of dried mint (optional)

1 pound carrots, peeled and cut
   into matchsticks

3 to 4 cups stock or water
   (see Note, page 144)

½ cup raisins

Yogurt for serving

Fresh green chilies (such as Thai)
   for serving

1. Put the rice into a large bowl, add cold water to cover generously, and swirl the rice with your hand until the water is cloudy. Pour off

the water. Repeat three times. Cover the rice with water a final time and let soak for 20 minutes.

2. In a large, heavy pot, heat the oil over medium-high heat until it shimmers. Add the lamb and cook, turning as needed to color evenly, until golden brown on all sides, 12 to 15 minutes.

3. Next, add the onions, cumin, salt, sugar, and the black pepper, white pepper, and mint, if using, to the pot. Gently and carefully mix together all of the ingredients for 1 to 2 minutes.

4. Add the carrots and mix well. Cook, stirring often, until the carrots begin to soften, about 7 minutes.

5. Add enough stock to just cover the lamb and the carrots. Scrape the bottom of the pot with a wooden spoon to make sure nothing is sticking. Taste and adjust the seasoning with cumin, salt, and sugar if necessary. Bring the liquid to a boil and then turn down the heat to low and let simmer.

6. Drain the rice and spoon it evenly over the meat with a wooden spoon, evening out the rice with the back of the spoon. Do not mix the rice into the meat mixture. Sprinkle the raisins evenly over the rice. Using the end of the spoon or a chopstick, gently poke a few holes through the rice. Cover the pot and simmer until the meat is tender and the rice is cooked, 30 to 40 minutes.

7. Watching out for the blast of steam, uncover the pot, then gently mix together all of the ingredients, lifting and folding from the bottom of the pot. Serve directly from the pot or spoon onto a platter. Accompany with the yogurt and green chilies.

NOTE

Lamb stock is ideal instead of water, but any type of stock would work well here.

5

Bolivia and the Andes

Cooking with Coca

"COME BACK AT NOON TOMORROW," Marsia Taha insisted as she leaned in to say goodbye with a gentle kiss on the cheek. "Tomorrow, you can taste your research."

Dominique, my wife, and I had just finished dinner at Gustu, a restaurant in La Paz consistently ranked among the best restaurants in Latin America, famous for pioneering a contemporary cuisine that relies almost exclusively on ingredients from the Andes and the Amazon. Gustu's staff had given us a tour of Bolivia through food—alligator ceviche, Altiplano corn stew, and bottles of Bolivian wine from Tarija as good as anything from Argentina, California, or France.

That afternoon, considerably more sober, I had come to Gustu to meet with Marsia, Gustu's executive chef, who, like her restaurant, is considered one of the best in Latin America.[1] Tall, in her early thirties, with long, undulating hair and glasses perpetually smudged from staring into steaming pots all day, Marsia exudes an unintentional elegance and listens unlike any other person I have ever met. Born in Bulgaria to a Bolivian mother and a Palestinian father, she spent her childhood in Bolivia, where she developed her love of cooking. In 2013, she joined Gustu as an intern and worked her way to the top spot ten years later. In the fall of 2024, she announced that she would be leaving Gustu to start her own restaurant, Arami, in La Paz.

Marsia is more than a chef. She is also a researcher and conservationist and a human rights activist at heart. Marsia has been at Gustu since its founding in 2013, when it was opened by the Danish celebrity chef Claus Meyer, who, with René Redzepi, cofounded noma, the world-famous restaurant in Copenhagen known for creating New Nordic cuisine, reviving local and foraged products. Meyer set out to make Gustu a Bolivian version, focused on Andean and Amazonian ingredients.[2] When Marsia took over as head chef five years later, she felt the restaurant had lost its trendsetting edge. "We were, of course, still serving exciting and unique food using local ingredients from the Andes, Amazon, and Altiplano," she told me, "but it wasn't fully connecting with communities growing those ingredients."

Sitting across from me on a broken-in black leather sofa in Gustu's airy and colorful foyer, Marsia described an urge she felt a few years earlier to immerse herself in Bolivia's pre-Columbian cooking cultures. She began splitting her time between Gustu's kitchen and traveling the country, securing invitations to meet Indigenous communities to learn about their ancestral ingredients and ancient cooking techniques, some of which Marsia learned were on the brink of extinction. "It was painful to hear about these beautiful things being lost," she told me. So in 2018, Marsia cofounded an organization called Sabores Silvestres with the Wildlife Conservation Society in La Paz. Today, the organization works across Bolivia to preserve both biodiversity and ancestral culinary cultures by working with local communities to identify new products with potential culinary uses and to link farmers with restaurants and markets to provide sustainably produced, high-quality ingredients. "I started researching on day one at Gustu, ten years ago," she said. "Since then, not a month goes by that we're not taught about a new ingredient."

Among the most unique components of Marsia's cooking is the coca leaf. It is dark green and oval, two to three inches long, with a tough vein running down its middle. It has a smooth, leathery texture with a polished sheen, giving the leaf an almost lacquered appearance. If you didn't know what it was, you'd easily mistake it for a bay leaf. The variety Marsia works with is grown by the Chari community in Apolobamba, on the border with Peru. She says it is sweeter and more fragrant than other varieties.

Sipping on soda water, Marsia explained that for at least eight thousand years, this plant has enriched Andean civilizations in ways that are hard to count.[3] Valued at times like gold, it was chewed and brewed and offered to the gods by Andean peoples long before the Incas. It is used as a medicine and a cure for altitude sickness. In a tea, it invigorates you like a double espresso without the jittery aftershocks. Studies show the coca leaf is packed with essential minerals like calcium, magnesium, and phosphorus as well as vitamins A, B_1, B_2, B_6, C, and E. There are also critical nutrients such as fiber and protein. According to the World Health Organization (WHO), the leaves also possess "positive therapeutic effects."[4]

Coca helped reshape the global economy in the seventeenth and eighteenth centuries. Imperial Spain learned that its Indigenous slaves mined more Andean silver when they chewed more coca. That stolen silver flooded global markets, transforming trade and economic power in ways still felt today. More recently in its history, coca was refined to create cocaine, which thrust the coca leaf into the center of the war on drugs, which has falsely equated coca, a sacred plant safely consumed for thousands of years by Andean communities, with cocaine. As a result, Indigenous communities have fought to maintain a connection to the plant's traditional uses.

But in the past few years, chefs and bakers in Bolivia and other Andean countries have found seemingly endless uses for coca in a bout of creativity and culinary resistance. Many dry the leaf and grind it into an electric-green powder, evocative in both taste and texture of Japanese matcha. They're mixing it into ice creams, cakes, and candies and using it to make mouthwatering chocolates. They're adding it to meat marinades and ceviches to impart a smoky, verdant depth to their dishes. Even brewers and distillers use it for new and herbaceous craft beers and botanical liquors.

. . .

Dominque and I returned to Gustu the next day at noon, as Marsia had instructed. We were greeted by Andrea Moscoso Weisse, the restaurant's effervescent manager and sommelier, who disappeared behind the bar to mix us both a margarita-like cocktail using *tumbo,* a slightly sweet and acidic yellowish-green oblong fruit, a cousin of the passion fruit.

A few moments later, Marsia emerged from the kitchen carrying two rough stone plates with a basket of tangy sourdough rolls the color of pale moss. "Please tell me what you think," she said while wiping her glasses clean with the edge of her black apron.

Half a dozen fried coca leaves were arranged like the backplates on a stegosaurus, rising out of a wavy dollop of soft greenish-brown butter infused with coca essence. Like many Americans, I had been force-fed false information about coca and cocaine. My first encounter with the plant and the narcotic was in the 1980s in Cleveland while in the fifth grade. The Catholic nuns invited uniformed police officers to my school to talk about drugs. They taped pictures of coca bushes and baggies of white powder to the chalkboard. For the next thirty minutes, the officers scared the shit out of two dozen ten-year-olds about the evils of cocaine and other drugs. It was Catholic school, so everything was evil.

Outside school, the message was different. In the 1990s, white mainstream American culture told me drugs were a harmless part of being young, something you "experimented" with in college. The party lives of rock stars and actors reinforced this. Cocaine enhanced their creativity; it made their music and movies better. Few called their drug use criminal; rather, it was an addiction to be medically treated. But when it came to Black and Brown people as well as gay men using cocaine, politicians scared us shitless again with racist and homophobic shrills of a looming apocalypse of crime, "crack babies," and AIDS.

It wasn't until I went to Afghanistan in the early 2000s that I came to directly understand how misguided U.S. foreign policy often amplifies the global illicit drug trade rather than mitigates it. A few times, I watched U.S.-backed Afghan police cut down fields of white, pink, and purple opium poppies, whose sticky sap makes up the main ingredient in heroin. In the Afghan conflict, heroin bankrolled the Taliban insurgency as well as corrupt American-allied warlords. Until the Taliban issued a drug ban in 2022, Afghanistan was the world's largest opium producer.[5]

For years, the central tenet of the U.S. counternarcotics policy in both Afghanistan and Latin America has been "source country eradication"—the simple idea being that if you eradicate coca and poppy crops at the source, you stop drug production and thus consumption. Multiple studies have concluded that eradication programs have produced more harm than good, causing environmental degradation, economic upheaval, and a sharp drop in public support for government officials as they sent impoverished rural communities, which often farmed coca and opium out of desperation, into the welcoming arms of insurgents and drug traffickers.[6]

In Afghanistan, as well as in Bolivia, U.S.-backed source eradication in the 2000s created an impossible situation for poor farmers. In both places, source eradication was paired with programs funded by USAID, the U.S. foreign aid agency, that incentivized farmers with cash to plant alternative crops for which there were often no local demand or markets. Making matters worse, at least for Bolivians, USAID's cash support was conditioned on farmers eradicating their entire coca crop first. In the end, the United States has spent billions eradicating coca at gunpoint or spraying toxic pesticides over plantations and peasant farmers' crops with no appreciable drop in supply or demand. Various analyses have concluded that it cost $240,000 for every kilogram of cocaine ultimately removed from the retail market through spraying, or more than five times the retail value of the drug. In other words, we export blame instead of dealing with our demand for dangerous drugs at home.[7]

"Some people think coca is the same as cocaine," Marsia told me. "They think if you just mix it around in your mouth, you'll produce cocaine." Coca is indeed the primary ingredient in cocaine. The reality, however, is that it takes three hundred pounds of coca leaves, and around a dozen highly controlled toxic chemicals, to make a single pound of cocaine. Bolivians will make this point by explaining you can't get high by chewing or cooking with too much coca, just as you can't get drunk by eating too many grapes.

Even so, more than a few Andean chefs told me that customers have stomped out when served coca. In a widely reported instance in the Colombian press, an outraged U.S. diplomat created a scene at Leo, a world-class restaurant in Bogotá, when his cocktail arrived with fermented coca leaf. In Bolivia, U.S. diplomats have reportedly been far more polite.[8] At Intrepid, a distillery in La Paz, a staffer told me during a tour that U.S. embassy officials visit from time to time, and when offered sips of Cocalero de Altura, an herbaceous, gin-like Bolivian spirit distilled with a dozen Andean and Amazonian botanicals, including coca leaf, "they're nice; they simply say 'No thank you' and stick to our other non-coca spirits."

Any lingering childhood apprehension melted away when I bit into the coca-leaf chips Marsia had made for us. It was a new taste: bitter, smoky, and slightly sweet, with a trace of citrus. Yet I instinctually recalled two other leaves that have left indelible marks on my culinary soul, the curry leaf and the makrut lime, often used in Indian Ocean cultures' cuisines. The fried coca leaf was delicate yet crunchy, like biting into a paper-thin potato chip or shiso tempura.

Marsia left the leaves whole, unadulterated, and gently fried them in butter so the flavor could speak for itself. Both the simplicity and the practicality of the recipe compel you to engage head-on with the plant—and your biases. Before that, I thought eating coca might be a gimmick, like flavored foam. But it wasn't. The coca-infused brown butter spread over the warm sourdough was nourishing and comforting. The chips were delicious. Between bites, I thought, *The recipe is saying, "This isn't strange. You, too, could cook this at home."* But because of the war on drugs, you actually can't.

On a clear winter day in 2023, the sunlight in La Paz had painted the city into high relief. The intense high-altitude light burst around the edges of buildings, creating a contrast between the cornflower-blue Andean sky and terra-cotta-orange brick buildings so sharp that everything appears to leap off the canvas. I stepped out of the hot glare and into the breezy, high-ceilinged foyer of Phayawi, a traditional Bolivian restaurant in a contemporary art deco setting.

Inside, Valentina Arteaga, the head chef and owner, took me by the elbow and guided me toward the staircase on my left. "Let's go upstairs to the bar," she said. "I'll make you a drink there." Sitting on a dark green velvet couch overlooking the dining room, I sipped a Bolivian Sunset, a punchy cocktail made with Cocalero de Altura. *Tumbo* and carrot juice gave the cocktail its reddish-orange color and sweetness to balance the assertive other ingredients. It was served in a martini glass and garnished with freshly dried coca leaves. Together, the red drink and the green garnish reflected the color of La Paz's city flag.

I was at Phayawi around La Paz Day, the July 16 holiday commemorating the city's role in liberating Bolivians from Spanish colonialism. Most of the celebration happens the night before, during what is called Verbena Paceña, when downtown La Paz becomes a massive, wildly colorful street party. On nearly every street, there are marching bands in full regalia and feathered top hats. They snake through crowds of people sipping *sucumbé,* an almost obligatory seasonal cocktail like eggnog that is made with egg whites, milk, a grape brandy called *singani,* and spiced with cinnamon and cloves. Phayawi, however, celebrated with the Bolivian Sunset.

Valentina opened Phayawi in 2020, building the menu around her grandmother's recipes, such as *sopa de maní,* a luscious peanut soup with pieces of tender beef, topped with fresh herbs and a tangle of shoestring potato fries. At the time, Bolivians weren't used to seeing their national cuisine elevated and celebrated; I had heard often that having a good restaurant meant you had to serve French, Italian, or Japanese. Never Bolivian. "I love our food. Whenever I dreamed of my own restaurant, it had to be Bolivian," Valentina told me. "A lot of people questioned what I was doing. They said no one would eat in a restaurant like this, no one would pay to eat *sopa de maní* in a nice place." But they did. And in late 2024, Phayawi was named one of best restaurants in Latin America.[9]

Before opening Phayawi, Valentina interned with Marsia Taha at Gustu, learning how to challenge Bolivians to reconsider not only the ingredients that made up their cuisine but also how it should look. Gustu's cooking has a strong Bolivian identity but it is experimental rather than traditional; customers expect something that looks and tastes different. But Valentina serves familiar dishes, executed to their greatest potential and made with the best ingredients. A La Paz chef told me, "Valentina is creating pride in our national cuisine. Serving our favorite dishes with the best ingredients, like *charquekan* [a plate of dried llama meat strewn atop hominy and native potatoes], in a beautiful place shows respect to our people and our food. That's how Phayawi earned respect."

Like Gustu, Phayawi's menu is built on the best local ingredients. "It's important that we use Bolivian ingredients like coca leaf. It's an important part of our culture we were told we should be ashamed of," Valentina said. "Coca leaf is not the main ingredient in our cooking here [at Phayawi]. Like other ingredients, it has its own unique flavors, so we only use it when it makes sense in a dish or drink. But it's also important that we use it because of what it means."

You can buy coca spirits like Cocalero de Altura, the coca liquor in the cocktail I was sipping at Phayawi, as well as a half dozen varieties of coca chocolates at La Paz's airport, which is especially frustrating because international customs officials are obliged to treat coca and cocaine the same, which means you can't bring your purchases back to the United States. The taboo has killed any legal markets outside the Andean countries for safe coca products like chocolates, spirits, and teas, meaning if you want to try Marsia Taha's coca chips and butter, you'll have to fly to La Paz. The whole thing is tragically ironic, because many of the coca products you can't bring home from Bolivia were actually born in America.

· · ·

With the exception of Cuba and Puerto Rico, by 1836 most Latin American countries had shaken off their colonial overlords. American and European travelers descended on these highly exoticized places. Many made their way to newly independent South American republics, returning home with euphoric tales of experimenting with coca leaf. Paolo Mantegazza, an Italian neurologist who spent time in Peru's coca-growing region, noted a sense of being "drenche[d]" in a "new strength," "as a sponge soaks itself with water."[10] Mantegazza also saw coca as a healthier alternative to tobacco, writing that "the air which you make unhealthy for you and uncomfortable for others, will regain all its purity; and if you choose good quality coca, you will see that a pinch of leaves chewing gently, is as good as a few cigars and will warm your heart inside and outside."[11] Sigmund Freud, who experimented early with both coca leaf and cocaine, reported feeling "more vigorous and capable of work."[12] Researchers and pharmaceutical companies seized on these testimonials, importing coca leaves to study the plant's properties.

Soon coca products like tonics, tinctures, cordials, beer, and soft

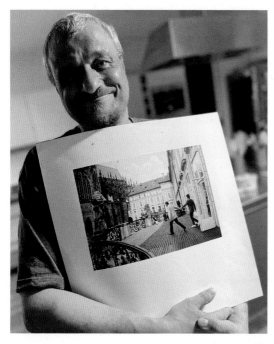

Roman Vaněk with a photograph of Václav Havel and Mick Jagger on the balcony of Prague Castle in 1990, right after the Velvet Revolution. For many Czechs and Slovaks, this photograph captures the moment when they emerged from behind the Iron Curtain to reclaim their rightful place in the West.

Photo: Michael Shaikh

Receptury teplých pokrmů or *Standards for Warm Meals* is the main cookbook that dictated the meals in communist-era eateries. Most Czechs and Slovaks were unaware of its existence. It was only after the Velvet Revolution that the public learned about the *Standards* and just how much the Communist Party of Czechoslovakia (KSČ) was dictating their culinary lives.

Photo: Michael Shaikh

Fresh blue swimmer crabs, the main ingredient in Eelam Tamil crab curry, at a fish market in Jaffna, Sri Lanka. Although the Tamil crab industry is back on its feet after the war, the best-quality crabs are reserved for export, which has priced many Tamils out of a cherished culinary staple.

Photo: Michael Shaikh

Stuffed rotis at New Kalyani restaurant in Scarborough in Ontario, Canada. Scarborough is home to one of the world's largest Eelam Tamil diasporas. New Kalyani owner and chef, Kumar Karalapillai, packs his version of this spicy short eat with a mixture of vegetables, curry leaves, and flakes of *maasi karuvadu*, a type of dried cured tuna often used in Eelam Tamil cooking to impart a deep savory flavor.

Photo: Michael Shaikh

Walking through Padmini's garden outside of Jaffna town in Sri Lanka.
Photo: Michael Shaikh

Rohingya cooks commonly use a knife called a *guwa dhaw*, which they use while sitting on the floor, steadying the knife under foot. Then meat, fish, fruit, or vegetables are cut by pulling the food toward their body through the blade. Here, a Rohingya refugee in Bangladesh uses a *guwa dhaw* to thinly slice *leyara*, a spindly spinach variety that is similar in form to asparagus.

Photo: Michael Shaikh

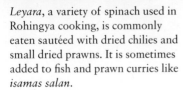

Leyara, a variety of spinach used in Rohingya cooking, is commonly eaten sautéed with dried chilies and small dried prawns. It is sometimes added to fish and prawn curries like *isamas salan*.

Photo: Ro Yassin Abdumonab

A typical kitchen in a family shelter in the Rohingya refugee camp in southern Bangladesh. The shelters are tiny and have two to three small rooms, ranging in total from 130 square feet to 500 square feet for a family of five to six people. Kitchens are dark and cramped and can function as sleeping areas at night as well.

Photo: Ro Yassin Abdumonab

Uyghur refugees in Istanbul learn to make noodles for *narin*, a nourishing soup made with lamb, onion, carrots, and cumin. Families, individuals, and institutions throughout the Uyghur diaspora have turned to cooking as a way to connect and protect that cherished part of their culture being erased by China's government.

Photo: Michael Shaikh

The disappearance of traditional Uyghur bakeries, which made traditional naan, was the first indication of the effort at cultural erasure by the Chinese in the Xinjiang region, which is home to ethnic Uyghurs.

Photo: Michael Shaikh

Marsia Taha's fried coca leaf chips in brown coca butter at Gustu in La Paz, Bolivia.

Photo: Michael Shaikh

Bolivian coca leaf.

Photo: Marcelo Pérez del Carpio

Juana Quispe (center) is a meticulous recordkeeper and incredible storyteller. Over cups of coca tea, Juana uses dozens of old newspaper clippings and pictures, to carefully navigate her daughter Dina (right) and the author (left) through the thicket that is the history of the drug war in the Chapare, Bolivia, and the emotional details of her arrest in 2003. This was the first time Dina heard her mother recount that experience.

Photo: Marcelo Pérez del Carpio

Marian Naranjo grinding amaranth and corn at the Flower Tree Permaculture Institute in the Santa Clara Pueblo, New Mexico. She has been central to contemporary efforts to reclaim and preserve vital aspects of Pueblo culture, and, for nearly three decades, has been at the leading edge of efforts to pressure the U.S. Department of Energy and the Los Alamos National Laboratory to take responsibility for the ongoing environmental and public health consequences of Manhattan Project–era explosive testing.

Photo: Michael Shaikh

Red amaranth growing at Ts'uyya Farm in Albuquerque, New Mexico. Ts'uyya Farm was founded by Reyna Banteah from the Zuni Pueblo; it is both a seed bank and farm that utilizes sustainable Pueblo farming methods to grow organic food for nearby communities.

Photo: Michael Shaikh

Ray Naranjo
Photo: Michael Shaikh

Manko, Ray Naranjo's food truck. Serving a fusion of Native American and New Mexican cuisine, Manko is known to have some of the best food around Santa Fe.

Photo: Michael Shaikh

Author learning to make tortillas in Mexico.

Photo: Bushman Photography

drinks infused with a coca-leaf extract, as well as chocolates, candies, and pâtés, could be found in the major American and European cities. Coca wines were extravagantly popular, which is not surprising, since alcohol enhances the effects of coca. The ethanol in the wine is a solvent, extracting the trace amount of the cocaine alkaloid from the coca leaf. When cocaine and alcohol mix inside a person, they create another drug called cocaethylene, which can make the drinker feel mildly euphoric.

Of all the coca wines, Vin Mariani was a culture-defining, runaway success. Writers like Mark Twain, Jules Verne, and Émile Zola all drank it. Rudyard Kipling, the most popular writer in the English-speaking world at the time, mused that Vin Mariani must be "compounded of the shavings of cherubs' wings."[13] Robert Louis Stevenson is said to have thought up his characters Jekyll and Hyde while drinking coca wine. The world's most famous actress, Sarah Bernhardt, was a fan. So were queens, presidents, and popes like Leo XIII, who carried a hip flask of Vin Mariani "to fortify himself in those moments when prayer was insufficient."[14]

Angelo Mariani, a Corsican chemist and bibliophile known for his lavish parties, developed his namesake wine in 1863 in France by infusing red Bordeaux with coca-leaf extract. Although he sold his product as Vin Mariani à la Coca du Pérou, Mariani sourced his leaves from Bolivia. In fact, he was the main importer of Bolivian coca leaf, using about twenty-two tons a year for his wine and other coca products his company made. It's hard to say what Vin Mariani tasted like, since it was banned more than a hundred years ago, but if it was anything like the version sold in the Coca Café outside Museo de Coca in La Paz, then it may have been slightly sweet with an amaro-like bitterness.

Vin Mariani's popularity inspired a range of imitators, most notably John Pemberton. Pemberton was a Confederate soldier in the

Civil War who was stabbed in the chest during a battle. He took morphine to deal with the pain but developed a dependency. Trained as a pharmacist, he allegedly weaned himself off morphine by blending fluid extract of coca leaf and wine. In the process, he founded Pemberton's French Wine Coca in Atlanta in 1885. But just as Pemberton's business took off, Georgia banned alcohol, rendering his beverage illegal because of the booze, not the coca. Pemberton replaced the wine in the formula with a sugar syrup, debuting his new drink in 1886 as "Coca-Cola: The Temperance Drink."[15]

Following the Civil War, America was in the grip of a disorienting cultural and technological shift, and coca became a palliative for a puzzling era. Americans were endlessly fascinated by exotic stimulant foods from their colonial holdings, like cacao, coffee, opium, sugar, rum, tea, and tobacco. But at the turn of the century, these were all proving too tame to cope with the pace of change.[16] Angelo Mariani marketed his tincture of Bordeaux wine and coca as having the ability to "brace body and brain" and "make the weak strong."[17] Others claimed their coca products would boost productivity and creativity. Coca-leaf extract soon became among the most widespread additives in popular remedies and tonics prescribed for a range of conditions, real and imagined.[18] By all accounts, these relatively mild coca-leaf products tasted good and were safe, if not harmless.

In 1860, in the early stage of the Western coca-leaf craze, Albert Niemann, a German chemist in Berlin, isolated the cocaine alkaloid. Working through thirty pounds of Bolivian coca leaf, he determined that cocaine constituted just about 0.25 percent of each leaf. Two years later, Emanuel Merck, one of the founders of the eponymous pharmaceutical giant, formulated cocaine hydrochloride—powdered cocaine—out of Niemann's discovery.

For the next twenty-five years, however, the science sat on a shelf until cocaine's medical value was finally proven in 1884 as a revolutionary and effective local anesthetic for surgeries. (Though in fairness to the Incas, they had used coca for its analgesic qualities for centuries.)[19]

Cocaine was a powerful drug; it was widely used in hospitals as an anesthetic during painful medical procedures. But it soon began circulating among the public alongside coca-leaf products. Then burgeoning, unregulated pharmaceutical companies pushed it on the masses through the patent-medicine industry.[20]

Mostly quack remedies, patent medicines were widely used at the turn of the twentieth century by just about everyone for their cure-all "secret formulas."[21] Their purveyors often plied these false medicines on the poor; they were cheap and could be bought without seeing a doctor. Cocaine-based patent medicines were peddled as panaceas for morphine addiction (not unlike the earlier version of Coca-Cola) and something called neurasthenia, a vaguely defined disease by today's standards but at the time widely diagnosed as a culturally oriented mental and physical illness brought on by the rapidly modernizing, disorienting American society.[22] But investigative journalists and doctors at the time routinely exposed them as often nothing more than colored water or alcohol mixed with large amounts of pure cocaine.

Then, in 1906, the federal government passed the Pure Food and Drug Act, the first anti-coca law, and forced patent-medicine manufacturers to disclose their formulas. The temperance movement sweeping the nation at the time prevented the Food and Drug Administration from distinguishing between high-potency *cocaine* products and low-dose *coca-leaf* goods. People like Angelo Mariani, the maker of Vin Mariani, pushed back, arguing that conflating cocaine products with coca-leaf ones was unfair and unwarranted. But Mariani failed, and within a decade, coca-leaf products disappeared from the United States.[23]

Next the government turned its attention to powdered cocaine, which by then had also become incredibly popular. Initially, the price of cocaine kept it in the hands of wealthier white people, lending this new party drug an air of legitimacy and exclusivity. Then, as prices dropped, the very people who had started the craze for cocaine grew into a powerful opposition force to ban it, often relaying sensationalist, racist fears about Black people abusing drugs. Stories with inflammatory headlines like "Negro Cocaine 'Fiends' Are a New Southern Menace," which ran in the main section of the Sunday edition of *The New York Times* in 1914, were clearly manufactured to terrify white people into supporting harsh drug policies.[24]

Rumors flew in the Jim Crow South that cocaine fiends were getting their fix at soda fountains.[25] As the historian Grace Elizabeth Hale points out, at the time, in Atlanta, Coke's home base, these were fashionable gathering places for middle-class whites as an alternative to bars and were where the drink caught on as an "intellectual beverage" among the well-off.[26] To get ahead of bad press, the company changed the drink's secret formula by removing all traces of the cocaine alkaloid from the coca leaves.

In 1914, Congress passed more anti-coca legislation with the Harrison Act. While that act didn't ban coca and cocaine outright, it did make it incredibly hard to obtain them without a license. The Coca-Cola Company, however, persuaded Congress to include an exception in the Harrison Act that permitted the use of "de-cocainized coca leaves or preparations made therefrom, or to any other preparations of coca leaves that do not contain cocaine." Only two companies—Merck & Co., Inc., and Maywood Chemical Works—were granted what were in effect monopoly licenses to import raw coca leaves. The

Coca-Cola loophole allowed Merck to import coca leaves for medicinal purposes, while Maywood (now the Stepan Company) was given permission to make Coke's secret formula.[27]

. . .

You don't often think of plants as audible beings, but coca has quite a noisy life in the Yungas, along the eastern slope of the Andes outside La Paz. The first time I visited a coca field outside the town of Coroico, a small town in the Yungas, I heard the crop before I saw it.

That day, Alberto rode alone at a fast clip ahead of our car on his lime-green motorcycle. Driving a few feet behind, I watched as he leaned muscularly into his turns, like a professional motocross racer, as he led us along winding high-mountain dirt roads. A jovial, short, and stocky Aymara man with jet-black hair in his early forties, Alberto is a *cocalero*, or coca farmer, who has occasionally sold his leaves to chefs and bakers in La Paz. In July 2023, he had invited me and Marcelo Pérez del Carpio, my translator and photographer, to walk the coca fields that have been in his family for generations.

Twenty minutes into our journey, Alberto slowed down, bringing his motorcycle alongside our car. Poking his smiling, chubby face through the passenger-side window, he instructed Marcelo and me to stop the car just ahead at a makeshift cul-de-sac. From there, Alberto said it would be ten minutes by foot as he led us into the brush along a gray rocky path. Halfway through the path, we found ourselves enveloped in a claustrophobic mix of tall grass the color of beach sand and spindly old gray mandarin trees with gnarled branches that looked like witch's fingers covered in lichen. Eventually we approached a clearing, and the sound of our feet scuffing over rocks was overwhelmed by a loud, persistent crackling, like kindling in a fire or light static electricity. A group of thirty *cocaleros* came into view directly ahead—old men, young women, some teenagers, some in their twenties, all lounging on the hillside. Off to one side, there was a tall woman with a small child, a girl she was holding by the arms, teaching her to stand. I saw they were talking, laughing, and listening to a radio. But I couldn't hear any of that over the fuzzy static all around us.

To my amazement, right beside me was the little source of that big sound, a three-foot-tall coca bush, its little dark-olive leaves fluttering in the breeze. The plant was a single instrument in a thousand-piece orchestra of coca covering miles of the steep, lush mountain valley. Once I understood the nature of the sound, the crackling static became something else: melodic, soothing, almost hypnotic; a soundtrack to the immense natural beauty of my surroundings. Marcelo and I sat down on a terraced part of the hillside a few feet from the woman playing with her child, and just listened to Alberto's coca field.

The Yungas is a subtropical forest in western Bolivia blanketing the high peaks that form a chain of jagged ridges undulating to the horizon, which you see only when the clouds give you permission. That day at Alberto's coca field, they had, and in spectacular fashion too. Alberto's field was roughly a quarter square mile, balanced precariously on a high ridge of a wide canyon plunging into a river thousands of feet below. From it you could see miles of creased mountainsides dotted with more coca fields, which the sunlight and cloud shadows that day had painted a million shades of green.

Alberto joined us a few moments later after briefly speaking with the *cocaleros,* wedging his stocky body between Marcelo and me to sit down. It was about 2:00 p.m. and my stomach reminded me I had eaten only a single orange for breakfast. Just then, Alberto passed a small plastic bag of dried, waxy-looking coca leaves to Marcelo and me. We thanked him and each took a small handful of ten to fifteen leaves, stacked and rolled them, and put them into our mouths between our cheeks and back teeth with a tiny bit of clay-like ash called *lejía*, which helps to release the trace amount of cocaine alkaloid in the leaves. After a minute or two of light chewing to soften the leaves, my mouth tasted grassy and sweet and my tongue was a little numb. A moment later the espresso-like buzz hit, slapping away my hunger pangs.

Before long, the group lounging on the hillside above Alberto, Marcelo, and me stood up and stretched before tying cotton sacks around their waists. Together the *cocaleros* ambled down the hill toward a terraced section of mountainside thick with coca plants, eventually funneling into a single line to go through the field's only entrance. As they moved deeper into the field, they fanned through the rows, each finding a spot to work. From above, the workers' colorful clothes set against the dark green coca field made me think of Jackson Pollock's *Convergence*, where the painter had flung bright primary colors onto a dark canvas. Soon the soft crinkling chime of coca leaves twisting in the wind in Alberto's field was overtaken by the sound of quick, syncopated snaps and cracks. At first, it was every second or two, but quickly the snapping was constant as the *cocaleros* found their picking rhythm.

Coca is mostly grown and harvested like this in two regions in Bolivia, the Yungas in the west and the Chapare in the east. The Yungas, where Alberto's field is located, produces approximately 60 percent of the country's coca crop. Since ancient times, Yungas families have grown just enough to meet their many quotidian needs, which were often deeply connected to cultural traditions. Under the Incas, however, coca was first cultivated at scale here on these terraced mountainsides to send to Cusco, the Incan capital.

The Spanish continued large-scale cultivation in the Yungas after conquering the Inca Empire in 1533. Initially, the Spanish banned coca as a pagan vice, but they took over its cultivation and trade in the colonial era to supply enslaved silver miners, who worked better with it. Their haciendas, or large feudal estates, continued to control Yungas coca even after Bolivian independence in 1825, until the Bolivian National Revolution of 1952 broke them up. Since then, the land has been owned by Indigenous families, like Alberto's, who grow coca, among other things, to supply domestic markets for chewing, tea, and medicines.[28]

The main variety of coca grown in the Yungas is called Huánuco; it was the plant the *cocaleros* were harvesting on Alberto's hillside. Each plant can live up to forty years and can be picked clean four to six times a year. The leaves of Yungas Huánuco are smaller than those of other coca varieties in Bolivia and are prized for their sweetness. One possible explanation for this is that Yungas Huánuco contains only 0.63 percent of the bitter cocaine alkaloid, whereas other varieties contain upward of 0.75 percent.[29] There's a polarizing debate, but some Bolivians consider Yungas Huánuco to be the best for chewing and teas, and it is the leaf that winemaker Angelo Mariani used in Vin Mariani in the nineteenth century. Most chefs, chocolatiers, bartenders, brewers, and distillers use this variety today.

With the rare exceptions of the coca leaf used in Vin Mariani and the thirty pounds that Niemann used to extract the cocaine alkaloid in Germany in 1860, Bolivia was never part of the global commercial coca trade that existed at the turn of the twentieth century.[30] In 1879, Bolivia lost its Pacific coastline in a war with Chile, making an already hard-to-reach country landlocked. Almost every American and European company, including Coca-Cola, went to Peru for its coca needs.

Even though it was a minor player in the global trade in the early twentieth century, Bolivia was still attuned to the United States' anticocaine politics. By the mid-1920s, Congress had banned all trade in coca and cocaine, as well as the production of cocaine in the country (the exception being Coca-Cola). But the United States wanted to take the ban global and in 1923 put cocaine on the world's agenda at the League of Nations (the precursor to the UN), where it attempted to designate the raw materials used to make illicit drugs as illegal themselves. Powerful coca growers in the Yungas were panicked, as was the Bolivian government in La Paz, which saw a stable source of tax revenue potentially disappearing.

A seasoned diplomat, Arturo Pinto-Escalier, was sent to Geneva, the headquarters of the League of Nations, to resist U.S. efforts to designate his country's indigenous coca an illegal international drug. Pinto-Escalier passionately defended the plant, attesting to the fact that in Bolivia there was neither a legitimate pharmaceutical cocaine industry nor an illicit one to speak of. And how could there be, he asked, when almost all of Bolivia's coca was consumed by its domestic market for chewing, brewing tea, and ceremonial uses? Any surplus that could theoretically be diverted to cocaine, he pointed out, was traded in Chile and Argentina, where it was chewed by miners. According to the transcripts, Pinto-Escalier was applauded for his remarks and for holding off America's nascent drug war for another few decades.[31]

●　●　●

By the end of World War II, America's breakup with coca was complete. Still, drugs were coming into the United States, and politicians in postwar Washington were panicked by reports of accelerating cocaine use by "alienated youth," "bohemians," and "urban minorities." Those in Washington saw this as another opening to take the domestic drug war global.

Yet the United States was unable to sell the idea that coca was a grave threat. To settle the question once and for all, the UN sent an expert commission to the Andes in 1950 to study coca. But the Americans stacked the commission with flunkies, who pushed the findings in profoundly biased and racially prejudiced directions. For instance, as its work was getting underway, Harry B. Fonda, a pharmaceutical executive who Washington handpicked to lead the commission, told journalists that coca chewing is "not only definitely harmful and deleterious, but is the cause of the racial degeneration of many population groups and of the decadence which is obvious in many native inhabitants, and even the half-castes, of certain regions of Peru and Bolivia." He went on to say, "Our studies will confirm the truth of our statements, and we hope to be able to submit a rational plan of action based on the realities of the situation and on experience in the field, to secure the total eradication of this pernicious habit."[32]

Ironically, the UN commission's final report ultimately stopped short of concluding that coca chewing was a form of addiction. However, the World Health Organization (WHO), which not only had sway over international drug policy, but was also heavily funded by the United States at the time, privileged the commission's racial biases over the factual lived reality of millions of Indigenous Andeans and concluded that coca chewing was the same as snorting cocaine. The WHO's decision eventually led the UN to designate coca leaf as a Schedule I drug alongside the most dangerous narcotics, such as heroin and cocaine, in the 1961 UN Single Convention on Narcotic Drugs.

But there was a catch. The Americans insisted that the Single Convention include the Coca-Cola loophole. Since the early twentieth century, the United States has ensured that this loophole has made it into every major piece of international drug-control legislation, making Coca-Cola the only consumer product that can legally be made with coca leaf and sold globally. In that regard, the government created a global monopoly for benign coca-leaf products. This still infuriates people throughout the Andean countries. Coca farmers and Indigenous groups, big and small business owners, and government ministers never failed to point out to me that Coke can sell and profit from safe coca products, but they can't.

With coca officially outlawed and conflated with cocaine at the global level, the United States and its South American partners have destroyed the prospects of millions of Andean and Amazonian farmers who could have made a living supplying a global industry making safe and enjoyable coca products. What's more, this pushed the cocaine business underground, spawning what is today a multibillion-dollar illicit cocaine economy. Not only did the drug war push the price of drugs to record lows, but it also sent drug use in new and perilous directions, unleashing horrifying violence and human rights abuses on low-income people of color across the Western Hemisphere. This war on the poor not only failed to curb U.S. demand for cocaine but also impoverished, wounded, and killed countless Bolivians, primarily Indigenous Andeans. A similar fate is still being inflicted on Colombians and Peruvians.

Today, the Single Convention remains the bedrock of the global international drug-control regime. It goes as far as requiring signatories to eradicate all coca bushes, even those that grow wild, as well as expressly banning coca leaf chewing—an ancient social practice that hasn't killed a single person in history. It's fair to say that the UN's decision to equate coca with cocaine was nothing short of a colonial crime perpetrated on South Americans.

. . .

Lush and green, with steamy valleys and rainforests, the Chapare region of Bolivia lies in the east of the country where the Andes meet the Amazon. A blast of polar air from the south, called the *surazo*, blew into Chimoré, a tiny town in the Chapare that sees more rain than sun, as I took refuge in the kitchen of Juana Quispe. Juana made a large pot of hot coca tea to keep us warm. In La Paz, coca tea is made simply by steeping dried coca leaves in hot water, giving it a faint green hue. But in the Chapare, Juana said, people prefer toasting their leaves before steeping them, turning their tea into beautiful shades of light gold and brown.

The Spanish referred to the Chapare as "La Ceja de la Selva" ("the jungle's eyebrow"). Residents call it "El Trópico de Cochabamba." At a nearly ten-thousand-foot drop in elevation from the high desert of La Paz, it is a wet and sultry place, with rainforest valleys sloping into the Chapare River, a distant tributary of the Amazon. In fact, the name "Chapare" is derived from the Quechuan phrase *ancha paran* ("it's really rainy"). The Chapareños, the people who live here, have a love-hate relationship with it. "The tropics can get cold without warning. Not everyone can handle the crazy weather, not to mention the mosquitoes," Juana said. "We have heat, humidity, and heavy, heavy rains. But it's home."

Juana had plucked the coca leaves for our tea a few days earlier. She had left them outside to dry on her patio on a tarp. In the first hours of drying, the air around them can be thick with an aroma of fermented citrus and mint. The leaves are dry enough for tea or chewing when their edges pucker and curl inward. But true *cocaleros* know they are dry by the soft tissue-paper sound they make. Juana switched on the stove and dropped a small handful of dried leaves into a saucepan.

On the wall of the kitchen were black-and-white murals of Che Guevara and Hugo Chávez, Juana's heroes. Her fourteen-year-old daughter, Dina, washed glasses for our tea in the kitchen sink as her mother steadied the saucepan, folding the coca leaves over one another with a wooden spoon to keep them from burning. The handful of greenish-gray leaves was nearly brown when Juana switched off the stove and poured over the hot water. She then added a heaping spoonful of turbinado sugar, which she told me smoothed out the tea's toasty bitterness. I took my first sips, waiting for the whisper of the coca's buzz to wash over me.

Much of Bolivia's recent history has taken place in the Chapare.[33] In the 1980s, the region was heavily militarized. In 1988, the UMOPAR (the Mobile Police Unit for Rural Areas), Bolivia's notorious counternarcotics police, trained and equipped by the United States, massacred a dozen unarmed coca farmers in Villa Tunari, the Chapare's largest town. Later the region was the site of Bolivia's Coca War, the brutal period of repression of coca farmers by U.S.-backed security forces from 1997 to 2003.[34] The Chapare is also the heartland of the MAS, the Movement Toward Socialism, the political party running Bolivia today. The party was formed in the Chapare in 1998 by Indigenous peasants and coca growers who organized to resist the war on drugs and who in 2005 catapulted Evo Morales, a fellow coca farmer, into the presidency. The MAS's stunning victory, partly based on the idea that some coca could be grown legally and that illegal coca could be eradicated peacefully, transformed and steadied the society, arresting decades of political chaos and countless coups.[35]

The Chapare is among the poorest regions of the country;

there are no high-end restaurants like Gustu here. Culturally and economically, the two places couldn't be further apart. Despite their distance, however, Gustu and the Chapare are deeply connected. The life-and-death political struggles, largely fought around the coca leaf by the people of the Chapare, created the space that allowed for a restaurant like Gustu to open. Gustu and the new Bolivian culinary movement would not exist without people like Juana Quispe.

I had to come to the Chapare not because Juana was a chef or a culinary historian or a home cook using coca leaf but because she had been closely involved with a groundbreaking movement as mayor of her town and later as a congresswoman who has changed the Chapare and Bolivia for the better. And because her activism had chiseled away at the notion that the "drug war" in Bolivia had to be violent or, indeed, a war at all.

"Would you mind if Dina stays with us?" Juana asked. "My daughter hasn't yet heard me tell the story that you came so far to hear." Juana gathered her hefty blue-and-white winter coat around her as she sat in a seat next to her daughter. I watched Dina's face blossom with curiosity as her mother unpacked tattered manila envelopes on the table in front of us. From each packet Juana carefully pulled dozens of black-and-white newspaper clippings, all from before Dina was born.

Juana handled each clipping like an old family heirloom. We watched as she moved her arms across the table like a maestro conducting an orchestra, carefully arranging and rearranging the clippings. She stood to get a bird's-eye view of the newspaper articles scattered across the smooth, worn surface of her kitchen table. Her eyes went searching, and then she cautiously lifted a yellowish sheet from the table. Sensing the worn page might disintegrate at any moment, she placed her hand underneath it. Her voice cracked as she read the headline: "Acusan cocalera de terrorismo" ("Female coca farmer accused of terrorism"). A single large tear rolled down her round, gentle face, which wore an unmistakable expression of defiance. "This one is about me," Juana said, reaching for her daughter's hand.

"It was a warm spring morning in September 2003. I was up early cooking that day. I was making potatoes, plantains, and some vegetables too, I think," Juana recalled. "Goni was in power then," she said, using the nickname for Gonzalo Sánchez de Lozada, the intensely pro-U.S. Bolivian president.[36] "We had a lot of family visiting. I was trying to get a head start on breakfast before everyone woke up." The next few moments were a blur, she said; then Juana and her five-month-old baby were in police custody.

The police had kicked down her door and dragged her from her kitchen; Juana was scared, but she was no stranger to this type of violence. For as long she could remember, the police had run roughshod over her Chapare community of coca growers. Known as "Leopards" for their camouflage uniforms, the counternarcotics police acted with impunity, barging into homes, abusing families, arresting farmers and then torturing them during interrogations. "It was a violent time," Juana explained as she rubbed Dina's hand.

• • •

Like Juana's family, most other coca growers in the Chapare are Quechua- or Aymara-speaking Indigenous peasants from the highlands who came here starting in the 1960s with the promise of free farmland. At the time, poverty was running high in their home communities, so the government encouraged migration to the Chapare to ease the pressure.[37] More migrants arrived in the 1980s during a severe economic crisis.

At the time, inflation was running at a staggering 16,000 percent. Driving some of this inflation was that the coca trade was funding the lavish lifestyles and spending of senior military officers who earned millions protecting drug traffickers. At the time, demand for cocaine in the United States and Europe was sky-high, Bolivia was the world's second-largest producer of raw and partially processed coca paste, and the Chapare was a hub of the regional drug trade. The illegal coca/cocaine trade—much of it based in the Chapare—at one point was making the country over one billion dollars a year, more than legal exports and foreign loans combined.[38]

To contain inflation, the United States and the International Monetary Fund (IMF) imposed a "shock therapy" plan developed by the American economist Jeffrey Sachs, which, most notably, required the government to close state-run mines. Although Sachs's shock therapy smothered hyperinflation, bringing it down to 10 percent within two years, it also killed off the working class's livelihood. Thousands of miners lost their jobs overnight. Homelessness soared and most families couldn't get enough food to eat. Miners and other newly jobless Bolivians were forcibly relocated to the Chapare, where the only work they could find was growing coca. Ironically for the United States and the IMF, shock therapy not only probably dampened the worst effects of the economic crisis but also may have unwittingly fueled Bolivia's cocaine economy.[39] Some scholars suggest the cocaine industry supported jobs for 10 to 20 percent of the Bolivian population.[40]

Given the magnitude of the illegal cocaine trade and the massive amounts of money sloshing around, it's easy to assume that coca farmers were driving Ferraris around the Chapare, living it up in gaudy narco-villas with gun-toting guards. But the reality was that most were living in flimsy wood shanties without running water or electricity. Hospitals and school buildings were nonexistent. "Schools were patches of dirt ground. Our children sat under a tarp or tree," Juana said. "Books?" she asked rhetorically, anticipating my question. "None."

Just as with poppies in Afghanistan, growing and selling coca leaves in the Chapare provided the only real source of income to keep families afloat. Coca is a wonder crop in many ways. It grows well at different subtropical altitudes. It has a long life (about four decades) and is resistant to pests. Crucially for cash-strapped farmers, it can be harvested four or more times a year.[41] And if dried properly, coca leaf doesn't rot, making it easy to store and transport. Farmers see their coca plots as "savings accounts," because in tough times they can sell their crops either to the legal markets in Cochabamba or to the illicit market. Selling coca into the legal market earns a farmer, on average, about four thousand dollars a year. Unsurprisingly, figures are murky, but a farmer may earn double that on the illegal market.

In 1998, Juana was in her twenties when the mousy-faced ex-dictator Hugo Banzer launched Plan Dignidad (The Dignity Plan), a blueprint for the total elimination of illegal Chapare coca within five years and the forced resettlement of a third of Chapare's population outside the region.[42] "When Banzer came here with Plan Dignidad, that's when the dirty war got worse," she said. She paused and then added, "That's when the DEA and the army started clearing our coca fields."[43]

Plan Dignidad may have been Bolivia's idea on paper, but it was America's project in practice. Unlike other U.S.-funded programs in Peru and Colombia, which aimed to convince coca farmers to switch to legal crops voluntarily, Plan Dignidad left farmers in Bolivia with no choice.[44] Under the plan, military conscripts directed by the Narcotic Affairs Section (NAS) of the U.S. embassy in La Paz fanned out over the Chapare, an area slightly larger than Connecticut, forcibly ripping out coca, a crop tens of thousands of peasants like Juana's family relied on as their only source of income.[45]

Juana became a local leader in the MAS opposition, a party that evolved out of the movement to defend coca growers from the violence of the U.S.-backed drug war. The MAS had become the second-largest party in parliament, and its leader, Evo Morales, an Indigenous Aymara coca grower and two-term congressman, made it clear he was coming for the presidency too. For decades, the Bolivian state had used violence to maintain a discriminatory system between light-skinned elites and the largely Indigenous majority. "They wanted to break the MAS by breaking me and my family. That's why I was arrested," Juana explained. Pausing to clasp Dina's hand in hers, she continued: "But they couldn't."

The Leopards had burst into her home before dawn, not once but several times. "They never knocked, only kicked their way in," Juana said. She described how the Leopards had once handcuffed her, beaten her, and then thrown her into a river. They did this to intimidate her into silence, she said, after she witnessed them murdering an unarmed farmer in his coca field during an eradication operation. Another time, she said, "they found a few dollars in the house, ten or twenty dollars, and accused us of being drug traffickers because they said only drug traffickers had dollars." They beat the men and sexually assaulted the women, including her young daughter at one point. "And they stole our food," she added.

These raids didn't just target her family. "Everyone in the Chapare experienced something similar," she explained. The type of "systematic terror policing" that Juana suffered at the hands of U.S.-backed drug police was so widespread that Bolivia's human rights ombudsman officially classified them as mercenaries, motivating the United States to push the government to grant immunity to its personnel in the country.[46]

But something was different that warm spring day in 2003 when police arrested Juana and her baby during breakfast. Rather than take her to the local army base for interrogation, they put mother and child on a plane to the capital, La Paz. "That's when the terror set in," she remembered. That's when Juana learned that President Lozada's government was charging her with terrorism and attempted murder. "They were going to send me to prison for thirty years," she said, still terrified by the thought. "Who would take care of my family, my children? That's all I could think about." She grasped Dina's hand even tighter as she wiped away another tear with her cuff.

This was the first time Dina had seen the article about her mother's arrest. The police told the journalist they had found dynamite and fuses in Juana's home. They accused her of plotting to blow up a local church and its congregation during Sunday service, when it would be most crowded. Juana didn't own any dynamite. The charges were absurd and concocted by lawyers working out of the NAS in La Paz.[47] Even the priest of the local church Juana was accused of attempting to blow up said as much. Eventually, MAS lawyers and congressmen like Evo Morales stepped in to help Juana get the charges dismissed.

• • •

In 2005, Evo Morales was elected president, promising a better deal for the nation's Indigenous people and an end to the drug war. Soon after he took power, he launched an audacious yet down-to-earth scheme to demilitarize the illegal coca eradication in places like the Chapare. The plan permitted farmers to grow a set amount of coca in specific zones for legal domestic consumption while allowing a modicum of space to self-police the limits, a concept officially called Community Coca Control.[48] At the same time, Morales continued to go after drug traffickers and cocaine producers.

In 2006, Morales's approach received unexpected support from a leaked UN report. In 1995, the WHO had conducted what is still probably the largest-ever study of cocaine use across the world. It sharply rebuked the United States, saying crop-destruction and law-enforcement strategies had failed. It singled out public anti-drug messages, saying they "perpetuate stereotypes and misinform the general public." Public health data, the WHO said, indicated that "occasional cocaine use does not typically lead to severe or even minor physical or social problems. . . . A minority of people . . . use casually for a short or long period and suffer little or no negative consequences." And finally, it said what Bolivians had known all along: The use of coca leaves appears to have no negative health effects. In fact, coca is a safe source of essential vitamins and even has "positive, therapeutic" effects.[49] The WHO report was never published because the U.S. representative to the WHO in 1995 threatened to withdraw U.S. funding for the organization unless it agreed to "dissociate itself from the conclusions of the study."[50]

Community Coca Control culminated in Bolivia's breaking entirely with the U.S. drug war in 2008 when Morales expelled the U.S. ambassador and the DEA from Bolivia. He kicked out USAID four years later.[51] The following year, Bolivia enacted a new constitution, incorporating one of the most comprehensive sets of rights for Indigenous communities anywhere in the world, including protection of coca as "cultural patrimony, as a renewable natural resource of the biodiversity of Bolivia, and as a factor of social unity." Notably, it also made explicit that "in its natural state, coca is not a narcotic."[52]

Most important, Community Coca Control ushered in a period of peace at the same time that government seizure of cocaine and destruction of drug labs steadily increased.[53] Violence and human rights abuses in the Chapare "stopped almost overnight," Juana told me. "We went from the darkness of night to living in the light of day." Today, compliance with the government's antidrug policies is enforced by community members and backstopped by a civilian, not a military, agency, generating almost no violence. Under the Community Coca Control scheme, Juana explained, "*cocaleros* and *campesinos* stopped being treated like criminals. Instead, we are treated like *compañeros,* like citizens." For the MAS and its many supporters, coca leaf became more than a centuries-long expression of Andean Indigenous culture and national sovereignty and unity; now it was also a resource to promote economic development.[54]

In 2009, Juana was elected to Bolivia's national parliament with roughly 90 percent of the vote. There she helped her party pass legislation to support the development of coca-leaf products. The law was based on the widespread distinction that millions of Bolivians make between coca and cocaine as a way to push coca leaf into a legal, safe market and away from an illegal, violent one. Since then, the Bolivian government has spent millions of dollars to incubate a market for coca products far beyond those for leaf chewing and ceremonial uses. Officials at Bolivia's Ministry of Agriculture told me there are at least twenty-one companies making coca-leaf products in the country today, products such as teas, wines, cakes, liquors, flour, energy drinks, candies, and even shampoos and toothpastes.

One such venture is El Viejo Roble, a distillery in the hills of western La Paz. It's hidden behind a corrugated-steel gate guarded by two big old dogs who are more likely to lick you to death than bite you. El Viejo Roble is managed by Adrián Alvarez Prieto, a tall, curious, and contemplative man with thinning gray hair and tinted glasses. El Viejo Roble has been in his family for three generations. It is a straightforward company, Adrián explained, one that makes affordable spirits that cater to the everyday person.

In the basement of the distillery, Marcelo and I looked on as Adrián pried the lids off two royal-blue fifty-five-gallon plastic drums. Inside each barrel, fifty pounds of coca leaves were submerged in alcohol, macerating to make a dark green, nearly black, viscous liquid. Adrián called us closer, gesturing to us to lean in and smell the concoction. I gently scooped the air over the barrel several times toward my face and inhaled. I braced myself to be bludgeoned by the blunt force of alcohol. Instead, I was kissed by the slightly sweet and piney aroma of the coca leaf.

Adrián put the lids back on the barrels and led us a few steps across the slippery distillery floor to a large, raised stainless-steel tank polished to a mirror shine. At the top, there was a small square hatch. Adrián pulled two small glasses from his soggy apron and submerged them in the tank, filling each with a crystal-clear liquid. "This was in the blue barrels. This is what happens to the coca leaf after distilling and filtering," he said, holding it up to the light above our heads. "*Salud,*" he said as he gently clinked his glass with ours. "This is Pachamama."

El Viejo Roble is one of a handful of distilleries in Bolivia using coca leaf in their spirits. Reminiscent of flavored vodka, theirs is named Pachamama (Mother Earth), after the widely revered Andean earth deity, who is the center of all life. Bolivia codified respect for Pachamama into law in 2012, establishing the land as sacred, a living system with rights to be protected from exploitation. To an outsider, it may appear tacky to name a bottle of booze after a deeply venerated being, but for many Indigenous Bolivians, coca leaves and alcohol are essential ritual offerings to her. Pachamama, the drink, embodies both, Adrián said through a smile.

Pachamama is distilled using organic coca leaves grown in the Yungas. It takes about twelve thousand pounds to produce five hundred bottles a year, Adrián explained.[55] Government regulations control how his coca leaf is procured, secured, and discarded to ensure that it doesn't end up in the illicit market. "It's an incredibly onerous process," he said. "But it's worth it; we wanted to make a truly Bolivian spirit, something different from *singani*," Adrián said, referring to Bolivia's brandy-like national spirit. "*Singani* is made with white grapes, which originally came from Spain. With Pachamama, we wanted to honor our own indigenous ingredient—the coca leaf—which is at the heart of Bolivia's identity."

Pachamama is a relatively new product for El Viejo Roble; production started eight years ago and has seen a moderate success. Adrián is eyeing the international market. He believes there's a lot of interest in his product abroad, but the UN convention makes it impossible to expand business beyond Bolivia. It's the same for Gustu's former chef Marsia Taha, who is often invited to cook abroad. "I dream of cooking coca in other countries," she told me. "People would love it. But you can't take it with you. You get arrested for having it in most places."

In May 2024, the WHO announced it would launch a scientific review to reconsider coca's status as a Schedule I narcotic, the same as cocaine. It is the first step in the formal process to decriminalize the coca leaf worldwide. Based on its findings, the WHO may recommend changes in coca's classification under UN drug-control treaties. The WHO recommendations would then be submitted to the UN Commission on Narcotic Drugs for approval, with voting likely in 2026. Washington has signaled openness to the WHO's study but not to legalization at this point.[56]

According to John Walsh and Martin Jelsma from the Washington Office for Latin America, a drug-policy and human rights organization, changing coca's status in the UN Single Convention would restore the rights of Indigenous peoples and even help open legal international markets for natural coca products, "fortifying Andean economies while bringing coca's benefits to increasing numbers of people around the world."[57]

A legal global coca-leaf market is not a panacea for the world's cocaine problems. But neither is criminalizing and maligning peasant coca farmers as the cause of cocaine misuse. Bolivia's community-control strategy is not without flaws, but it does prove you can make headway on curtailing illicit coca without committing human rights abuses.

That said, culinary and other natural uses of coca don't demand a lot of leaves. And there is a risk that removing coca from the UN drug treaties could turn into a Pyrrhic victory. A sudden glut of legal coca could tank its price, which would be bad for hundreds of thousands of farming families who live off the leaf. But there are possible solutions, like South Africa's agreement between the Khoisan people and the industry behind the herbal tea rooibos, under which a percentage of profits are paid to the Indigenous people who used the plant before production was industrialized. The challenge will be doing this at scale with coca without repeating the tragedies of earlier alternative-livelihood programs.

• • •

Light had suddenly flooded Juana Quispe's home. I could see through the window a large break in the rain clouds. The *surazo,* the cold front that had smothered the Chapare, was finally moving on.

Sitting at her kitchen table, Juana told me she had once been invited to Gustu, the restaurant in La Paz. She asked me if they were still cooking with coca leaf. I opened my phone to show her the pictures I had taken of Marsia's coca-leaf chips and butter.

I asked Juana how she felt about a restaurant that catered to wealthy Bolivians and tourists cooking with coca when most people in the Chapare couldn't afford to eat there.

She thought for a moment before replying. "Why should I be angry?" she said. "In fact, I am proud. That's what we fought for."

Juana's Mate de Coca

(Coca Leaf Tea)

Makes 4 to 6 servings

This is the tea Juana made for me at her home in Chimoré, in Bolivia's Chapare region. It is the perfect antidote to altitude sickness or a cold day and a wonderful alternative to an espresso. Unfortunately, there are no substitutes for coca leaf. You might just have to go to Bolivia for this tea.

30 to 40 dried coca leaves, plus
more for serving (optional)
4 to 6 cups water

Honey and/or lemon wedges
for serving

1. Put the coca leaves into a small saucepan, place over low heat, and toast the leaves until they darken to the color of chocolate, 1 to 2 minutes, shaking the pan now and again to prevent the leaves from burning.
2. Add the water to the pan—using the smaller amount for a stronger tea and the larger amount for a weaker tea—increase the heat to high, and bring to a boil. Turn down the heat and simmer until the water turns dark gold, 3 to 5 minutes. Turn off the heat and let sit for 10 minutes.
3. Strain the tea through a fine-mesh sieve into cups. Add a couple of leaves from the sieve to each cup or add a fresh dried leaf to each cup if desired. Serve with the honey and/or lemon to taste.

Marsia's Terrina de Demi y Ñames de Hongos con Payuje y Ensalada de Palmito

(Mushroom and Yam Terrine with Payuje and Heart of Palm Salad)

Make 3 to 4 servings

A few days before I submitted this book to my publisher, Marsia Taha was named Latin America's Best Female Chef of 2024 by 50 Best Restaurants. A few days later, Marsia announced she was leaving Gustu to open her own restaurant in La Paz called Arami, which in Guaraní means "a shard of heaven." At Gustu, Marsia cooked with ingredients from across Bolivia, but at Arami, she will focus on ingredients from the Bolivian Amazon.

Arami is scheduled to open at the end of 2024 and this terrine will be on the menu. Mushrooms are the star ingredient of this dish. This mushroom terrine is topped with a rich mushroom vegetarian demi-glace that is balanced with a heart of palm salad spiked with banana vinegar and served with a twist on *payuje,* a traditional sweet banana-based drink from Beni, a region in the Bolivian Amazon. In Marsia's version of *payuje,* the bananas are roasted for hours in the oven at very low temperature, producing a sweet and toasty, almost nutty flavor. I never imagined bananas and mushrooms working well together, but they do in this recipe.

I find this dish emblematic of contemporary Bolivian cuisine, mixing cultures, cooking, and ingredients in surprising ways. It doesn't include coca leaf, but it does call for two other (somewhat) hard-to-find ingredients: banana vinegar and fresh hearts of palm. With some work you can find both online. Sadly, canned hearts of palm don't really work here; they just don't have the necessary crunch. But don't let this deter you from making the terrine. I've found that green papaya works as a decent substitute for fresh hearts of palm. If you can't find fresh hearts of palm or green papaya, you can easily serve the terrine with a bright, tangy green salad with a few berries.

You can bake the terrine in your oven, or you can cold-smoke the mushrooms and cook the terrine on a grill. This is a time-consuming recipe, so you might wait for a weekend to make it, but it's worth the effort. So is going to La Paz and eating Marsia's food, as well as visiting the city's other tremendous restaurants.

PAYUJE

3 large or 5 medium firm bananas
    or plantains, peel kept on
    (see Notes, page 184)

6 tablespoons unsalted butter
2 tablespoons whole milk
¼ teaspoon kosher salt

TERRINA DE DEMI Y ÑAMES DE HONGOS (MUSHROOM AND YAM TERRINE)

3 ounces dried mushrooms, such
    as matsutake
2 tablespoons olive oil
½ carrot, coarsely chopped into
    chunks
1 small white onion, ½ coarsely
    chopped and ½ finely diced
Kosher salt and freshly ground
    black pepper

½ yam, peeled
½ pound fresh mushrooms, such
    as lion's mane, trumpet,
    oyster, or shiitake
7 tablespoons unsalted butter,
    plus more for serving
3 garlic cloves, minced
2 tablespoons heavy cream

ENSALADA DE PALMITO
(HEART OF PALM SALAD)

¼ pound fresh hearts of palm
½ cup sliced seasonal berries,
    such as blueberries,
    raspberries, or strawberries
    (see Notes, page 184)

1 bunch mint leaves
1 tablespoon banana vinegar, plus
    more as needed
Kosher salt

1. Make the payuje: Preheat the oven to 175°F. Line a sheet pan with parchment paper and roast the bananas until the peels are black with a slightly reddish hue, 6 to 8 hours, until the skin feels rubbery and springy when pressed with a finger and the inside feels soft but not mushy. Start checking after 6 hours. Don't worry about rotating the bananas but the skins should turn black within the first hour. Resist the temptation to take them out of the oven—they need time to develop their flavor. Remove the bananas from the oven and let cool for a few minutes (see Notes, page 184). Carefully remove the peels and add the banana to a blender along with the butter, milk, and salt. Blend on low until you get a smooth and creamy but slightly thick mixture, stopping to scrape down the sides of the blender jar as needed, 30 seconds to 1 minute. The payuje can be made up to 2 days in advance and stored in an airtight container in the refrigerator.

2. Make the terrina: Place the mushrooms in a large bowl and cover with 8 cups of filtered water for 8 to 12 hours or overnight. Strain the rehydrated mushrooms through a fine-mesh sieve into another large bowl, reserving the mushroom water. Rinse the mushrooms gently and set aside.

3. In a large skillet over medium heat, warm the oil. Add the carrots and the chopped onion and sauté until the carrots have caramelized, 10 to 12 minutes. Add the reserved mushroom water, ½ teaspoon salt, and a few grinds of pepper and bring to a boil over medium-low heat. Cook until the carrots and onion are softened, stirring occasionally, about 15 minutes. Using a slotted spoon, remove and discard the carrots and onions. No solids should remain in the pot. Continue to simmer the broth until it has thickened to the

consistency of a thin syrup and is the color of balsamic vinegar, 1½ to 2 hours.

4. While the broth simmers, bring a medium pot of water to a boil. Add the yam and cook until soft. Remove from the heat and strain the yam through a fine-mesh sieve. Once cool, grate the yam pieces on a Microplane into a bowl.

5. Using a food processor or knife, finely chop the rehydrated and fresh mushrooms. In another large skillet over medium-low heat, melt the butter. Add the garlic and cook until golden brown, about 3 minutes. Add the diced onion and cook for another 5 minutes, until both alliums are golden. Add the chopped mushrooms along with ½ teaspoon salt and a few grinds of pepper. Mix thoroughly and cook until the mushrooms absorb all the butter and the pan is beginning to dry, about 10 minutes, then remove from the heat.

6. Preheat the oven to 350°F and line a loaf pan with parchment paper. In a bowl, combine the cooked mushrooms with the grated yam and mix in the heavy cream. Transfer the mixture to the loaf pan and bake for 20 minutes or until the top is beginning to crisp. Alternatively, smoke and bake on a grill (see Notes).

7. Make the ensalada: Using a vegetable peeler, slice ribbons of heart of palm and then slice the strips even finer with a knife. Alternatively, use a mandoline. In a medium bowl, toss the heart of palm with the berries, mint leaves, banana vinegar, and the salt to taste. Set aside for a few minutes to let the vinegar and berries mingle. (The salad should be bright and tangy to balance the richness of the mushrooms.)

8. Let the terrine cool to room temperature. When ready to serve, cut it into thick slices. In a large skillet over medium heat, melt a tablespoon of butter and, working in batches, fry each terrine slice until golden spots form, about 1 minute on each side. Place each slice in bowl. Drizzle with the mushroom demi-glace and top with the ensalada. Serve with a dollop of the payuje on the side.

NOTES

I have made this recipe at home a few times and have learned that in a pinch, you can skip roasting the bananas in the oven if you have good-quality ripe bananas or plantains. The *payuje* won't be as nutty or deep as intended, but it will work if you're short on time.

You need a combination of fresh sweet and tart berries for the salad. For the best flavor, you'll need to slice them into small pieces. It can be tedious, but it will help release their juices and allow the berries to macerate and mingle better with the strands of palm heart (or green papaya), making each bite tastier.

To bake the terrine on a gas grill, prepare a cold smoker device, like a smoke tube. Transfer the cooked mushroom mixture to a grill-safe pan, place the pan on the grill next to the smoker, close the lid (but don't light the grill), and cold smoke for 1 hour. Open the lid and remove the pan and smoker device from the grill. Then light the grill and preheat to 350°F. In a bowl, combine the smoked mushroom mixture with the grated yam and mix in the heavy cream. Transfer the mixture to a loaf pan and return to the grill. Close the lid and cook until the top is beginning to crisp, 20 to 25 minutes.

6

The Pueblo Nations

Amaranth and the Return of the Fourth Sister

THE FIRST TIME I remember tasting amaranth was in Ray's tortillas at the Indian Pueblo Kitchen in downtown Albuquerque in the summer of 2021. Ray was the executive chef then, and he had used a combination of amaranth and corn flour to make me a stack of floppy, round tortillas, each the size of a large sand dollar, to eat with a plate of bison ribs he had braised in juniper. Dusty and faintly golden, they were heavier than their size suggested and tore perfectly with just the right amount of resistance without leaving a frayed edge. When I bit into one, the tortilla momentarily hugged my teeth in a warm embrace before giving up its nutty, malty, and subtly sweet flavor.

Ray Naranjo is a Native American chef from Santa Clara Pueblo in northern New Mexico. He's a big, affable man with a wide, warm smile, built more for a football field than his food truck, Manko. After leaving the Indian Pueblo Kitchen a few years ago, Ray opened Manko, a food truck and catering business serving a fusion of Native American cuisine—mostly from his Pueblo traditions—and New Mexican and Western food. A regular fixture of festivals and food events across the state, Manko is arguably New Mexico's most beloved food truck. "When Ray was a boy, we didn't have much money most days," his mother, Marian Naranjo, a famous potter and Indigenous activist, told me. "Once in a while, the kids had to fend for themselves. They were all responsible for the house and each other when I was working," she recalled. Ray, she said, hated to clean, so he cooked. The second youngest of her four children, Ray was her most sensitive but also her most curious child. "Ray would just walk around Santa Clara, sometimes eating from trees, using old knowledge," she told me at her home on the Santa Clara reservation outside Española, New Mexico. "Learning to eat well from the earth."

Ray was around ten years old when he first thought of becoming a chef. "When I was a little kid, instead of going on a hunting trip with the elders, I stayed home and cooked Thanksgiving dinner. My mom was a hunter because we were part of the hunter clan, and when they came home, I had cooked a pretty big dinner. I am pretty sure I knew I wanted to be a chef then," Ray told me.[1] "I used to watch cooking shows on TV as a kid. There's no way we could afford the ingredients on those shows. But I would kinda get creative with what we had back then and try to re-create versions of what I saw on TV, like stuffed burgers."

Today, Ray is in his mid-forties and has been a professional chef for most of his adult life. After culinary school, like many other Indigenous chefs of his generation in the United States, Ray cooked in the kitchens of reservation casinos before focusing on his own Pueblo cuisine and working his way into the top job at the Indian

Pueblo Kitchen at the Indian Pueblo Cultural Center in Albuquerque. Then, in May 2022, Ray set off on his own to start Manko. In Tewa, Ray's ancestral language, *manko* means "come and eat."

Ray's home, Santa Clara Pueblo, sits in the shadow of Los Alamos, on the banks of the Rio Grande. In Tewa, Santa Clara Pueblo is called Kha'Po Owingeh (Singing Water Village). There are nineteen Pueblo tribes in New Mexico today; each is a sovereign nation on a federally recognized reservation with its own government. The Pueblo tribes share a common history, as well as aspects of culture, but remain diverse peoples, speaking several different languages and dialects. Hundreds of years ago, the Pueblo homeland reached from its heartland in New Mexico into Colorado and Arizona, but today, most Pueblo reservations are located, like Santa Clara, along the upper reaches of the Rio Grande in New Mexico.

Over the past few years, Ray has patiently introduced me to Pueblo cuisine. Traditional, pre-European Pueblo food follows the seasons and is deeply rooted in the land of the nineteen nations. At the heart of its culinary philosophy is the belief that people are *within* and *part* of their ecosystem, not separate from it. Pueblo cooks use corn, beans, and squash, as well as wild onions, mushrooms, purslane, and juniper. Piñon nuts and pumpkin seeds add texture to dishes. Bison, elk, deer, fish, and regional birds are important animals. Honey and berries like currants, chokeberries, and blueberries add sweetness. Dishes are flavored with epazote, sage, mint, *cota,* and wild parsley and seasoned with native chilies and, most important, salt that the Pueblo people traditionally harvested from the Zuni Salt Lake and the Estancia Valley, both in New Mexico.

Wheat, dairy, beef, pork, chicken, and spices like black pepper are not part of heritage Pueblo cooking, as most of these were introduced by Europeans. But Ray, like other Pueblo chefs, often incorporates them into his contemporary fusion cooking. Ray also cooks with amaranth, another ancient precolonial ingredient often used in Pueblo cuisine. In one form or another, amaranth is usually on the menu at Manko, as in the Native Berries and Bird Seed Salad—a colorful and gratifying bowl of spinach tossed with quinoa, heirloom tomatoes, feta, and sunflower and pumpkin seeds, dressed in vinaigrette made with local berries, and then topped with popped amaranth to add a malty crunch.

· · ·

Amaranth is sometimes referred to as the Fourth Sister to the sacred Three Sisters—corn, beans, and squash—which are at the heart of not only Pueblo cuisine but also the cooking of many Native American nations.[2] In her book *Braiding Sweetgrass*, Robin Wall Kimmerer, a botanist and a member of the Citizen Potawatomi Nation, talks about the grammar of animacy among Indigenous languages to address the nonhuman living world, like plants and animals, as well as objects, places, and landscapes imbued with sacred meaning: "Imagine seeing your grandmother standing at the stove in her apron, then saying of her, 'Look, it's making soup. It has gray hair.'" She points out that in English, we never refer to anyone, especially not a family member, as "it." That would, of course, be deeply disrespectful. "*It* robs a person of selfhood and kinship, reducing a person to a mere thing." In most Indigenous languages, she says, "we use the same words to address the living world as we use for our family. Because they are our family."[3]

Amaranth is not my family in that sense. But I have spent so much time with her, and with people for whom she is family, that I can't help but show her that same grammatical respect. She has many varieties, but I am most familiar with *Amaranthus cruentus* (red amaranth). She is an endearingly beautiful plant with a tall, slender, but sturdy red stem decorated with wide, flat, fluttering mint-green leaves that taper toward the top, giving way to bundles of soft, finger-like flowers the color of plums or an old brick path soaked by rain. These flowers always seem to lean in your direction, seeking your attention, wanting to gently stroke your head as you walk by.

The human relationship with amaranth is ancient. Grown all over the world but native to the Americas, amaranth was first cultivated by the Olmec and the Maya some eight thousand years ago, not only because of the plant's beautiful plumes but also because of what they contained within. Each of her bright, floppy crimson fingers contains thousands of highly nutritious pinhead-sized seeds. Her nutrient-dense, peppery leaves can be eaten like spinach.[4] Friends with roots in Tamil Nadu in South India often make *pooriyal,* a stir-fry of fresh amaranth leaves, chilies, and coconut.[5]

Gardeners adore amaranth for her ornamental flowers, which remain bright long after they're dried. The plant's name is derived from a Greek word meaning "unfading" or "immortal."[6] Health food enthusiasts proclaim her yet *another* "superfood," and as they did avocados, quinoa, and goji berries, they have turned amaranth into a billion-dollar industry.[7] Climate activists also evangelize the plant as a food for the future because she resists drought, grows fast, and tolerates tough soils. In fact, amaranth is right at home in a high New Mexico desert, in a crack in a New York City sidewalk, or even in space, where NASA grew some in the 1980s. Big Ag fears varieties of amaranth as an existential threat to industrial crops, since the plants are unperturbed by the industry's arsenal of weed killers.

Like her relative quinoa, amaranth is technically a pseudocereal and is naturally gluten-free. The seeds contain all nine essential amino acids, making amaranth among the most protein-dense edible plants on earth. The seeds are also rich in lysine, an amino acid lacking in corn. So when Ray toasts and grinds amaranth seeds into a flour, or masa, and mixes it with a corn masa, the result is not only a delicious tortilla but also a far more nutritionally balanced food.

Braised bison with amaranth tortillas is a dish Ray is particularly proud of—one that displays the diversity of Native cuisines in North America: bison meat, a staple of Great Plains nations like the Arapaho, Crow, and Sioux; juniper, a common ingredient in Pueblo and Diné (Navajo) cooking; and amaranth and corn tortillas, a tradition dating back thousands of years to the ancient Maya.[8] The Ancestral Puebloans, Ray's ancestors, who lived across the northern Southwest until the arrival of the Spanish in the sixteenth century, also had a tradition of eating amaranth and corn tortillas. The Ancestral Puebloans had grown corn for thousands of years, but amaranth is a relatively recent addition to Pueblo food, something they started growing only about eight hundred years ago.[9]

Like corn, amaranth was venerated in Indigenous societies in the Americas before the European invasions. Colonial Spanish Catholics outlawed amaranth five hundred years ago across their "New World" colonies. Believing it was sacrilegious, they attempted to decimate it throughout the Americas with a myopic crusading zeal akin to today's drug war to eradicate the coca leaf. "Amaranth was embedded deeply into our ancestral culture. It was an important part of our cuisine that also connected us to our Creator. But the Spanish took it from us, and then the United States came and changed things even more," Ray explained during one of our first conversations, referring to the back-to-back colonialisms the Pueblo people have endured since the late 1500s. "It's only really in the past few years that we've been able to really bring amaranth back now," he said, with a sense of pride.

The Pueblo people point out that New Mexico is the oldest colony in what is today the United States. Since the late fifteenth century, their nations, as well as other Indigenous nations, have had their land occupied almost continuously, first by Spain, then briefly by Mexico, and finally by the United States. Although the Pueblos' experience with each colonial power was distinct, the common element is that they all intentionally divided Indigenous people not just from one another but also from their cultures.

Much like the people who first grew amaranth on the continent, the plant itself endured centuries of violence and erasure. Perhaps what's most important about this story is that the heroic persistence of the Pueblo people to remain, now and forever, in their world proves beyond all doubt that saving a food culture is the same thing as saving lives.

. . .

A graceful and warm woman in her seventies, Marian Naranjo, Ray's mother, is many important things. An elder of the Santa Clara Pueblo nation, she is, as a friend described her, "a serious activist and antinuke campaigner, not to be fucked with." Marian has battled Los Alamos National Laboratory, the site of the Manhattan Project, for dumping nuclear waste on nearby sacred Indigenous land. She is also a proud grandmother of eight who let slip one night that, in her younger days, she had once partied backstage with Alice Cooper and Redbone.

In 2004, Marian founded Honor Our Pueblo Existence (H.O.P.E.), an organization based on her reservation and aimed at strengthening her community through environmental- and cultural-protection projects. On a cold, windy afternoon, the kind where the sunlight flickers from the low clouds racing over the mesas, Marian, Ray, and I warmed ourselves by a fire in the corner of a long adobe building next to their home on the Santa Clara Pueblo. It was a special place with deep meaning for Marian and Ray's community. A few years earlier, Marian, along with friends and relatives, had built the house by hand. Today, it is where Marian teaches younger generations to make an ancient bread called *buwah*.[10]

Adorned with buffalo skins and elk and deer antlers, the house was a ceremonial space as much as a teaching one. Dug into the earthen floor in front of us was a shrine, a shallow round hole filled with freshly ground cornmeal. Four ears of corn, each a different sacred color—red, blue, white, yellow—pointed outward from the circle in the directions of the four cardinal mountains that delineate the Tewa Pueblo world, on top of which are sacred sites. In a tone just above a whisper, Marian explained: "It symbolizes our universe."

As we took in the sweet, earthy aroma of the resinous piñon wood cracking in the fire, Marian explained how *buwah* is made. She pointed across the room to a row of a dozen or so wide, flat stones, each a different shape and size. Some had a rugged look; others seemed intentionally formed into rectangular slabs. On top of each flat stone was a smaller one shaped like a rolling pin. "In Tewa, they are called O', and they came from our sacred mountains," Marian said. And like mortars and pestles, they are used to grind corn or amaranth into flour for *buwah*.

Buwah is a thin and flaky bread, almost like phyllo, that shatters in your mouth. It takes tremendous skill to grind blue corn and amaranth into flour fine enough to achieve that tissue-paper thinness. Marian showed me how she does it. I stood mesmerized as she moved her arms rhythmically over the O'. The energy flowing from her core was calibrated by her shoulders, elbows, and wrists, while the pestle-like stone had almost become an extension of her hands. With every motion, I watched how she adjusted its pressure and angle ever so slightly to ensure an even grind and a powdered sugar–like fineness.

Once ground, the amaranth and corn flours are mixed with juniper or corn-husk ash and water to make a thin batter. *Buwah* batter is always made with blue corn flour, but some will add amaranth flour directly to the batter, while others will use it just to add color to the bread. With the latter method, cooks soak amaranth flowers in water overnight to make a maroon dye. In the morning, the dye is added to the batter, giving the bread a deep purplish hue.[11]

Marian guided me through a wooden door at the end of the long room and into another small single-room building, which she entered with the reverence of a temple. Inside, on the far wall in each corner, were two clay ovens licked black with flames. In front of each oven were two heavy, flat cooking stones, noticeably larger than the grinding stones in the other room. We stood in silence for a moment, almost in prayer, before Marian told me we were in the *buwah tewha*, a kitchen built for the singular purpose of baking *buwah*.

"Our ancestors used stones like these to make *buwah*," she said. She explained they were occasionally seasoned like a cast-iron pan with the oil of ground squash seeds to keep them in good cooking shape. To bake *buwah*, the stones are heated from underneath with hot coals, then lightly greased with elk or deer brain. The bluish-purple batter is spread thinly across the stone as if making a crêpe or a *dosa*. In seconds, a paper-thin sheet of bread forms and must be removed quickly yet gently. Then a second sheet is made. Right before the second sheet is finished, the first sheet is layered on top for a few seconds to soften. Both sheets are then removed from the stone and gently folded together into thirds, making a parcel the size of a tamale. *Buwah* can be eaten alone or held longways and dipped into stews like an edible spoon. The *buwah* that Marian made for me had a subtle, earthy flavor and were slightly sweet with a gentle tang.

. . .

There's a chapter in the historian Roxanne Dunbar-Ortiz's book *An Indigenous Peoples' History of the United States* that forever altered my understanding of roads and highways in North America. At the time of the European invasions, she explains, Indigenous peoples had occupied and shaped every part of the North and South American landscape. Colonial settlers didn't come upon virgin forest or empty deserts and prairies. Rather, they arrived on continents that had already been carefully sculpted to sustain human and nonhuman life, to foster communication and trade among Indigenous societies from the Amazon to Alaska and from the Great Lakes to the Great Plains.[12]

Dunbar-Ortiz, citing work by other scholars, also describes how early European explorers were mesmerized by the spacing of trees, how their horses could gallop safely through a forest without stopping, and how the forests "could be penetrated even by a large army." But the trails and roads they found were not dirt paths in the woods winding along animal tracks. Nor were they well-worn routes used by nomadic people during seasonal migrations. They were intentionally created by the Indigenous peoples as "an extensive system of roadways that spanned the Americas, making possible short, medium and long distance travel." Later the roadways were "adopted by the early settlers and indeed were ultimately transformed into major highways."[13]

The ancestors of today's Pueblo peoples also built hundreds of miles of roads radiating out from northern New Mexico. Averaging thirty feet wide, these roads cut straight through rocky terrain, connecting dozens of Pueblo communities living along the Rio Grande to one another and to other networks of roads leading into the wider world. One of them was the roughly 1,600-mile road that connected South America with the Southwest. Known today by its Spanish colonial name, Camino Real de Tierra Adentro (Royal Road of the Interior), it is far older than its name suggests. For centuries before the Spanish, it facilitated trade in everything from seeds to ideas, and it was likely on this intercontinental highway that amaranth found its way to the Pueblos.

At the northernmost edge of the Pueblo road system is the Taos Pueblo, the longest continuously inhabited community in the United States. Sitting in the shadow of the Sangre de Cristo Mountains, the southernmost range of the Rockies, and close to several rivers, Taos was an important trading center, drawing people and goods from the Pacific Ocean to the west and the Great Plains to the east, from the Canadian Rockies to the north, and from as far south as Central America. At Taos, turquoise from the Pueblo and Diné lands in the Southwest and buffalo products from the plains could be traded for tropical birds, feathers, copper, shells from the Caribbean, and chilies, vanilla, cacao, and amaranth from Mexico.

Amaranth had a profound impact on pre-European Pueblo society. Porter Swentzell, a historian from Santa Clara Pueblo and Marian's relative, told me that corn arrived in the Southwest from Mexico about four thousand years ago. Initially, he explained, corn wasn't as prized as it is now. Among the reasons, corn lacked lysine, a critical amino acid, making it hard for humans to digest. That changed a thousand years later when amaranth, along with other lysine-rich foods such as beans and squash, made its way into Pueblo lands.[14] The Pueblos found that when corn was paired with a lysine-dense food such as amaranth, it became both more nutritious and easier to eat.

What's more, Porter sees a connection between the appearance of lysine-dense foods in Pueblo cuisine and New Mexico's iconic adobe architecture. "It's not surprising to learn that agriculture became important around here with the arrival of these crops," he writes, referring to amaranth, beans, and squash. Porter's writing points out that these foods led Pueblo communities to settle along the upper reaches of the Rio Grande, where villages started out as groups of pit houses dug into the ground, later graduated to stone buildings, and then eventually developed into the architectural style of red multilevel adobe settlements that Spanish conquistadores would name *pueblos*.[15]

· · ·

When Hernán Cortés arrived in the Valley of Mexico in the fall of 1519, the Aztecs were cultivating nearly a million acres of amaranth, an area five times the size of Los Angeles, making it among the most important and valuable crops in the world at the time. Montezuma, one of the last Aztec rulers, demanded twenty thousand tons of amaranth annually as tribute.[16]

Along with corn, beans, and chia, amaranth was important to the Aztecs, as well as other Mexica people. The Mexica popped amaranth seeds, boiled them like a cereal, and ground them into a flour for tortillas and tamales.[17] The Mexica also considered amaranth a divine plant. It was used in dozens of Aztec and Mexica rituals, large and small.[18] At birth, infants were anointed with an amaranth paste and were presented with edible figurines molded from a sweet, sticky mixture of popped amaranth and agave sap or honey. These amaranth figurines, called *zoales,* would be in the shape of a deer or a bow to foretell the child's future as a fast runner or a skilled hunter.[19]

We have a good idea of what *zoales* tasted like too. Whenever I am in Mexico I stock up on packages of *alegrías,* round and crunchy confections of popped amaranth welded together with agave. The food writer Ligaya Mishan describes them as "a proto–Rice Krispies Treat."[20] With a name meaning "happiness" or "joy," *alegrías* likely feel and taste almost identical to a *zoale.* Light and soft, with a delicate crunch from a few unpopped grains of amaranth, *alegrías* have a gentle, nutty sweetness like brown rice kissed by vanilla.

Some *zoales* were life-size, some even larger, with human blood as an added ingredient. According to Aztec cosmology, Huitzilopochtli, the god of sun and war, was forever battling the darkness of night, and if the darkness won, the world would end. So, to keep the sun in the sky, the Aztecs nourished Huitzilopochtli with human blood during ritual offerings.

Here amaranth played an important role. To honor Huitzilopochtli, Aztec priests constructed enormous replicas of the god out of an amaranth dough moistened with human blood. These giant *zoales* were carried in procession through Tenochtitlán to the Templo Mayor, the Aztecs' largest and most sacred temple, where it was consecrated as the flesh and bone of Huitzilopochtli and "broken up and distributed among the people who ate them with a mixture of reverence and fear."[21]

The Spanish Catholics were concerned that the Aztecs were mocking their holy sacraments; Aztec parents anointing their newborns with amaranth hewed way too closely to baptism. At the same time, the celebration of Huitzilopochtli seemed like a satanic insult to their sacrament of the Eucharist, in which a loaf of bread, like an amaranth *zoale,* is consecrated as the body of Jesus Christ and eaten alongside wine drunk as his blood.

Seeing the work of the devil among the Aztecs, Cortés and his Catholic priests leveled Tenochtitlán, murdered most of its population, and banned amaranth, declaring it pagan. Some accounts even suggest Cortés executed those found growing the plant or even just saving its seeds.

. . .

Imperial Spain's conquest of the Americas is often presented as an accident of geography, a serendipitous misstep by Christopher Columbus on his way to India. But consider this: Columbus's very first business venture in the Caribbean involved sending 550 people packed on four ships back to Europe to be sold in Mediterranean slave markets. Soon after the conquistador Hernán Cortés landed in Mexico, he also asked the Spanish Crown for permission to subjugate the Aztecs and sell them as slaves.[22] In fact, Cortés would go on to become the largest slave owner in colonial Mexico, at points buying and selling hundreds of enslaved people in a single day.[23]

Whenever the conversation turns to slavery, we typically imagine enslaved Africans, but rarely do we consider what historian Andrés Reséndez calls "the other slavery," the nearly five-hundred-year trade in Native slaves initiated by imperial Spain in the Americas.[24] In fact, Spain, as Reséndez points out, was to Native slavery what Portugal and England were to African slavery, namely the original architect and beneficiary. Indigenous slavery and Black slavery coexisted for nearly three hundred years. From Columbus to the nineteenth century, this secretive industry may have ensnared five million Native people, numbers approaching the cataclysm that was the transatlantic slave trade.[25] As with Black slavery, the legacy of this violence continues to shape societies.[26]

When Spain conquered Mexico, it occupied land so rich in silver that Spanish America became the world's leading supplier.[27] At the time, Spain's currency, the silver *real,* was on its way to becoming what the U.S. dollar is today, the principal way in which nations stored their wealth. Pulling it from the earth was brutal. Silver ore was buried deep underground or in mountains, and shafts had to be dug by hand, often through hundreds of feet of rock. Spain needed vast amounts of manpower.

During the early phases of the invasion of Tenochtitlán in 1521, Aztec soldiers heroically withstood Spain's superior weaponry and horses for weeks, unnerving Hernán Cortés. It's conceivable he linked the Aztecs' resilience, at least in part, to their diet of amaranth. In fact, the seeds may have comprised up to 80 percent of the Aztecs' calories then.[28] Scholar Katarzyna Beilin suggests the Spanish learned that without amaranth, the Native people "would be weakened and easier to control" when it came to mining silver, for example. And "if corn survived while amaranth disappeared, it was because corn sustained life while amaranth sustained a civilization both materially and, in the Aztecs' case, spiritually," writes Beilin. "Allied with elites and gods, amaranth disappeared altogether with them."[29]

· · ·

In 1598, following the same ancient desert highway that brought amaranth into the Southwest, Spanish conquistadores came to search for silver in New Mexico. Instead, they saw huge profits in the extraordinary number of Native people who could be captured and enslaved.[30] Among them were large, vibrant societies of artisans and farmers living in dozens of compact adobe homes along the upper reaches of the Rio Grande. The Spanish applied the name *pueblo,* their word for "village," to these diverse and dynamic communities.[31] They would eventually impose the names of Catholic saints, like "Santa Clara," the name of Marian and Ray's pueblo, on these communities to differentiate them.

Like Columbus in the Caribbean and Cortés in Mexico, Juan de Oñate, New Mexico's first colonial governor, quickly transformed the Pueblo lands into a supply center for enslaved people and goods for silver-mining towns in Mexico.[32] The Spanish established dozens of missions, some nothing more than sweatshops where Native people manufactured goods for export.[33] When Mexican mines were short on enslaved labor, New Mexican governors stuffed not just Pueblo but also Apache and Diné people into wagons heading south down the Camino Real, turning an ancient Indigenous trade highway into a slave route.

As Indigenous slaves were sent south, foreign foods came north. Spaniards feared that eating indigenous foods like amaranth and corn would turn them into godless Natives.[34] As they did everywhere they went in the Americas, the Spanish colonists changed the food landscape of New Mexico, creating farms and ranches worked by enslaved people, who were forced to dig up their crops of amaranth, corn, beans, and squash and replace them with foreign plants, especially wheat and grapes, foods necessary for the Catholic sacraments. The amaranth ban came north along with livestock to support the new colony, and Pueblos were pressured to raise cattle, sheep, chickens, and pigs, which would eventually begin to replace bison in their food culture.

In the first few years of colonization, the Spanish relied on the

Pueblo for sustenance. By the end of the first decade, however, the Pueblo were depending on the colonists for food, so much so that Native women were reported to have followed carts carrying corn from the pueblos to the colonists' city of Santa Fe in the desperate hope of scavenging a stray cob that might fall on the road.[35] By 1680, a combination of famine, disease, and overwork had brought the Pueblo to the brink of extinction. Just eight decades after Oñate's arrival, the Pueblo population had fallen from eighty thousand to just around seventeen thousand, an 80 percent collapse.[36]

On the full moon of August 10, 1680, the Pueblo communities along the Rio Grande revolted. Led by Po'Pay, an influential shaman, the Pueblo attacked their Spanish overlords, razing haciendas and churches and seizing guns and horses. The warriors laid siege to Santa Fe, forcing the entire Spanish population to flee New Mexico to where they eventually established today's sister cities of El Paso, Texas, and Juárez, Mexico.[37]

The Spanish returned to reconquer New Mexico in 1692 and did not leave until they were forced out during the Mexican War of Independence in 1821. By then, the Pueblo had acquired tastes for certain imported colonial foods, namely the chili, which, as Pueblo historian Porter Swentzell writes, was most likely carried into New Mexico by enslaved Indigenous people from Mexico. The Pueblo also saw value in certain Spanish farming techniques, such as the use of horses and oxen to plow fields, the management of orchards, beekeeping, and animal husbandry, all of which form the basis of today's New Mexican cuisine.

At Manko, his food truck and catering business, Ray blends ancient Pueblo ingredients with colonial ones—such as in his Native Berries and Bird Seed Salad, which incorporates two of the Four Sisters, amaranth and squash seeds, and dairy products like feta cheese, which were not part of precolonial Indigenous diets—to create his "Native American Fusion" food. He also serves Gangsta Meat Tacos, for which he folds shredded rib-eye steak spiked with lime juice (both cows and limes were brought by the Spanish) and Hatch green chili into a warm amaranth and corn tortilla, which he tops with fresh red cabbage for crunch.

After Spain left, New Mexico and the Pueblo homeland were briefly incorporated into the new country of Mexico, but the United States invaded Mexico in 1846, taking most of what is today the American West. New Mexico became a U.S. territory in 1850 and a state in 1912. At the time, the government didn't view the Pueblos as a military threat and so didn't wage war on them or force them off their land onto distant reservations, as it did many other tribes. That's why today the Pueblo are something of an anomaly: Unlike most other reservations in the United States, each Pueblo nation sits on or very near its original land in New Mexico.

This is not to say the Pueblo didn't lose land. In fact, they lost far more land to the U.S. government and courts within a hundred years of New Mexico's becoming a territory than they had under a quarter of a millennium of Spanish and Mexican rule.[38] Rather, much of America's violence against the Pueblo people took the form of a gradual yet relentless erosion of their culture through assimilation projects like the Native American boarding school system, which, as boarding school historian Margaret Jacobs points out, was charged with forcibly erasing the heritages of multitudes of diverse Native Americans, Alaska Natives, and Native Hawaiians and replacing them with a singular white Christian culture.[39]

For 150 years, between 1819 and 1969, the federal government, along with the complicity of churches and civil-society organizations that had deceptive names like "Friends of the Indian," forcibly separated Native children from their families and took them to boarding schools hundreds or even thousands of miles away. Once ensnared in the boarding school system, Native children were subjected to "systematic militarized and identity-alteration methodologies," as they were described in a 2022 U.S. government investigation.[40] Native children as young as four years old were pressured to forget every aspect of their culture. Their spiritual beliefs were banned as superstitions. Names were changed. Braids were cut. Language suppressed. Native clothes burned. Like inmates in prison, some children were even forced to wear government-issued clothing with two-digit numbers that corresponded to their white names.[41]

Although Native American boarding schools varied by location, tampering with the culinary heritage of Native American, Alaska Native, and Native Hawaiian communities was not just a common feature of this assimilation atrocity but a core component of it. School curricula were designed to interfere with the transfer of life-sustaining Indigenous food-related knowledge—like heirloom recipes and medical properties of plants—from one generation to the next to break what is among the most significant connections humans have to their cultural identity. At the Santa Fe and Albuquerque Indian schools, Pueblo children were not just forced to prepare Anglo-European recipes as part of the curriculum but taught to favor a Western industrial diet based on sugar, dairy, and wheat, a diet now known to be linked to diabetes and other diseases.

Unsurprisingly, Native parents fiercely resisted boarding schools and the breakup of their families. When they did, military personnel and police forced their way onto Native reservations and into homes, taking children until the schools were filled. Parents were cornered to comply in other ways too. In 1830, President Andrew Jackson signed the Indian Removal Act, expelling Native Americans from their lands and forcing them west along the infamous Trail of Tears. Ironically, as legal scholars point out, Jackson justified this genocidal act by arguing that tribal lands could no longer sustain life, precisely because of the damage caused by American occupation to tribal food culture.[42] Forced onto reservations, Native Americans were also forced into reliance on army food rations to survive. When parents refused to hand their children over to boarding schools, the government stopped these food rations, leaving them with the impossible choice between starving and losing their children.

The mastermind behind the boarding schools was General Richard Henry Pratt, a veteran of the American Indian Wars and the 1864 Red River Campaign. He claimed to have successfully "civilized" seventy-one prisoners of war taken from the Red River battle and incarcerated at Fort Marion, in St. Augustine in the Florida Panhandle.[43] He convinced the federal government that a similar pattern of prolonged abuse could work at an industrial scale with children, a mission he bluntly summarized as "Kill the Indian in him, and save the man."[44] In 1879, the government approved Pratt's plan and established the first boarding school, the Carlisle Indian Industrial School, on an army base in Pennsylvania.

Sun Elk, from the Taos Pueblo, was among the first children taken to Carlisle, spending seven years there starting in 1883. Later, as an adult, he told his story:

> They told us that Indian ways were bad. They said we must get civilized. I remember that word too. It means "be like the white man." I am willing to be like the white man, but I did not believe Indian ways were wrong. But they kept teaching us for seven years. And the books told how bad the Indians had been to the white men—burning their towns and killing their women and children. But I had seen white men do that to Indians. We all wore white man's clothes and ate white man's food and went to white man's churches and spoke

white man's talk. And so, after a while we also began to say Indians were bad. We laughed at our own people and their blankets and cooking pots and sacred societies and dances. I tried to learn the lessons and after seven years I came home.[45]

In May 2022, Congress held hearings on the legacy of the Native American boarding school system. Having waited sixty-seven years to tell his story, Jim LaBelle, an Inupiaq man, vividly detailed how he survived a decade of his life in two boarding schools in Alaska between 1955 and 1965. Like other survivors who also testified that day, Mr. LaBelle recalled the importance of his Inupiaq culinary heritage and how it was intentionally stripped away when he was a young child. "We were used to eating traditional foods such as moose, caribou, salmon, reindeer, berries, and grains," he recounted as his voice cracked under the emotional weight of his words. "Now we were forced to eat industrial foods in one-pound cans. We had severe stomach issues, diarrhea, vomiting, sometimes all at once. We soiled our pants and beds, and the Matrons would force us to clean our own mess."

The assimilation efforts of the Native American boarding school system went as far as targeting Indigenous food production itself. Boys were compelled to learn to use industrial farm machinery to grow crops like wheat and raise cattle, while girls were obliged to be subservient to men and trained to be domestic workers and cooks in white households. "Today," because of these policies, Mr. LaBelle concluded, "I cannot speak my language, nor could I conduct all of those wonderful traditional activities we call subsistence farming, hunting, fishing, and gathering."[46]

Every survivor of Native American boarding schools whom I spoke to or whose testimony I read mentioned that physical abuse was a rampant feature of these institutions. Severe overwork coupled with a poor diet contributed to many Native children dying of malnourishment at these schools. When confronted with their neglect, school officials insidiously blamed the children for being picky eaters. Thousands, maybe tens of thousands, of Native children never returned home and lie in unmarked graves. At the National Archives, there's an attendance book from 1909 from the Santa Fe Indian School in New Mexico that includes a diagram of a "grave-yard plot" and the locations of twenty-five graves, all but two of which belonged to students.[47] As the historian Margaret Jacobs chillingly observes, the salient difference between Indian boarding schools and other schools of that era was the presence of a cemetery.[48]

The physical, sexual, and emotional abuse endured by Native children at those schools has been carried by survivors into adulthood. In fact, a 2022 investigation into the Native American boarding school system initiated by the U.S. Department of the Interior under Secretary Deb Haaland (who is Laguna Pueblo from New Mexico) found that Native adults today who were intentionally cut off from their culture by those institutions are physically and mentally unhealthier than Native Americans who were freer to live their own culture as children.[49] This is even more terrifying when you consider that this is happening to Uyghur children in China right now.

Tiana Suazo is the former executive director of the Red Willow Center, a working farm and community center dedicated to the well-being of the Taos Pueblo in northern New Mexico. Surrounded on three sides by the Sangre de Cristo Mountains, the farm is remarkably serene. It's not hard to see why Tiana described it as a place of healing for her community. Part of the healing process, she explained, is training younger generations of Native Americans how to grow traditional foods harmed by colonialism.

"Our goal is to both preserve and restore elements of our heritage and traditional cuisine," Tiana told me. The heart of Red Willow's mission is to restore and preserve Pueblo traditional food culture. That, Tiana explained, often requires the cooperation of her elders, who understand, for instance, how native plants like amaranth were used in traditional ceremonies. "Thankfully, some of the elders have this knowledge, but the issue is that some are afraid to pass it on now," she said.

"They're mistrustful because of what's happened to them," she went on, referring to the boarding schools. "They think [their knowledge] will be mishandled, stolen, or given away. So they're guarding it." Tiana let a few moments of silence pass. "The elders' instincts, they are completely understandable and justifiable given what's happened," she said. "We have to be sensitive but also work fast to earn their trust, to prove that we can both use it for our people and safeguard it before they go. It's a labor of love, but it's how we survive."

·   ·   ·

For Native chefs like Ray Naranjo, as well as farmers and food activists like Tiana Suazo, the ultimate goal of their work is reversing the disastrous health effects of the Western diets forced on their people for the past several hundred years. Today, Native Americans are diagnosed with obesity 60 percent more often than White adults. Indigenous people have more type 2 diabetes—which often leads to paralysis, amputation, and blindness—than any other race or ethnic group. According to the 2014 edition of the Indian Health Service's report *Trends in Indian Health,* diabetes causes death in Native Americans at a rate 177 percent greater than in other Americans.[50] A scholar and citizen of the Lower Brule Sioux

Tribe, Nick Estes, describes this "forced diet" as "one of the deadliest diseases imposed by colonizers."[51]

In 2014, Marian and Ray Naranjo's relative Porter Swentzell, then in his late thirties, was diagnosed with heart disease. "I was overweight, and the doctors told me I was going to die if I didn't change the way I eat," he told me during the winter of 2022. "They told me I wasn't going to see my kids graduate from high school. That kind of scary stuff."

Porter and I were talking at the Tower Gallery on the Pojoaque Pueblo, just north of Santa Fe. The gallery house was built to display the work of Roxanne Swentzell, Porter's mother and a world-renowned artist, author, and food activist. Sitting among Roxanne's powerfully expressive clay and bronze sculptures, Porter told me that his doctor told him to improve his diet and showed him a picture of the USDA food pyramid. For decades, the food pyramid was plastered on the walls of doctors' offices and classrooms, colorfully displaying the junk science of "all fat is bad" and "carb loading is good." The USDA knew for years that the pyramid was the product of lazy government policy but abandoned it only after it was clearly linked to rising rates of obesity in the United States.[52]

"For years, it was doing violence against our own tribal ideas about what is healthy, what is good. It was saying indirectly that our way of living wasn't right. It was attacking our Native way of life through the pyramid. The USDA was saying, 'We, not you, are going to tell you what's healthy for you—what's good for you,'" Porter explained as he wiped his gold-framed glasses clean with the edge of his shirt.

"The shape of the pyramid," he said, "directed us to eat a lot of the wrong kinds of stuff and didn't include any Native foods." At the time, the USDA, astonishingly, recommended eating between six and eleven servings per day of grain products, and though it said that several of those should be whole-grain servings, it suggested foods often made with enriched white wheat flour, the same crop that replaced Pueblo crops during Spanish times and that today is subsidized by U.S. industrial agriculture policies.[53]

Porter wasn't the only one at Santa Clara Pueblo with health troubles. His mother, Roxanne, struggled with her weight and had high cholesterol, high blood pressure, and other diet-related health problems unusual for her age. Porter's eight-year-old son had been diagnosed with prediabetes, while other relatives were diabetics battling obesity, autoimmune diseases, chronic fatigue, and depression. Marian Naranjo told me she was "headed for stroke and other problems" at the time.

When the doctor told Porter that following the food pyramid would solve his problem, Porter recalled thinking, "It was the same solution they had been giving to other tribal members with the same problems. And none of them got healthier." And that's when he remembered: "It was the same pyramid on the cans of commodity foods."

· · ·

Commodity foods are packaged, shelf-stable foods (like white flour; sugar; processed peanut butter; dried pasta; processed cheese bricks; canned juices, meats, and vegetables; and powdered eggs and milk) provided to low-income Native communities by the Food Distribution Program on Indian Reservations (FDPIR). The program is run by the U.S. Department of Agriculture (USDA) and serves about one hundred thousand people a year with roughly $150 million worth of food, with most recipients residing in the western United States.[54] For some, it provides essential lifesaving nutrition that staves off hunger.

The FDPIR is an outgrowth of the food stamp program created in the 1960s to address hunger and food insecurity among low-income people. Today, more than 25 percent of all Native Americans are enrolled in federal food-assistance programs like the FDPIR.[55] Commodity foods in general have historically tended to favor those products with powerful congressional lobbies, like soy, corn, milk, poultry, and beef, rather than foods that are more culturally relevant for Indigenous people but receive few or no government subsidies, such as amaranth, lentils, beans, and nuts.[56] The FDPIR prioritizes calories over culture and even nutrition, so food is often highly processed and stripped of much of its nutritional value. Scholars say USDA programs like the FDPIR have become "dumping grounds" for a glut of unhealthy commodities.[57]

For many Native Americans, the FDPIR is reminiscent of the notorious rations provided to tribes in the nineteenth century after they were forced onto reservations and into reliance on food from the same people waging war on them. Rations like flour, beef, coffee, and sugar, all foreign to tribal diets, were often insufficient and arrived rotten, inducing illness, malnutrition, and starvation. The Diné journalist Andi Murphy writes that commodity foods are "seen as the latest incarnation of a violent and unequal historical relationship between tribes and the federal government."[58]

Until the 1940s, Porter Swentzell explained to me, most Pueblos had a fair amount of control over their food. Because they weren't moved to reservations, they were able to farm more readily than some other Native tribes. World War II, however, changed that when the government took control of millions of acres of Indigenous and New Mexican land to build military bases, missile ranges, and R&D facilities, like Los Alamos National Laboratory on the Pajarito Plateau, where the atomic bomb was developed during the Manhattan Project. The war economy caused tectonic shifts in New Mexico:

The population boomed, and the state went from a barter economy to one based on cash. People turned to wage labor, and subsistence farming declined as Pueblo farmers took up ranching; fields that had once grown food for people were now growing feed for cattle.[59]

This was "a watershed event" for Pueblo cuisine, Porter said. In the decades following the war, Los Alamos gentrified with an influx of highly educated scientists, becoming one of the wealthiest towns in the country, while poverty took hold below in Pueblo communities. In turn, the Pueblo increasingly had to turn to government assistance programs, among them the FDPIR, to feed themselves. On paper, commodity foods were described as fighting poverty among Native Americans, but in practice, they were a harmful solution to a problem for which the federal government was entirely responsible.

That said, Andi Murphy urges caution when thinking about commodity foods. Andi has reported extensively on the FDPIR and, like many Native Americans, grew up eating canned commodities. "It's understandable that many people see it as just another version of colonial rations and the [federal] government's mistreatment of the tribes, and they're not wrong," she told me in the winter of 2022. But she was quick to point out that some of the remotest places in the United States are reservations. "Families just don't have running water or electricity, which means that canned [commodity] foods, which are shelf-stable, by the way, are a necessity for many people."

Despite their tainted legacy of culinary destruction, commodity foods have also inspired ingenuity.[60] The most iconic example of this is the Indigenous taco (sometimes called the Navajo or Indian taco). What gives the taco its "Indigenous" identity is its frybread base. Fry bread was created by Diné women with rations provided while they were interned at Bosque Redondo in New

Mexico in the 1860s, after the Long Walk.[61] Commodity foods a century later helped make this survival food ubiquitous throughout Native American culture.

For many, fry bread's history is painful and complex, but its recipe is simple: Mix oil, wheat flour, baking powder, salt, maybe a little sugar, and milk. Fry the dough in hot oil. As the Diné food writer Ungelbah Dávila sums up: "They are European ingredients, but this is an Indigenous food."[62] To make an Indigenous taco, a piece of fry bread is topped with beans, meat, chili, shredded cheese, lettuce, diced tomato, and onions. Ray Naranjo has a Frybread Friday special at Manko that includes an Indigenous taco based on his grandmother's recipe.[63]

Nevertheless, Native Americans have long pressured the USDA to make changes to the FDPIR, but their suggestions have often fallen on deaf ears. In 1990, Charles "Red" Gates, a member of the Standing Rock Sioux Tribe in North Dakota and a tribal FDPIR liaison, forced this issue in testimony he gave to Congress:

> **Charles Gates:** At this time, I would like to open a couple of these cans, and show you what some of the people are forced to eat because that is all they have.
>
> **Congressman Hall:** Now, what is this? Is this canned meat?
>
> **Charles Gates:** This is canned beef, supposedly. We get reports saying that it is supposed to be real good for us.
>
> **Congressman Faleomavaega:** Is this USDA-approved?
>
> **Charles Gates:** Yes.
>
> **Congressman Dorgan:** This is sent through the commodities program from USDA; is that correct?

Charles Gates: Right. You can see the top of the can here, with the fat on it.

Congressman Hall: Why don't you bring it up here? Why don't you take it up and show it to us? It does not look too good.

Charles Gates: No, it does not. If you dump it out in a plate, you will see blood vessels.

Congressman Dorgan: Do you have a plate? Let us take a look at it. Do you have a stronger scooper?

Congressman Faleomavaega: If the chairman will yield, I will wager the chairman that dog and cat food probably have more nutritional value than what this is offering.[64]

Red Gates's activism continued until his death in 2023, and he was instrumental in bringing changes to the FDPIR, like getting the USDA to include more fresh fruits and vegetables in commodity food packages. Today, tribes are going further, pressuring the USDA to cede to tribes control over where their food comes from. In 2021, the USDA launched the FDPIR Self-Determination Demonstration Project, a $3.5 million pilot allowing tribes to bypass the USDA and buy healthier food more aligned with their cultural preferences directly from their own sources, including from within their own tribes. Only eight tribes are part of the initial phase, but Congress is considering expanding the program, building hope that it could eventually be extended nationwide.[65]

While changes to the FDPIR are welcome, they're not coming quickly enough. As public health scholars point out, through rations and commodity foods, "Indigenous people were the first Americans to be pressured to consume large amounts of processed foods."[66] Like Porter Swentzell and his relatives at Santa Clara, they have since become an unwitting canary in the coal mine for the rest of America about the catastrophic health consequences of agricultural subsidies: Within a few generations, dependency on USDA commodity foods contributed to skyrocketing rates of diabetes and obesity, which were almost nonexistent in Native American communities until they were pressured to adopt Western diets.

"Unlike the Spanish, who came pointing swords at the Pueblos," Porter said, "the Americans came with free stuff: canned foods, farm machinery, money for substandard housing." After pausing for a moment to reflect, he continued, "In some ways, this was a far more insidious type of colonialism. It fostered a reliance on unhealthy food and fucked with our health."

. . .

Around the time Porter Swentzell was in the doctor's office, his mother, Roxanne, noticed something curious happening at Santa Clara Pueblo. In 1987, Roxanne founded the Flowering Tree Permaculture Institute to preserve and share the Pueblo people's traditional sustainable gardening and farming practices. Over the years of watching her crops, such as varieties of amaranth, corn, and beans, she saw that "only certain plants—mostly our Pueblo crops—thrived in this high desert landscape," while others that didn't belong "always died or struggled endlessly to survive."[67]

Native Pueblo plants were thriving while the health of their Santa Clara Pueblo community was failing. "We're living in our homeland and eating as if we're on Mars," Roxanne thought.[68] Both she and Porter heard from their elders that the people at the pueblo had been far healthier only a few decades earlier. Porter researched and reconstructed the diets of his ancestors, going as far back as the Ancestral Puebloans before the introduction of European food and cooking techniques. He and Roxanne then experimented with reassembling the diet to understand if it could be done today.

Roxanne cooked while Porter, the patient and guinea pig, ate. He cut out dairy, wheat, and refined sugar. He ate boiled and grilled food instead of deep-fried things. He ate more berries, nuts, and seeds, such as currants, piñon nuts, pumpkin seeds, and amaranth, mostly grown in Roxanne's garden. Porter did this for several weeks before stepping on a scale. When he did, he saw that he had lost dozens of pounds; he felt better and looked better. Porter told me that when he returned to the doctor's office, the physicians were dumbfounded. "The doctors didn't believe it when I told them what I did," he said. Porter and Roxanne didn't keep a daily log of the experiment to offer statistical proof to the doctors, but they knew they were onto something profound.

Two years later, the Swentzells launched a larger experiment. This time, Roxanne and Porter were joined by twelve other members of Santa Clara Pueblo, ranging from six to sixty-five years old; some were overweight and had been diagnosed with diabetes. Others had heart disease, autoimmune disorders, inflammation, allergies, high cholesterol, and even depression. Before the trial, each participant was weighed by a physician and had their blood tested for cholesterol and blood sugar levels and other biomarkers. Then for three months, the fourteen volunteers ate only what their ancestors would have eaten before Spanish enslavement and American assimilation, before boarding schools, before commodity foods.

Marian and Ray Naranjo also took part in the Swentzells' experiment. Marian, as an elder, acted as a spiritual leader, helping steady the group over the rockiest parts of their journey. Chef Ray not only created the recipes but also came up with new ways to cook them; dishes included soul-warming savory elk meatballs simmered with fresh zucchini and corn and Marian's piñon nut cookies, sweetened only with cacao and currants. "We ate what our ancestors ate, but we couldn't always cook their way, over an open fire, for example," Ray told me. "We had to adjust it for how we live now in modern kitchens."

Twelve weeks later, all fourteen members of the group were weighed and had their blood tested again. But no one needed a scale to tell them their health had improved. They all felt energetic and effervescent. Roxanne had lost fifteen pounds, and her cholesterol levels had normalized. Porter had lost more weight. Marian and Ray were also healthier. Annette Rodríguez, another participant, noticed a marked improvement in her lupus symptoms, writing later that eating her ancestral food did something that "prescribed medications hadn't been able to do." Returning, even just briefly, to their precolonial Pueblo diet resulted in weight loss, blood sugar control, lower cholesterol, clearer thinking, more energy, and deeper connections to their community and Mother Earth. In short, the decolonized diet appeared to mitigate many of the diseases the Pueblo and other Native Americans have been dying from during the last century.

The Pueblo Food Experience, as this remarkable event has been named, is memorialized in a cookbook by the same name. Edited by Roxanne Swentzell and Patricia Perea, *The Pueblo Food Experience Cookbook* documents, in almost poetic terms, the heroic stories behind their return to their original cuisine, along with recipes. Ray's amaranth and corn tortillas are not in the book (the recipe for them is on page 224), but even so, he says the Pueblo Food Experience exposed more people to amaranth who now see it as the ancestral food it has always been.

Beata Tsosie-Peña participated in the Pueblo Food Experience and has since developed a strong and spiritual bond with amaranth. Soft-spoken and deeply earnest, with long jet-black hair, Beata believes that, like the Three Sisters (corn, beans, and squash), "amaranth is a teacher, an elder we can learn from," she told me. "For thousands of years, humans coevolved with these plants. We have these special living relationships with them." Today she is part of a growing network of Indigenous women who have been sharing ancestral knowledge of how to grow and prepare amaranth. But what sets her work apart from that of others is her focus on reinvigorating the ancient highways and relationships that first brought amaranth into Pueblo lands.

In 2008, a friend introduced Beata to Qachuu Aloom, a collective of Indigenous Maya Achì women from Rabinal, a small, forested town a few hours north of Guatemala City. The Spanish also outlawed amaranth in Guatemala when they set upon the Maya in 1524. Nearly 450 years later, U.S.-trained state forces deliberately targeted the Maya people during Guatemala's civil war from 1960 to 1996, during a genocide called the Silent Holocaust. To protect their food culture during the war, Maya farmers hid handfuls of amaranth seeds in glass jars and buried them in their fields or under floorboards in their homes. In 2006, Qachuu Aloom, "Mother Earth" in the Maya Achì language, was formed by survivors to restore plants nearly lost to war.

Over the years, Beata's relationship with the women of Qachuu Aloom blossomed. "Our shared story of colonial violence," she said, "threaded our communities together." Beata has traveled to Guatemala, and the women from Qachuu Aloom have come north to New Mexico and shown her how to plant "the offering" they had carried with them: handfuls of tiny cream-colored amaranth seeds. Today "the descendants of those first amaranth seeds" Beata was given are now tall, flowering red plumes in the Española Healing Foods Oasis, a public garden built by Pueblo women just out-side Santa Clara Pueblo.[69]

The garden was conceived during a downpour. In 2012, Beata was stuck in her car in the library parking lot, her eyes trained on a hill behind Española City Hall. "I was just watching the rainwater wash the hill away," she said. Rainstorms repeatedly washed dirt down the hill; then the city would hire bulldozers to push it back up. "All that effort just to protect a parking lot," Beata remarked.

At the time, Beata was working with Tewa Women United (TWU), a nonprofit organization founded by Pueblo women to end the intertwined problems of environmental injustice and vio-lence against Native women and girls. "The problem [with the hill] then," she said, "was the city saw the water as a liability when it was actually a resource and a source of life."

Beata and TWU approached city officials with a plan to build a garden. By 2016, TWU had secured the funding and approvals to break ground on the Española Healing Foods Oasis, now a thriv-ing community garden with dozens of species of native trees and edible plants. Woven among them are dozens of floppy amaranth plumes. "Having amaranth in the Oasis is something of a home-coming," Beata said through a soft smile.

While the Spanish amaranth ban is history, its legacy is still alive. Beata explained that colonialism intentionally divided Na-tive people in New Mexico. For Beata, growing amaranth has helped in small but meaningful ways to bridge some of that divide. "It's a communal plant in the way it's harvested and processed," she said. "It forces people together to talk, which helps you cut through the layers of trauma."

By working with chefs like Ray Naranjo, Beata hopes to return amaranth and those relationships to Pueblo kitchens, where they help reestablish ties to an older but healthier culinary culture.

"Restoring amaranth by itself isn't going to save us from colonialism and generations of trauma," she told me. "It is just one aspect, just one step in the restitution of the entire Indigenous ecological system."

· · ·

In the winter of 2023, Ray invited me to sit in on a private cooking class he was teaching at Roxanne Swentzell's Flowering Tree Permaculture Institute. Ray was teaching members of his pueblo how to cook with the Four Sisters: corn, beans, squash, and amaranth. Three generations of Swentzells, three generations of Naranjos, and a few other relatives gathered quietly around a large wooden table to watch Ray's demonstration of making a hearty dish of tofu with Pueblo black beans. But the formality quickly crumbled, giving way to a warmth and ease of the family affair that, after all, it really was.

Ray retreated into the kitchen to start a red chili sauce for a Frito pie. Eventually the guests gathered in the kitchen as well, talking, snacking, and hovering around the chef. Marian took a seat at the counter overlooking Ray and the stove. I picked up a copy of *The Pueblo Food Experience Cookbook* off the counter and landed on a page with a photograph of Roxanne Swentzell, whom, at that moment, I could see over Ray's shoulder rolling out tortillas. The photographer had captured Roxanne squatting calmly over a clear plastic box, cleaning dozens of velvety magenta plumes of amaranth. I felt Marian turn toward me. "It is important to remember something we learned about our culture after many generations," she said. "Things like amaranth don't always disappear. Sometimes they are just waiting to be remembered."

Ray's Po'Pay Bisque

Makes 4 to 6 servings

Named after Po'Pay, the leader of the 1680 Pueblo Revolt against Spanish colonizers in present-day New Mexico, this dish is a tribute to an event that ensured the survival of the Pueblo people. Po'Pay's given name was Popyn, which in Tewa means "ripe squash," so for this recipe Ray uses the bluish gray Taos Pueblo Hubbard squash, native to New Mexico. It tends to be larger than other Hubbard varieties and has a harder shell, which protects it against the sometimes bitter cold of a New Mexico winter.

The bisque is garnished with amaranth leaves and popped seeds and squash blossoms. Amaranth leaves are sold at some farmers' markets, well-stocked grocery stores, and Asian and Mexican markets. Look for the popped seeds (aka puffed seeds) at the same sources as well as natural-foods stores and online. If you can't find amaranth leaves, you can substitute microgreens, but don't forgo the puffed amaranth—it really adds a wonderful toasty flavor as well as a very pleasing, delicate crunchy texture to this dish. If you can't find puffed or popped amaranth online or at your local specialty market, you can easily make your own. And keep in mind that amaranth seeds are often sold as "whole grain amaranth." Fresh squash blossoms are seasonal and available from late spring through early fall. They can be found in some farmers' markets, Mexican markets, or perhaps in your own garden or your neighbor's. As Ray says about the ingredients in this dish, "Flowers to seeds to new plants symbolize the generations."

Lastly, this recipe calls for Zuni salt, which Native American communities harvest from the Zuni Salt Lake. It's not an easy ingredient to find. You can substitute it with high-quality flaky sea salt.

One (3-pound) Taos Pueblo
Hubbard squash or other
winter squash like red kuri or
kabocha

8 cups water
Zuni salt or high-quality flaky
sea salt

FOR GARNISH AND SERVING

3 to 4 tablespoons puffed or
popped amaranth seeds,
storebought or homemade
(see Note)

16 small amaranth leaves or
½ cup microgreens

4 to 6 fresh squash blossoms,
stamens and pistils removed

Ray's Amaranth and Corn
Tortillas for serving
(page 224)

1. Rinse the outside of the squash well. Then cut off the stem end and cut the squash into quarters. Scoop out the seeds and stringy flesh from each quarter and set aside.

2. In a medium saucepan, combine the squash pieces and water and bring just to a boil over medium-high heat. Turn down the heat to a gentle simmer and poach the squash until it is soft when pierced with a fork, about 30 minutes for most varieties.

3. While the squash cooks, preheat the oven to 300°F. Rinse the squash seeds, discarding any strings, flesh, or other bits; then pat the seeds dry. (The seeds can be roasted in or out of the shell. The entire seed is edible.) Pile the seeds onto a sheet pan and sprinkle with a large pinch of Zuni salt or regular-size pinch of sea salt and toss to coat evenly. (The seeds are naturally oily so you don't need to toss with additional oil.) Spread the seeds in a single layer. Roast, stirring the seeds halfway through, until they begin to pop and are lightly browned, about 15 minutes. Remove from the oven and set aside.

4. When the squash is ready, remove the pan from the heat and, using a slotted spoon or tongs, carefully transfer the pieces to a cutting board. Let the pieces cool until they can be handled. Then peel away and discard the skin from each piece and return the pieces to the poaching liquid in the pan. Add 2 tablespoons Zuni salt or 1 tablespoon sea salt and, using an immersion blender, puree the

squash with the poaching liquid until smooth. (Alternatively, transfer the poaching liquid and squash to a food processor or in batches to a blender and puree until smooth, then return the puree to the pan.) Reheat the bisque over medium-low heat until hot, stirring occasionally to prevent scorching.

5. Ladle the bisque into bowls and garnish each serving with the roasted squash seeds, amaranth seeds and leaves, and squash blossoms, dividing them evenly. Serve immediately, accompanied with the tortillas.

NOTE

To make your own puffed or popped amaranth seeds, warm a dry saucepan over medium heat for 2 minutes. Add a tablespoon of amaranth seeds and cook until they puff, 1 to 2 minutes, then immediately transfer to a bowl. Repeat with another tablespoon of amaranth seeds. Leftovers can be enjoyed as a snack.

Ray's Amaranth and Corn Tortillas

Makes 12 to 16 tortillas

These are the tortillas Ray Naranjo made for me the first time we met. This recipe calls for a single tablespoon of amaranth flour, which is just enough to spread its nutty flavor throughout each tortilla. This recipe is incredibly flexible. You can dial up or dial down the ratio of amaranth flour to masa harina as you'd like. (I like the taste of amaranth and will often make tortillas with equal amounts of amaranth flour and masa harina.) You'll notice, however, that the tortillas become denser as you add more amaranth.

1½ cups masa harina, plus more as needed

1 tablespoon amaranth flour

¼ teaspoon salt

2 tablespoons lard, melted, or olive oil

1 cup hot water, plus more as needed

1. In a large bowl, whisk together the masa harina, amaranth flour, and salt. Add the lard, then the hot water, stirring with a wooden spoon until the ingredients come together in a ragged dough. Then, using your hands, continue to work together all of the ingredients until the dough is evenly hydrated and pliable. If the dough seems too stiff, add a little more hot water, a tablespoon at a time, or simply work the dough with a wet hand. If the dough seems too wet, add pinches of more masa harina until the consistency improves. Cover the bowl with a kitchen towel and let the dough rest for about 10 minutes.

2. Turn the dough out onto a work surface, divide it into 12 to 16 equal portions, and shape each portion into a ball. Cover the balls with the kitchen towel.

3. Just before you shape your first tortilla, line a dinner plate with a second kitchen towel and set the plate near the stove. Then heat a comal, griddle, or cast-iron skillet over medium-low heat for 5 minutes.

4. You can shape the tortillas with either a tortilla press or a rolling pin. If using a tortilla press, line the two plates of the press with plastic wrap. (Or cut open a plastic bag along the seams and use the halves to line the plates.) Place a dough ball on the bottom plate and close the press, flattening the ball to about ⅛ inch thick. If using a rolling pin, place a dough ball between two sheets of plastic wrap and roll out the ball into a round roughly ⅛ inch thick.

5. Shape a tortilla as directed, add it to the hot pan, and cook until brown, toasty marks appear on the underside, 40 seconds to 1 minute. Flip the tortilla and cook until brown spots appear on the second side, 15 to 30 seconds longer. Transfer the tortilla to the towel-lined plate and cover with the towel to keep warm. Shape and cook the remaining tortillas, stacking them as they come off the pan and covering them with the towel. Serve warm.

The United States

Eating the Atomic Bomb

THE FIRST TIME I ate at Manko, Ray Naranjo's food truck, I didn't know what to order, so I asked him for a recommendation. Ray thought for a few moments, and then a wide smile lit up his face as he leaned out the window, tapping emphatically a couple of times on a sign taped to the front of the truck.

MOTLEY

Inside Out Green Chile Cheeseburger

Grilled Buns & Burger with Roasted Garlic Aioli Finished with
Green Chile Cheese Sauce $10

SERVED WITH RUBBER GLOVES

"I just put it on the menu today. You'll be the first to try it. Let me know what you think," he said with a laugh as he slipped back through the truck window into the kitchen.

"What's up with the rubber gloves?" I asked.

"The burger is smothered in the green chili sauce," he said. "They make it easier to eat with your hands. It's messy, but it's really good."

"I thought they were to guard against radiation," I quipped. It was an embarrassingly corny joke; we were in downtown Los Alamos, a couple of miles from Los Alamos National Laboratory, where J. Robert Oppenheimer and his team designed and produced the atomic bomb.

"Nah, man," he chided me. "Rubber gloves won't protect anyone from that shit."

· · ·

The town of Los Alamos sits on top of the Pajarito Plateau on a series of high, finger-like mesas splayed out from the Jemez Mountains, with deep ravines carved by intermittent streams lined with ponderosa pines that eventually feed into the mighty Rio Grande, the state's largest river. The Pajarito Plateau is a profoundly sacred place for the Pueblo people, like Ray. For thousands of years, long before Europeans even knew about the Americas, the ancient Pueblos built shrines here, making it a sacred source of "crucial ceremonial materials like spring water, medicines, minerals and clay," according to author and oral historian Sara Sinclair.[1] "That land is our church; it is our Mecca," Marian Naranjo, Ray's mother, told me.

Los Alamos before the Manhattan Project is often depicted as an empty, abandoned place. But when it was taken over by the government, it was alive and imbued with meaning not only for Native Americans but also for generations of Nuevomexicano ranchers who were forced off the plateau at gunpoint.[2] In fact, during the Great Depression, the plateau was a major source of beans for Americans, who relied on them as an affordable source of protein. When the Manhattan Project arrived in New Mexico in April 1943, the U.S. Army established both a nuclear laboratory and an explosives test site on the plateau of land belonging to the people of the San Ildefonso Pueblo. Today, the lab is officially known as Los Alamos National Laboratory (LANL), and its operations affect not only San Ildefonso, but also half a dozen other nearby Pueblo nations—Cochiti, Jemez, Santa Clara, Pojoaque, Tesuque, and Nambé.

Today, much of that sacred land is a Superfund site. For decades, the lab experimented with radioactive explosives on the plateau, littering the land with debris and fallout, some of which was directed away from the lab and over civilians living outside the fence.[3] "We often heard the explosions up there but never a word from the lab about the fallout they sent over our heads," a farmer in his seventies from a nearby pueblo told me. It wasn't until the 1990s, around the time the Clinton administration began declassifying materials related to Los Alamos operations, that communities nearby got a glimpse of the toxic tragedy unfolding on the plateau.[4]

The United States is the most nuclear-bombed country on earth, with over one thousand nuclear weapons detonated on its territory. According to Joseph Masco, author of *The Nuclear Borderlands,* "Most of us have some level of radioactive toxins in our bodies directly derived from the U.S. nuclear complex."[5] The National Cancer Institute has said that, on average, everyone alive in the United States between 1945 and 1963 received two rads of iodine 131, a radioactive isotope linked to thyroid cancer, from nuclear testing. Americans who drank milk probably received far more than that, children especially.[6] And as of late 2021, trace amounts of fallout from nuclear testing in the 1950s and '60s were showing up in jars of American honey.[7]

Area G is the lab's primary nuclear waste dump on the plateau, which it built in 1957 after bulldozing sixty-three acres of ancient Pueblo sites.[8] The dump is a toxic wasteland of leaking, unlined shallow pits and shafts containing potentially millions of cubic feet of radioactive garbage generated by nuclear weapons research during the Manhattan Project and the Cold War. Among the hazardous materials buried at Area G is tritium, a radioactive element used in the cores of nuclear weapons to amplify their explosive power.[9] Tritium is carcinogenic, and while it's unknown just how many containers of the substance are at Area G, local advocates are particularly concerned that tritium has long since made its way off the plateau.[10]

In the 1970s, the lab had two major tritium accidents, which released more than fifty thousand curies of tritium into the air over New Mexico.[11] In 2001, trace amounts of it were found in water supplies, including near San Ildefonso Pueblo, which shares a property line with the lab.[12] Then in 2016, the lab worried that at least four of Area G's old barrels of tritium had built up enough hydrogen and oxygen inside to explode.[13] The lab wanted to relieve the pressure by releasing the radioactive tritium gas into the air. The lab, however, was forced to stop after Tewa Women United and several other advocates warned the public about tritium gas and its ability to rapidly convert into tritiated water and enter the food chain.[14]

Today, tritium and other toxins are ubiquitous in Los Alamos's ecosystem. Honeybees and honey collected from hives around Area G have shown high levels of tritium contamination, as have rodents and owls.[15] Elk, which are a staple of Pueblo cuisine and graze on Los Alamos property, have been found to have high levels of strontium 90, a carcinogenic radionuclide, in their bones. And piñon trees on the plateau, once a source of food for local communities, "now maintain plutonium in their circulatory system at a rate one hundred times greater than background levels, as do local grasses."[16] At one point, corn, beans, and squash, the Three Sisters and staples of Pueblo cuisine, which lab scientists grew on lab property for testing purposes, all revealed radionuclides, such as plutonium 238, 239, and 240, absorbed from the soil at levels dangerous to humans.[17] Lab officials say they test the plants and animals every three years and there is no health risk to humans.[18]

In January 2004, the U.S. Department of Energy (DOE), which oversees the lab, discovered an underground plume of hexavalent chromium, a toxic chemical and carcinogen (the same one made infamous by the 2000 film *Erin Brockovich*) that had been used in the lab's non-nuclear power plant. For two decades, between the 1950s and the 1970s, the lab had simply flushed water containing hexavalent chromium down the canyons of the Pajarito Plateau as a means of disposal. The DOE failed to report its discovery to the New Mexico Environment Department, as required by law, until December 2005, nearly two years later.[19] The plume, now one mile long, half a mile wide, and a hundred feet deep, has since seeped into an aquifer, threatening the safety of the public's drinking water.[20] Twenty years later there is still no accepted plan to clean it up.

One night, over dinner, I asked Ray Naranjo how the nuclear legacy shapes how he thinks about food. "I get a little concerned about what I'm buying from the farmers' markets, because those fruits and vegetables might be grown around the lab," he replied. "People try to take care around here, but you never know." A few moments later, he added, "But we do have to think twice about what soil and water our seeds will grow in. When you think about Pueblo cuisine and something like the Pueblo Food Experience—where we're trying to grow our own ancestral food on our own land to heal ourselves from the past and from things like commodity foods—and then think about all that in the context of the lab. It feels one step forward, two steps back."

Tina Cordova is a seventh-generation New Mexican. She grew up in Tularosa, one of a cluster of small Nuevomexicano towns in the southern part of New Mexico, near the White Sands Missile Range, roughly two hundred miles south of Los Alamos. Tina was born in the 1950s, and as a kid, she often heard stories about the Trinity test, the first detonation of a nuclear bomb, which was conducted at White Sands. Around 5:30 a.m. on July 16, 1945, local people were just starting their daily chores when they saw a blinding flash of light, followed by an enormous blast. It was still dark when the bomb's shock waves passed through their bodies. "They didn't know what was happening; they thought it was the end of the world," Tina told me. Forty miles away from Tularosa, J. Robert Oppenheimer, whose lab designed the bomb, stood in awe of the purple-and-orange ball of fire rising seven miles into the summer sky. At the same time, Tina said, families were on their knees, terrified, praying the Hail Mary.

At daybreak, a single massive black cloud blew toward Tularosa. For days that July, members of Tina's community later detailed in testimony, it rained gray ash on farming communities nearby. Children opened their mouths to the sky to catch ashes on their tongues like summertime snowflakes. Tina's grandmother dusted and dusted, but the ash kept falling, clogging cisterns and dirtying clothes, covering their animals, gardens, and orchards with filth.[21] Soon chickens and dogs in the area were dead. Local newspapers reported that an ammunition depot had exploded, but no one explained the peculiar snow.[22]

It wasn't until after the bombings of Hiroshima and Nagasaki a few weeks later that people in Tularosa learned that the ash cloud that had enveloped their towns was from the world's first nuclear explosion. It wasn't until years later that they learned that scientists from Los Alamos had secretly slipped in and out of the area, testing the fallout. They had determined that the radiation levels were so dangerous that people should have been evacuated, but they never were.[23] Louis Hempelmann, the health director for the Manhattan Project, would later reveal that "a few people were probably overexposed, but they couldn't prove it and we couldn't prove it. So, we just assumed we got away with it."[24]

Radioactive fallout from a nuclear explosion is created by the fireball, the iconic symbol of the atomic age. The fireball rises rapidly, sucking up and vaporizing soil, water, whatever is around. The radioactive debris that is created by the fireball is then dispersed by wind and deposited on the ground. We can absorb radiation from fallout through our skin or by breathing it in, but scientists believe we are mainly exposed by eating contaminated food. According to several radiological health experts writing in the *American Scientist*, plants can be contaminated "when fallout is directly deposited on external surfaces of plants and when it is absorbed through the roots of plants."[25] People can also be exposed by consuming meat and milk from animals grazing on contaminated plants.

"The fallout from the Trinity test got into everything," Tina said. "It got into our water, into the animals we ate, into the milk we drank. Then the cancers started showing up. For years, people suspected they were exposed [to radiation] through their food. But no one could prove it." Then, in 2010, the Centers for Disease Control and Prevention confirmed that the snow-like fallout had indeed contaminated the food system at the time. Moreover, it determined that among the primary ways the public would have been exposed to radiation from the test was by eating contaminated food. In fact, eating foods with high levels of radiation has been linked to cancer, stillbirth, and birth defects.

"Both of my grandmothers developed cancer. My father died of cancer. My aunts, uncles, a few cousins, my niece, they all were diagnosed too. It's not a short list," Tina said. Then she told me some of her story. "I was thirty-nine when I was diagnosed with thyroid cancer. I am the fourth generation in my family to have had cancer since 1945, and that's typical of families around Tularosa," she said matter-of-factly. "When the doctors told me, I knew almost right away how I got it." A few moments passed. Then Tina added: "The bomb, it affected more than our health. It changed our culture too."

I asked her how.

"We are farming families. Hunting families. Fishing families. We lived off our land. We took care of that land," she replied. "All of these activities informed our food culture, our rituals, our way of life." Tina, who is also an avid outdoorsperson and hunter, continued: "I am worried about hunting now. I am worried about eating the meat of the animals we kill. And I am not the only one. The Native communities here [in New Mexico] worry about this too. It [the Trinity test] tainted our rituals. It tainted our way of life. The explosion happened eighty years ago, and it is still taking things from us. This changed us forever—and we never had a say in any of it."

In 2005, Tina cofounded the Tularosa Basin Downwinders Consortium (TBDC), a group dedicated to raising awareness of the public health effects of the Trinity test on downwind communities and pressuring Congress to include New Mexico residents left out of the Radiation Exposure Compensation Act (RECA), a law compensating people sickened by exposure to radiation through nuclear weapons testing and uranium mining during the Cold War.

Part of Tina's work with the TBDC is surveying downwinders about the types of cancers and other diseases they've experienced.

For a decade, she traveled the state compiling roughly a thousand health surveys. Downwinders often mentioned how the fallout from the Trinity test turned their own culture against them. The things that had once defined the downwinders' way of life—hunting, farming, fishing—killed them or made them sick. In May 2024, Mike Johnson, the Speaker of the House, pulled a vote to reauthorize RECA, turning Congress's back on the world's first victims of an atomic bomb.

It's not just downwinders who report heightened rates of cancer and illness; Pueblo nations around the lab at Los Alamos do too. Studies indicate higher rates of bone, brain, and esophageal cancer among former lab workers, but few efforts have been made to work with Pueblo nations to study the lab's impact on them, despite some communities having documentation of increased rates of cancer going back to the start of the Manhattan Project.[26] Leaders of Pueblo health organizations told me that they don't have the resources to use this data for their own peer-reviewed studies, yet the burden of proof remains on them. "The irony is the lab does cutting-edge cancer research," a former lab employee told me. "The MRI was invented up there."

New START, the treaty between the United States and Russia that is the last major bulwark against nuclear weapons proliferation, is scheduled to expire in 2026.[27] In the meantime, all nine nuclear powers are rushing to upgrade their arsenals with new weapons.[28] Over the next thirty years, it will cost the United States roughly $1.7 trillion to upgrade and maintain its nuclear stockpile. This military spending spree, W. J. Hennigan, an expert on America's nuclear weapons program, wrote in *The New York Times,* will cost taxpayers "almost $57 billion a year, or $108,000 per minute for three decades."[29] Right now, Congress is sending billions to Los Alamos to produce new nuclear warhead cores, suggesting it is prepared to move from simply updating an ostensibly aging arsenal to expanding it.[30]

Congress has authorized Los Alamos to produce "pits," grapefruit-sized plutonium triggers for nuclear bombs, at an industrial scale in the coming years.[31] Some analysts expect this new production to "generate levels of radiological and hazardous waste that the lab has not experienced."[32] This ramp-up could mean more waste and accidents in the lab's production facilities, potentially subjecting the public to unwittingly breathing, drinking, and eating ever more radioactive contaminants.[33]

These fears are not unfounded. In 2023, the U.S. National Nuclear Security Administration (NNSA), the federal agency responsible for safeguarding the country's nuclear facilities, cited Los Alamos for a "significant lack of attention or carelessness" in protecting workers and the public after four accidents, including one where too much fissionable material was concentrated in the same place, a near miss that could have started a nuclear chain reaction and a deadly burst of radiation.[34] What's more, Alicia Inez Guzmán, an investigative reporter covering Los Alamos, found nearly one hundred other, smaller accidents at the lab's plutonium pit handling facility, resulting in a mix of safety incidents, including fires, floods, and worker contamination.[35]

Nuclear experts fear things could get even worse. Since taking office in January 2025, President Trump and his top adviser, Elon Musk, have moved to drastically cut the federal workforce, including crucial posts at the NNSA. Already understaffed, the NNSA has lost huge numbers of scientists, engineers, and safety experts due to layoffs and buyouts, including nearly a dozen staff members who oversee plutonium pit operations at Los Alamos.[36]

· · ·

In 2021, the lab found traces of per- and polyfluoroalkyl substances (PFAS) in the soil and sediment on its property.[37] PFAS, often called "forever chemicals," since they don't readily break down inside our bodies or in the environment, are used on military bases across the country to extinguish incredibly hot fires from weapons testing. They are linked to cancer, liver damage, thyroid disease, and lowered immunity. While the lab says its PFAS problem does not threaten the public, PFAS from Cannon Air Force Base in eastern New Mexico have already forced dairy farmers in Clovis County, one of the country's leading sources of milk, to euthanize entire herds to keep the chemical out of the U.S. food supply.[38]

The DOE says it will cost about seven billion dollars and take another twenty years to clean up the toxic detritus of the Manhattan Project.[39] In the meantime, the lab will make more bomb cores while trying to assure the public that the food and water in the area are safe. Recently, a Pueblo elder told me that he and others from reservations around the lab have stopped hunting elk out of concern they might be grazing in contaminated areas on the plateau. Echoing a sentiment of hunters like Tina Cordova, he made it clear he was articulating a widely held sentiment. "Hunting is now a dying tradition," he said. "We know what they drink, and we're too afraid to eat their meat."

It's fair to say there's almost no faith among those who live in the cities, towns, and reservations around Los Alamos that the federal government will clean up its mess. Some call the cleanup a "forever problem" because of the scale and the expense. Few trust the estimates, and fewer trust the DOE, because of its foot-dragging incompetence. In fact, the Government Accountability Office in July 2023 called the DOE's cleanup effort weak and faulted it for failing to come up with a "comprehensive approach to prioritizing cleanup activities in a risk-informed manner."[40]

"We have seen this movie before. And we can't let it play out the same way," Tina Cordova told me, referring to New Mexico's people again playing the leading role in a new nuclear era. "It's exhausting, but that's why we're staying organized and speaking out about the consequences of nuclear arms. If we don't, we will always be worrying about whether our air is safe to breathe, our water safe to drink, and our food safe to eat."

At the beginning of this book, I described how violence often persists after the atrocities are over; how it can sink its ugly tentacles down into time, moving from one generation to another, menacing us, changing who we are. I mentioned the violent Partition of India and Pakistan in 1947 and its impact on my father, and how years later its legacy was still stealing precious aspects of my family's culture. I also described how in Kabul, at my dear friend Tamim's dinner table, I witnessed how decades of war were robbing Afghans of their culinary culture, one recipe at a time. In Albuquerque, where Tina and I were talking on that cold December day, I saw those tentacles again. I saw the violence of the Manhattan Project, alive and well, and accountable to no one, prowling the land, stealing both the lives and the culture of countless New Mexicans.

· · ·

But then there's H.O.P.E., the organization Marian Naranjo runs to help tackle public and environmental health issues affecting her Santa Clara Pueblo community. It was founded right around the time Los Alamos officials belatedly revealed to the public that they had discovered the chromium plume. Marian told me that she was hoping to launch a new Pueblo food-sovereignty initiative with other Tewa women. The goal is to grow their ancestral foods on a scale that could feed most people at the Santa Clara Pueblo. H.O.P.E. has already secured a mobile kitchen for the initiative so it can process and cook what it grows. Eventually, H.O.P.E. wants to work with Roxanne Swentzell to conduct phase three of the Pueblo Food Experience for the entire pueblo, not only to help heal some of the older adults but also to teach children about their own cuisine and help set healthier eating habits at an early age.

"We want to take what we learn from the project and share that with the other pueblos too," she said. "But first, before we plant any seeds, we need to test the soil to understand what is there from Los Alamos. Radioactivity does not go away; it's within our system." She reminded me that the half-life of plutonium contamination is twenty-four thousand years, and it has been only eighty years since it first showed up on the plateau. "Our Tewa people have always been here and will always be here, so we will always know radioactivity."

I asked her what they'd do if they found contaminants in the soil. Would it set back their project?

"No," she replied. "If the soil is not ready, we'll just build raised beds and greenhouses."

Marian paused for a second, then, in a reassuring tone with a notable hint of defiance, offered: "There's no alternative to justice—the lab has to take responsibility for what it has done, for the desecration of our bodies and our land. But we can't wait forever for it to clean up its mess. This place is our church, and it always will be. We must do what we can now."

Marian took another moment and then calmly said, "We will do what we have always done: persist."

Tina's Chicken Posole

"Serves a lot of people"

Before her activism for Trinity Test survivors, Tina Cordova owned a restaurant in Albuquerque called Mi Hitas. This is the recipe for her famous posole, which the restaurant sold out every day. Mi Hitas is now closed, but Tina told me that back then, in the mornings, when she would start making this dish, "the pot of water with the chicken, garlic, and oregano boiling would fill the entire restaurant with the wonderful smell of posole." She added, "It is an amazing aroma that still reminds me of kitchens where all the women before me cooked. Women like my mom, my grandmothers, and my aunts!"

4 skinless chicken breasts or 8 boneless, skinless chicken thighs, or a combination of breasts and thighs

5 garlic cloves, chopped, plus more as needed

1½ tablespoons dried Mexican oregano, plus more as needed

One 110-ounce can of hominy, drained

One 14-ounce tub red chili puree or 14-ounce can red chili sauce

2 tablespoons chicken bouillon base

Kosher salt

Chopped white onion, for garnish

Ray's Amaranth and Corn Tortillas (page 224) or flour or corn tortillas, for serving

Saltine crackers, for serving

1. In a large stockpot, combine the chicken, garlic, and oregano with water just to cover the chicken, and bring to a boil over medium-high heat. Turn down the heat to medium and simmer gently until the chicken is cooked through, 25 to 30 minutes.
2. Turn off the heat and, using a slotted spoon or tongs, transfer the chicken to a cutting board. Let the chicken cool until it can be handled, then cut into bite-size pieces.
3. Add the hominy, red chili puree, bouillon base, and cut-up chicken to the pot and bring to a boil over medium-high heat. Turn down the heat to low and simmer, uncovered, for 30 minutes to heat the hominy and blend the flavors.
4. Season with salt to taste, then add additional garlic and oregano if needed. Ladle into bowls, garnish with the onion, and serve, accompanied with the tortillas. Ray's amaranth and corn tortillas work especially well with this dish.

Marian's Cacao, Currant, and Piñon Nut Cookies

Makes 18 cookies

These are Marian Naranjo's cookies made strictly from precolonial ingredients from the Americas. She developed the recipe for *The Pueblo
Food Experience Cookbook*, a cookbook by the Pueblo peoples of New
Mexico that tells the story of their original foodways through both recipes and essays. The cookies are spectacular, and they are best when made
with the native New Mexico piñon nut, which is more buttery and sweeter
than other species of pine nut. Cacao powder and cacao nibs are both
made from cacao beans, but cacao powder is processed at a much lower
temperature, so it retains more nutrients. Look for it or cacao nibs in your
local supermarket or natural foods store. This recipe can easily be halved.

½ cup cacao powder or cacao
   nibs
1½ cups water
½ cup dried currants or dried
   strawberries

1 cup white, blue, or yellow
   cornmeal
1 cup shelled piñon or pine nuts,
   or shelled pumpkin or
   sunflower seeds

1. Preheat the oven to 350°F. Line a sheet pan with parchment paper.
2. In a medium saucepan, combine the cacao powder and water, and
   bring to a boil over medium-high heat. Boil for 1 minute then
   remove from the heat and strain through a fine-mesh sieve into a
   medium heatproof bowl. Discard the contents of the sieve.
3. Return the strained liquid to the saucepan, add the currants, and
   bring to a boil over medium-high heat. Turn down the heat to

medium and boil gently until the currants soften, about 2 minutes. Remove from the heat and transfer the contents of the pot, including the liquid, back to the bowl.

4. In a small bowl, stir together the cornmeal and nuts. Add the cornmeal-nut mixture to the warm cacao liquid and stir with a wooden spoon until the mixture is the consistency of cookie dough. Drop the dough by rounded 2-tablespoon portions onto the sheet pan, spacing the cookies about 4 inches apart.

5. Bake the cookies until the center is set, about 10 to 15 minutes. Let them cool on the pan for about 10 minutes before serving. The cookies will keep in an airtight container at room temperature for 3 or 4 days.

ACKNOWLEDGMENTS

Food is powerful. But I have always been reluctant to ascribe it mystical powers. However, this book has forced me to admit now that food is indeed something of a skeleton key. For most of my life, food has, in one way or another, opened new areas of the world, revealing people I would never have otherwise met, making me a more fulsome person along the way.

Having an idea about food and war and turning it into a book was far harder than I could have imagined. Without Alice Whitwham, my literary agent at the Cheney Agency, this book would not have been written. Alice is a paradigm of brilliance and grace. Since the outset, she has been my strongest advocate, an impenetrable flak jacket, and a dependably honest friend. If I am afraid of failing anyone with this book, it's Alice.

Two longtime friends, Nimmi Gowrinathan and Nick McDonell, have helped with this project in more ways than I can describe. These two writers have long been intertwined in my personal and professional lives, deeply enriching both. I've tried to emulate their intelligence and sensitivity both in my writing and in life but never seem to come close.

Two families, the Baker-Samees—Aryn, Tamim, and Zolakhya—and the ad hoc family that Keiko Kawagoe built for me at Kimamaya in Miyazaki, Japan, have patiently taught me to see beauty in places often overlooked. My time with them, always too short, inevitably unearths things about life, culture, and myself I never knew.

Being pulled into Madhulika Sikka and Crown's orbit has been life-changing. Madhulika understood the concept of this book from day one. She is a supremely compassionate editor and now friend. During an unexpected rough patch in this process, she found me the most precious thing in life: time. This would be a far lesser book in anyone else's hands.

I am forever indebted to the hundreds of people who spoke to me for this project—who shared parts of their lives with me—in some instances for the first time. You've met many of them by name in these pages, while others were present in the ideas, but everyone gave generously of themselves for no motivation other than to help us understand their universe.

In the Czech Republic, I'm forever grateful to the Pecha family— Václav, Michaela, Vašek, and Barbara—as well the Krykorkas— Jan and Zuzana—for allowing me into their homes and lives over these many years. Dr. Václav Pecha sadly passed away while I was writing this book. He was a good friend, hooking me early on the beauty of the Czech lands. But his infectious love of life and good food, as well as his superb sense of humor, all live on in his family and friends, including the wonderfully gregarious and generous Lojza Slepánek, to whom I also owe a great deal for showing me the soul of Czech food. Similarly, I thank Roman and Jana Vaněk, who have more recently opened up their home to me. Without them, I could never have written chapter 1, and without them most Czechs wouldn't be eating as well as they do today. I'm also indebted to another great chef, Jan Punčochář, and his staff at U Matěje in Prague for showing me the past and present of Czech cooking. My deep gratitude also goes to Pavel Žáček, Vanda Thorne, Martin Franc, Iveta Hajdáková, and Anna West for putting Czech and Slovak cuisine in both a historical and a political context for me. I thank David Farley for reading draft chapters, as well as Vera Lich and John Sobol for showing me the umbilical connection between

Cleveland, my hometown, and early fights for Czech and Slovak independence.

The chapter on Sri Lanka and Eelam Tamil cuisine wouldn't have been possible without the exceptional Mario Arulthas and his deep knowledge of Tamil history, politics, and culture as well as his impeccable fact-checking. The wisdom of Anushani Alagarajah, Karunyan Arulanantham, Ahilan Arulanantham, Parthi Paramsothy, Jeeva Perumalpillai-Essex, Sanathanan Thamotharampillai, and the late Ethir Verasingham shaped my thinking from the outset, and for that I'm grateful. I was aided by many people on many trips to northern Sri Lanka over the years. Among those I can safely name are Suhirrthavathy Thiruchelvam and Kumanan Kanapathipillai, both of whom translated and photographed for me. In Canada, Babu Rajakulasingam, Yalini Rajakulasingam, Roshan Kanagarajah, Kumar Karalapillai, and Suganthy Muthukumar generously gave their time and cooking, as did many other spectacular home cooks and chefs. I'm particularly indebted to Rajiva, and people like her, whom I cannot mention by their true names. I might never have known the glories of Eelam Tamil cuisine if not for them.

Generosity defines Rohingya culture. There may not be a better example of that than this: As I began writing these acknowledgments in August 2024, historic flooding submerged eastern Bangladesh; countless people struggled to find food and clean water. To help their Bangladeshi hosts in their time of need, Rohingya refugees locked in the camps donated food from their constantly dwindling rations to the flood victims. Despite this display of humanity, the Bangladeshi government was, at the same time, turning away Rohingyas at the Myanmar border, who were fleeing in what some observers believe may be have been more genocidal violence. If that signals anything, it is this: It's time to close camps in Bangladesh, and it's time for Myanmar, and regional countries, and rich countries alike, to extend Rohingya citizenship once and for all.

There are many Rohingya people across the world who have generously helped me understand their culture. Several people have played an outsize role in helping with this book. First is the supremely skilled photojournalist Ro Yassin Abdumonab. Ro's research, translation, and filming assistance were invaluable. He's among the best colleagues I've ever had the privilege of working alongside. I'm equally indebted to Sharifah Shakirah, the founder of the Rohingya Women's Development Network (RWDN), who for years, has graciously guided my understanding of both Rohingya human rights and her cuisine. I'm similarly grateful to Syedah Husain at RWDN in Malaysia, Sahat Zia Hero and his organization, Rohingyatographer, in Bangladesh as well as Sam Naeem in the U.S. I thank the poets Mayyu Ali, Ahtaram Shin, and Shahida Win for opening a window on Rohingya culture that too few have the opportunity to look through. Most of all, I'm grateful to Maryam and her family (whom I can't mention by their true names) for letting me into their lives; it's an honor I hold dear every day.

Outside the Rohingya community, Richard Horsey and Matthew Smith have long been shining a light on Myanmar's politics and human rights. Their comments on early drafts undoubtedly made the chapter on Rohingya cuisine better. David Palazón, Shahirah Majumdar, and A. K. Rahman were invaluable in helping me see the role international aid agencies should (and shouldn't) play in protecting culture in times of crisis. I could never have experienced Myanmar the way I did without the hospitality of Adam Cooper, Isabell Poppelbaum, Susanne Kempel, Laurent Meillan, and Karin Zarifi, who graciously housed and fed me in Yangon and Bangkok over the years. Maya Lazić is a rock, to whom I am forever indebted, for keeping my head above water in very stormy seas while at the UN.

The chapter on Uyghur cuisine was among the most challenging to write, since I didn't travel inside Xinjiang for this book. It was simply too risky for interviewees. Rather, I relied on my notes and memories from my time there as well as the testimony of Uyghurs who left or escaped China more recently. I'm especially grateful to Tahir and Marhaba Izgil and their family for generously sharing their memories with me. I'm similarly indebted to Gulchehra Hoja, Zubayra Shamseden, and dozens of other Uyghur journalists, activists, chefs, and home cooks in China, the U.S., the E.U., and Turkey who similarly sat and spoke with me. I wish I could name you. I stand in appreciation for James Millward, Darren Byler, and Jonathan Loeb for sharing their knowledge of Xinjiang as well as their comments on various drafts. I also thank an old friend and diplomat, whose name is best left unsaid.

There's something extraordinary happening with Bolivian food and drink right now. Indicative of this trend are Valentina Arteaga, Sebastián Giménez, Alexandra Meleán, Andrea Moscoso Weisse, Juan Pablo Reyes, and Marsia Taha. I owe them a great deal for exposing me to modern Bolivian cuisine, as well as La Paz's morning markets and its nightlife. Arguably, modern Bolivian cuisine wouldn't have come about if not for the cultural and political space created by extraordinary women like Doñas Juana Quispe and Roxana Argandoña; it was an honor to be welcomed into their homes to hear their stories. Those interviews would've been incomprehensible to me if not for Marcelo Pérez del Carpio's patient translation, as well as his spectacular photography. I'm deeply grateful to the anthropologist Carol Conzelman, who allowed me and my wife to crash her holiday in the La Paz Yungas, where she patiently answered my questions about her decades of research on coca in the Andes. Nearly the same can be said for the anthropologist and author Thomas Grisaffi, who found time during his research travels around the Chapare. Above all, I'm indebted to Kathryn Ledebur, the executive director of the Andean Information Network in Cochabamba. Not only is she among the most intrepid human rights activists I know, but she's among the most gracious. Kathryn gave me hours upon hours of her time to edit and fact-check. I'm still dumbfounded by her generosity.

I also traveled to Colombia and Peru for my research on coca. While I don't discuss these countries at length in this book, the people I met in these places deeply influenced my thinking. In Colombia, I thank Diego García-Devis and Alejandro Osses for introducing me to dozens of activists, politicians, chefs, brewmasters, chocolatiers, and cheesemakers reshaping public attitudes toward coca there. In Peru, Cleto Cusipaucar and Jan Brack graciously spent hours walking the hillsides around Moray, discussing their work to preserve rare ingredients. I'm indebted to María Elena García and David Greenwood-Sánchez, two brilliant academics based in the U.S. Both were coincidentally in Peru during my trip in the summer of 2023, and both took time from their own tight research schedules to educate a stranger on the politics of Peruvian cuisine.

I stand in awe of the Pueblo Nations now in New Mexico. Being shown life from their perspective, even for a brief moment, has been among the greatest privileges of my life. At Santa Clara Pueblo, Marian Naranjo and her son Chef Ray, as well as Roxanne Swentzell and her son Porter, showed me a whole new way of eating, if not living. *The Pueblo Food Experience Cookbook* has made me healthier—for that I will forever be grateful. At Santa Clara, I am also indebted to Nathana Bird, Beata Tsosie-Peña, and other current and former staff of Tewa Women United, as well as the brilliant and immeasurably kind Dimitri Brown, who reviewed a draft of the chapter. At Ohkay Owingeh, Chef Ryan Rainbird Taylor added much needed depth and texture to my rudimentary understanding of Pueblo cuisine. At Taos Pueblo, I wish to thank Tiana Suazo, the inspirational farmer and food sovereignty activist; it was a privilege to be entrusted with your story. I am also indebted to the passionate farmer and activist Reyna Banteah from Zuni Pueblo for introducing me to my first amaranth plant.

Beyond the Pueblo Nations, I owe special thanks to Andi Murphy (Diné) for her time in Albuquerque, answering countless questions, as well as her *Toasted Sister* podcast, which was an invaluable, and immensely enjoyable, way to learn about Indigenous foodways. Similarly, I'm appreciative of four extraordinary chefs, Ben Jacobs (Osage), Sean Sherman (Oglala Lakota Sioux), Camren Stott (Anishinaabe), and Brian Yazzi (Diné) for speaking with me often at a moment's notice and in the freezing cold about their inspiring work. I thank Kristie Orosco (Kumeyaay) and Stan Rodriguez (Kumeyaay) for introducing me to the rich history, culture, and food of Native California, which left an indelible mark on my thinking and writing. I'd be remiss if I didn't say the same about the exceptional Kealoha Domingo and his native homeland of Hawai'i.

In terms of the Epilogue, I still remember the white-hot horror I felt when I encountered that black shadow on those stone steps in Hiroshima—when I learned it was a person permanently scorched into the stone by the heat of the atomic bomb. To take nothing away from the Hibakusha's stories, memories, and their righteous work to rid the world of nuclear weapons, most of us are taught that the first victims of the atomic age were Japanese, when in fact they were ordinary New Mexicans. It was an honor to spend all those hours with Tina Cordova and Marian Naranjo, who walked me through their respective family histories to remind us of all of the injustices committed against countless New Mexicans by the Manhattan Project—injustices that the U.S. government continues to ignore. I couldn't have written the Epilogue without the help of

Alicia Inez Guzmán, one of the most talented investigative journalists I've ever met. I'd also like to thank the Native Americans and Nuevomexicanos who recounted their personal experience living near Los Alamos National Laboratory, who urged me to share their stories but asked not to be named.

There also exists a special group of people composed mostly of my former colleagues at Human Rights Watch, International Crisis Group, and Center for Civilians in Conflict, who deserve thanks, specifically Sarah Yager, Candace Rondeaux, John Sifton, Robert Templer, and Saman Zia-Zarifi, all of whom went through versions of this book, providing crucial advice and encouragement at different stages. Similarly, I am indebted to Katia Bachko, whose crucial late-stage editorial advice unquestionably made this book better, as well as Krista Kowalczyk, who photographed me for this project. That said, this book is based primarily on oral accounts. While I've made every effort to confirm facts from each account, it also was necessary to enlist professional researchers and fact-checkers. It was an honor to work with Lucie Koenig, as well as several others, who prefer not to be named.

I'm deeply indebted to Chef José Andrés and Richard Wolffe for their friendship, partnership, and willingness to open doors to parts of the food and humanitarian worlds I never could.

The Crown Publishing Group is a special place. I have worked with editors my entire career, but none like Sohayla Farman, Fariza Hawke, Hilary Roberts, and Sharon Silva, all of whom I found to be supremely thorough, thoughtful, and kind. Dare I say they made what is often a tedious process enjoyable.

There were also many others who helped me fill up blank pages with their connections, encouragement, inspiration, appetites, and/or hospitality. Here I'd like to thank Michael Archer, Joni Arends, Dureyshevar and Malik Arshad, Martha Barry and Curtis

Cravens, Kim Barker, James Berzi, the late Jan Black, Cari Borja, Jiffer Bourguignon, Belinda Bowling, Shay Buchner, Kate Carey, Mark and Nitya Chambers as well as Tarun and Rana Chambers (who were impeccable recipe testers and food critics on many occasions), Nick Conway and Corey Stoughton, Sarba Das, John Dempsey, Carol Dysinger, Sophie Erikson, Justin Fraterman, Noriyuki Fujimoto, James-Henry Holland, Jonathan Horowitz and Leslie Bailey, Anadil Hossain, Margaret Jacobs, Marissa Jackson, May Jeong, Sidney Jones, Marla Keenan, Ashfaq Khan, Stephanie Kleine-Albrandt, Carolyn Kormann, Ana and Alastair Leithead, Eva and T. J. Lindeman-Sánchez, Rita Mestokosho, Saad Mohseni, Sahr Muhammedally and Russ Dyk, Ayesha Nadarajah, Bill Namagoose, Robert Nickelsberg, Anna and Timur Nusratty, Daisy Parker, Gretchen Peters, Balakrishnan Rajagopal, Sophie Richardson, Lev Rukhin, M. Salaam, Haroun Samei, Farouq Samim, the Shaikh, Chambless, and Gary families, Zolaykha Sherzad, Alexandra Sicotte-Lévesque and Ralph Mamiya, David Stevens, Edwina Thompson, Kirthika Umasuthan, James Walsh, Hinori Watanbe, and Thin Lei Win.

Lastly, my greatest thanks go to three people. Dominique, my wife, has been more important to this project than she knows. Almost every story and idea here we talked through or witnessed together. Dominique was a constant encouraging and thoughtful force who consistently reminded me that writing this book was worthwhile no matter what it took. And to Leah and Ali, my parents. Words will always feel inadequate in expressing my love and gratitude for you both. You always understood when I needed a helping hand or a hard kick in the ass. That is why this book is dedicated to all of you.

NOTES

Prologue: The Language of Food

1. Aanchal Malhotra, *Remnants of Separation: A History of the Partition Through Material Memory* (Noida, Uttar Pradesh: HarperCollins India, 2017).

2. *Palaw* is also spelled *polo, pilaf, pilau, pulao,* and *plov,* depending on the origin.

3. Sadly, something similar can be said for Palestinian olive farmers in the West Bank. Like fishing for Gazans, the olive harvest is central to Palestinian life and culture. In October 2024, the United Nations accused Israel of using "war-like" tactics against Palestinians in the West Bank, citing killings by soldiers and attacks on Palestinian olive groves by Israeli settlers. In 2023, according to the UN, approximately 23,000 acres of olive-cultivated land across the occupied West Bank remained unharvested due to Israeli-imposed restrictions. This resulted in millions of dollars of losses for Palestinian olive farmers and olive oil producers. A panel of UN experts concluded that "the Palestinian people's relationship to olive trees, which can live for hundreds of years, is also about their relationship to their ancestors and to their future. Restricting olive harvests, destroying orchards and banning access to water sources is an attempt by Israel to expand its illegal settlements." See "Israel Must Stop Violent Settler Attacks on Palestinian Farmers That Threaten Their Olive Harvest, Say UN Experts," UN Office of High Commissioner for Human Rights, October 16, 2024, ohchr.org/en/press-releases/2024/10 /israel-must-stop-violent-settler-attacks-palestinian-farmers-threaten-their.

4. In January 2025, the U.S. House of Representatives passed the Illegitimate Court Counteraction Act, a bill requiring the executive branch to impose targeted sanctions on a wide range of individuals connected to the International Criminal Court (ICC), which investigates the most serious violations of human rights, like genocide and war crimes. The sweeping bill would require the U.S. government to impose asset freezes and visa bans on foreign persons who conduct or assist any ICC investigation of U.S. persons or persons from certain allied countries. Basic human rights work like documenting and sharing evidence of potential international crimes would be sanctionable under the House bill. What's more, under the bill, family members of human rights investigators could also lose their U.S. visas or be banned from obtaining them. The bill, H.R. 23, passed by a vote of 243 to 140, with 45 Democrats joining Republicans in backing the

measure; 30 Democrats and 20 Republicans didn't bother to vote; 1 Republican abstained. On January 28, 2025, the Senate voted against moving the bill forward. On February 6, 2025, however, President Donald Trump issued an executive order authorizing asset freezes and entry bans on ICC officials, their families, and others supporting the court's work, effectively bringing the bill into force.

Chapter 1: The Czech Republic

1. Other writers have recently pointed this out too. For example, see Elizabeth Smith, "The Communist Cookbook That Defined Prague's Cuisine," *Atlas Obscura*, August 29, 2018, and David Farley, "How Prague's Top Chefs Are Reviving Austro-Hungarian Cuisine with a Modern Twist," *Travel + Leisure*, September 1, 2024.

2. Peter Demetz, *Prague in Black and Gold: Scenes from the Life of a European City* (New York: Hill and Wang, 1997).

3. The manuscript Vrabec submitted was for *Jihočeská Houbařská Kuchařka*, or the *South Bohemian Mushroom Cookbook*, which covered cooking with foraged mushrooms. It was eventually published in 1986.

4. Martin Franc, "Socialist Luxury on a Fork: Haute Cuisine in Czechoslovakia, 1948–1969," *Czech Journal of Contemporary History* 28, no. 3 (2021): 619–47.

5. Quoted in Alan Cowell, "Memories of Wartime Brutalities Revive Czech-German Animosity," *New York Times*, February 9, 1996.

6. Elizabeth Smith, "The Communist Cookbook That Defined Prague's Cuisine," *Atlas Obscura*, August 29, 2018.

7. David Farley, "A New Bohemia Is Evolving in Prague," *Afar*, September 24, 2012.

8. Smith, "Communist Cookbook."

9. Kenny Dunn, "Keeping That Local Flavor: A Deeper Look at Lokal," *Eating Europe*, February 9, 2016.

10. Lizzie Collingham, *The Taste of War: World War II and the Battle for Food* (New York: Penguin, 2012), 7.

11. Smith, "Communist Cookbook."

12. Approximately 263,000 Jews living within the borders of Czechoslovakia were murdered by the Nazis in the Holocaust. See "The Holocaust in Bohemia and Moravia," published by the United States Holocaust Memorial Museum. The food historian Lizzie Collingham points out that "starvation is a slow and excruciating process and the National Socialists [Nazis] discovered that starving unwanted groups to death was slower and less efficient than they had expected." Therefore, they decided to eliminate as many "useless eaters" as possible by sending almost ninety thousand Jews from Terezín to extermination camps in the Baltic states and Poland. By the end of the war, only one thousand Jews may have remained alive in the Czech lands. "Thus," as Collingham writes, "food is

implicated in the decision to speed up the Holocaust." Collingham, *Taste of War*, 7. The ninety thousand figure was given by the Czech Jewish novelist and dissident Ivan Klíma, who was interned at Terezín. Quoted in Cowell, "Memories of Wartime Brutalities Revive Czech-German Animosity."

13. Matthew Sedacca, "Why the Nazi Party Loved Decaf Coffee," *Atlas Obscura*, November 15, 2017.

14. Lizzie Collingham points out, "The lack of fat, combined with the very limited quantity of animal protein in the form of meat, eggs, or cheese in virtually all wartime diets resulted in a nagging sensation of hunger, even if the food contained sufficient calories." She later adds, "A lack of sugar and sweetness in the diet also provoked sometimes unbearable cravings." *The Taste of War*, 13.

15. Thomas McEnchroe, "From Cream to Pig's Blood: How Cooking Evolved During the Protectorate," Radio Prague International, January 4, 2019.

16. The 1945 Potsdam Agreement endorsed the expulsion of the German population from Czechoslovakia.

17. Six thousand more deaths were unexplained or listed as suicides. These figures come from a joint Czech-German historical commission. The death toll may have been far higher, but the precise numbers are disputed. See Brian Kenety and Martin Mikule, "Expulsion of Czech Germans: Bitter Memories and Disrupted Relations," Radio Prague International, May 9, 2005; and Robert Tait, "The Germans and Czechs Trying to Deal with Ghosts of the Past," *Guardian*, November 11, 2016.

18. In the Czech and Slovak languages, the Communist Party of Czechoslovakia is called Komunistická strana Československa, or KSČ for short.

19. Franc, "Socialist Luxury on a Fork."

20. Franc.

21. Smith, "Communist Cookbook."

22. Author interviews with Martin Franc, Prague, August 2022, and Roman Vaněk, Prague, September 2024.

23. Vrabec was incredibly active in retirement, continuing to write and teach across the country and internationally. Franc, "Socialist Luxury on a Fork."

24. Anna West, "When They Came for the Family Farms," *Are We Europe*, July 2022.

25. West, "When They Came."

26. Slavenka Drakulić, *Café Europa Revisited: How to Survive Post-Communism* (New York: Penguin, 2021).

27. Author interviews with Czech and Slovak academics. See also Franc, "Socialist Luxury on a Fork."

28. Author interviews. See also Franc.

29. Author interviews. See also Franc.

30. Author interviews. See also Franc.

31. Author interviews. See also Franc.

32. Author interviews. See also Franc, and Pavla Horáková, "Foreign Influences in Czech Cuisine," Radio Prague International, October 15, 2005.
33. Smith, "Communist Cookbook."
34. Drakulić, *Café Europa Revisited*, 62.
35. Henry Kamm, "Prague Leaders Home," *New York Times,* August 27, 1968.
36. Author interviews with Czech and Slovak academics. See also Franc, "Socialist Luxury on a Fork."
37. Smith, "Communist Cookbook."
38. František Syrový and Antonin Nestával, *Receptury teplých pokrmů* (Prague: Merkur, 1979), 661.
39. Streisand changed her name from "Barbara" to "Barbra."
40. Václav Havel, "The Power of the Powerless" (1978), trans. Paul Wilson, in *The Power of the Powerless: Citizens Against the State in Central Eastern Europe,* ed. John Keane (Armonk, NY: M. E. Sharpe, 1985), 43.
41. According to a 2017 survey by the Pew Research Center, just 29 percent of Czechs reported believing in a higher power. Another Pew survey published in 2019 found that just 9 percent of Czechs said religion is very important in their daily lives, one of the lowest percentages on this measure in the world. See "Eastern and Western Europeans Differ on Importance of Religion, Views of Minorities, and Key Social Issues," Pew Research Center, October 29, 2018.
42. Author interview with Iveta Hajdáková, January 2023. See also Iveta Hajdáková, "Gastronauts of Eastern Europe" (PhD diss., Charles University, Prague, 2005).
43. Since the fall of communism, Czechs are not only eating better food but also eating differently. During the communist years, Czechs experienced one of the highest rates of deaths related to coronary heart disease in the world. But after the Velvet Revolution in 1989, doctors began reporting an inexplicable drop in the incidence of heart disease. Only recently have medical researchers been able to offer an explanation. For most of its time in power, the KSČ subsidized meat and dairy products, which comprised a large portion of the communist-era diet. In 1991, Václav Havel's government ended this policy. The researchers found that ending subsidies "put immediate pressure on the budgets of the majority of families," compelling them to change their diets for the better. The downward trend continues today and has already added seven years to Czech life expectancy. See R. Poledne et al., "Rapid Drop in Coronary Heart Disease Mortality in Czech Male Population—What Was Actually Behind It?," *Biomedicines* 10, no. 11 (2022): 2871, doi.org/10.3390/biomedicines10112871.

Chapter 2: Sri Lanka and the Tamil Diaspora

1. For more on the significance of *kanji* among Eelam Tamils today, see Pallavi Pundir, "The Fearlessness of Kanji," *Eater,* January 2, 2024.
2. In Tamil, the word *aru* means "six," and *suvai* means "taste." In Tamil the

six tastes are *inipu* (sweet), *pulipu* (sour), *kasapu* (bitter), *kaarpu* (spicy/pungent), *uvarpu* (salty), and *thuvarpu* (astringent). That said, the concept of *arusuvai* is not unique to Tamil cuisine. It is also found in other South Asian culinary traditions such as Ayurvedic cooking.

3. S. J. Tambiah, *Sri Lanka: Ethnic Fratricide and the Dismantling of Democracy* (Chicago: University of Chicago Press, 1986).

4. Neil DeVotta, "Standardization and Ethnocracy in Sri Lanka," WIDER Working Paper 86 (2022), doi.org/10.35188/UNU-WIDER/2022/217-1. For more on the relationship between language and the civil war, see Neil DeVotta, *Blowback: Linguistic Nationalism, Institutional Decay, and Ethnic Conflict in Sri Lanka* (Stanford, CA: Stanford University Press, 2004).

5. E. Valentine Daniel, *Charred Lullabies: Chapters in an Anthropography of Violence* (Princeton, NJ: Princeton University Press, 1996).

6. HALO Trust, "Sri Lanka," n.d., halotrust.org/where-we-work/south-asia/sri-lanka/.

7. Cassava was sometimes used in short eats when potatoes were hard to come by during the war.

8. The army is composed of more than 210,000 personnel in a country of 22 million. See Adayaalam Centre for Policy Research and People for Equality and Relief in Lanka, "Normalising the Abnormal: The Militarization of Mullaitivu" (report, October 4, 2017).

9. Steven M. Goode, "A Historical Basis for Force Requirements in Counterinsurgency," U.S. Army, March 25, 2010.

10. Nimmi Gowrinathan and Kate Cronin-Furman, "The Forever Victims? Tamil Women in Post-war Sri Lanka," Deviarchy.com, August 28, 2015.

11. Paisley Dodds, "Dozens of Men Say Sri Lankan Forces Raped and Tortured Them," Associated Press, November 8, 2017.

12. Maarten Bavinck, "Fishing Rights in Post-war Sri Lanka: Results of a Longitudinal Village Enquiry in the Jaffna Region," *Maritime Studies* 14, no. 1 (2015): doi.org/10.1186/s40152-014-0019-0.

13. For more on women fighting the liberation struggles, see Nimmi Gowrinathan, *Radicalizing Her* (Boston: Beacon Press, 2021).

14. International Crisis Group, "The Sri Lankan Tamil Diaspora After the LTTE" (Report No. 186, February 23, 2010).

Chapter 3: Myanmar and Bangladesh

1. Chitrita Banerji, "The Bengali *Bonti*," *Gastronomica* 1, no. 2 (2001): 23–26.

2. Banerji, "The Bengali *Bonti*."

3. Jane Perlez, "Rise in Bigotry Fuels Massacre Inside Myanmar," *New York Times*, March 2, 2014.

4. Azeem Ibrahim, *The Rohingyas: Inside Myanmar's Hidden Genocide,* revised and updated edition (London: Hurst, 2018).

5. International Crisis Group, "Myanmar: The Politics of Rakhine State" (Report No. 261, October 22, 2014).

6. Lizzie Collingham, *Curry: A Tale of Cooks and Conquerors* (Oxford: Oxford University Press, 2006).

7. Ibrahim, *Rohingyas,* 25.

8. Ibrahim, 27.

9. International Crisis Group, "Myanmar."

10. For more on this UN official, see "Myanmar Rohingya: UN Recalls Top Official Lok-Dessallien," BBC, October 11, 2017; Oliver Holmes, "Top UN Official to Leave Myanmar amid Criticism of Rohingya Approach," *Guardian,* October 12, 2017. See also Hannah Ellis-Petersen and Emanuel Stoakes, "UN Report Condemns Its Conduct in Myanmar as Systemic Failure," *Guardian,* June 17, 2019.

11. Shayna Bauchner, "'Nothing Called Freedom': A Decade of Detention for Rohingya in Myanmar's Rakhine State," Human Rights Watch, June 10, 2022.

12. *Isamas salan* is the most common Rohingya spelling, though some might spell *salan* as *salon.* You won't find many results on Google because most people outside the Rohingya community don't know of it and not much about Rohingya food has been translated into English. Until recently, Rohingya was mostly an oral language. The only book that has identified and translated *isamas salan* is *RWDN Cookbook: Recipes and Stories from Our Kitchen to Yours* (Kuala Lumpur: RWDN, 2019), likely the only Rohingya cookbook in existence, from the Rohingya Women Development Network. For the spellings of Rohingya dishes in this book, I relied on the wisdom of Sharifah Shakirah, the founder of the RWDN; the spellings listed in the RWDN's cookbook; and the wisdom of Ro Yassin Abdumonab and his elders.

13. According to Rohingya sources and various human rights organizations, the Myanmar military has abducted and forcibly recruited more than one thousand Rohingya Muslim men and boys from across Rakhine State since early 2024. See Human Rights Watch, "Myanmar: Military Forcibly Recruiting Rohingya" (report, April 9, 2024).

14. World Bank, "Myanmar Economic Monitor: Livelihoods Under Threat" (report, June 2024).

15. Jessica Olney and Ali Ahmed, "Rohingya Face Fresh Uncertainty in Myanmar," United States Institute of Peace, May 8, 2024.

16. To get a sense of the physical space the Rohingya are confined to in Bangladesh, see Mohammed Hussein and Hanna Duggal, "What Is Life Like Inside the World's Biggest Refugee Camp?," Al Jazeera, August 25, 2023.

17. Hujjat Ullah, "Cultivating Hope, Harvesting Survival, Nourishing the Community," *Rohingyatographer,* no. 3 (December 2024).

18. Ullah, "Cultivating Hope."

19. In 2023, Bangladesh's home minister, Asaduzzaman Khan, defended his government's actions to Radio Free Asia, saying: "The number of Rohingya in Cox's Bazar is now several times higher than the locals. In this situation, if the Rohingyas are allowed to move freely, it will be difficult for us to handle the situation." He continued: "If anyone says they are worse

off here than in Myanmar, it would be totally wrong." John Bechtel and Ahammad Foyez, "Rohingyas Face Prison-like Conditions in Bangladesh Camps: Report," Radio Free Asia, September 22, 2023.

20. Michael Shaikh, "On Genocide in Myanmar and the Loss of Rohingya Foodways," *Literary Hub*, March 29, 2021.

21. This statement was made by a government official from the Awami League, Bangladesh's ruling party. In the summer of 2024, student demonstrations brought down the Awami League government and replaced it with a caretaker government. At the time of this writing, in December 2024, there is no discernible policy difference between the previous Awami League government and the caretaker government with regard to Rohingya refugees. In fact, there are signs the caretaker government may be taking an even harder line against the Rohingya. In August 2024, extreme violence in Rakhine State, across the border in Myanmar, forced more Rohingya to flee to Bangladesh for safety. Some of the violence reportedly included targeted attacks on Rohingya communities. Reports from eyewitnesses I spoke to at the time indicated that Bangladesh's border guards were blocking the refugees from entering the country. See also Human Rights Watch, "Myanmar: Armies Target Ethnic Rohingya, Rakhine" (report, August 12, 2024). In September 2024, in the midst of the violence, Mohammad Shamsud Douza, a senior Bangladeshi government official in charge of refugees, told Reuters that "Bangladesh is already over-burdened and unable to accommodate any more Rohingya." See Ruma Paul, "Thousands of Rohingya Flee to Bangladesh from Violence in Myanmar, Official Says," Reuters, September 3, 2024. See also "Bangladesh: End Rohingya Refugee Pushbacks," Fortify Rights, November 19, 2024.

Chapter 4: China and the Uyghurs

1. According to Kate Winslow and Guy Ambrosino, "onions most likely originated in Central Asia in the area around present day Iran, Pakistan and Uzbekistan, and have been grown and harvested since at least 5000 BC, making them one of the oldest cultivated plants we know." Kate Winslow and Guy Ambrosino, *Onions Etcetera: The Essential Allium Cookbook* (Minneapolis: Burgess Lea Press, 2017), 12.

2. In 1946, Abdurehim Ötkür, the father of Uyghur modern poetry, wrote "Män aq bayraq amäs" ("I am no white flag"), an intricate poem celebrating the Tängri Tagh and their tallest peak, Khan Tengri. Ötkür wrote the poem during his time of political imprisonment for supporting Uyghur independence in a rebellion in Ghulja. Today, his poem is widely read as a metaphor for his people. Because of the poem, the Tängri Tagh have become a symbol not only of Uyghurs' resilience but also of their ancient and unbreakable connection to their land.

3. For more on fat-tailed sheep, see Anne Ewbank, "For Thousands of Years, People Have Been Obsessed with Fat-Tailed Sheep," *Atlas Obscura*, February 5, 2019.

4. James A. Millward and Peter C. Perdue, "Political and Cultural History of the Xinjiang Region Through the Late Nineteenth Century," in *Xinjiang: China's Muslim Borderland*, ed. S. Frederick Starr (Armonk, NY: M. E. Sharpe, 2014).

5. Darren Byler, *Terror Capitalism: Uyghur Dispossession and Masculinity in a Chinese City* (Durham: Duke University Press, 2022).

6. Sean R. Roberts, *The War on the Uyghurs: China's Internal Campaign Against a Muslim Minority* (Princeton, NJ: Princeton University Press, 2020). See also Rian Thum, "The Spatial Cleansing of Xinjiang: Mazar Desecration in Context," in *Xinjiang Year Zero*, eds. Darren Byler, Ivan Franceschini, and Nicholas Loubere (Canberra, Australia: ANU Press, 2022).

7. Darren Byler, "The Future of Uyghur Cultural—and Halal—Life in the Year of the Pig," *Art of Life in Chinese Central Asia* (blog), March 9, 2019.

8. Darren Byler, the esteemed scholar of Uyghur oppression, also came to this conclusion. Byler, "The Future of Uyghur Cultural—and Halal—Life."

9. For more on this, see Barbara Demick, *Eat the Buddha: Life and Death in a Tibetan Town* (New York: Random House, 2021).

10. For more on this, see Human Rights Watch, "In the Name of Security: Counterterrorism Law Worldwide Since September 11" (report, June 29, 2012).

11. Author interview with Darren Byler, September 2022.

12. Tahir Hamut Izgil, *Waiting to Be Arrested at Night: A Uyghur Poet's Memoir of China's Genocide* (New York: Penguin, 2023), 157.

13. Urumchi is also spelled as Ürümqi. I have chosen to use the spelling that is closer to how the word sounds in Uyghur. The dictionary spelling is based on Mandarin and can be considered antiquated.

14. Tahir Hamut Izgil recounted these events to me in person over several meetings. But he also tells about them with poetic clarity in his book, *Waiting to Be Arrested at Night*.

15. Izgil, *Waiting to Be Arrested at Night*, 29.

16. Izgil.

17. Izgal, 51.

18. Tahir Hamut Izgil, "One by One, My Friends Were Sent to the Camps," *Atlantic*, July 14, 2021.

19. Izgil, "One by One," and author interviews.

20. Izgil, *Waiting to Be Arrested at Night*, 35.

21. Izgil, 83.

22. Izgil, 84. For more on Aséna's story, listen to a "A Uyghur Teen's Life After Escaping Genocide," *The Experiment* (podcast), August 18, 2021.

23. For more on the "Three Illegals and One Item" campaign, see Chang Xin, "Own a Compass or Boxing Gloves? You May Be a Terrorist," *Bitter Winter*, February 9, 2019.

24. Xin, "Own a Compass."

25. Josh Chin and Clément Bürge, "Twelve Days in Xinjiang: How China's Surveillance State Overwhelms Daily Life," *Wall Street Journal*, December 19, 2017. See also Steven Melendez, "In Locked-Down Xinjiang, China

Is Tracking Kitchen Knives with QR Codes," *Fast Company*, December 20, 2017.

26. Li Zaili, "How CCP Is Destroying Businesses in Xinjiang," *Bitter Winter*, November 11, 2018.

27. Josh Chin and Liza Lin, *Surveillance State: Inside China's Quest to Launch a New Era of Social Control* (New York: St. Martin's Press, 2022). See also Roberts, *War on the Uyghurs*.

28. Darren Byler, *In the Camps: China's High-Tech Penal Colony* (New York: Columbia Global Reports, 2021), 21.

29. United Nations Office of the High Commissioner for Human Rights, "China: Xinjiang's Forced Separations and Language Policies for Uyghur Children Carry Risk of Forced Assimilation, Say UN Experts" (press release, September 26, 2023).

30. Byler, *In the Camps*, 21.

31. For a list of the seventy-five activities in both Mandarin and English, see Xinjiang Documentation Project, "Identifying Religious Extremism," xinjiang.sppga.ubc.ca/chinese-sources/online-sources/identifying-religious -extremism/.

32. For more on this, see Byler, *Terror Capitalism*.

33. "Xi: 'Hold Together Tightly Like Pomegranate Seeds,'" *People's Daily Online*, July 4, 2022.

34. Amnesty International, "'Like We Were Enemies in War': China's Mass Internment, Torture and Persecution of Muslims in Xinjiang" (report, 2021), 31.

35. This statement draws on a conversation with Darren Byler as well as his post "The Future of Uyghur Cultural—and Halal—Life in the Year of the Pig," *Art of Life in Chinese Central Asia* (blog), March 9, 2019.

36. Byler, *In the Camps*.

37. Sayragul Sauytbay's June 4, 2021, testimony to the Uyghur Tribunal at uyghurtribunal.com/statements/.

38. Ted Regencia, "Uighurs Forced to Eat Pork as China Expands Xinjiang Pig Farms," Al Jazeera, December 4, 2020.

39. I know some readers will say I shouldn't be cavalier and use the term "cultural genocide," because it isn't a legal term defined anywhere in human rights law. My answer to that: It should be. In fact, Raphael Lemkin, the Polish lawyer who conceptualized the crime of genocide, originally had cultural destruction in mind. Lemkin argued that genocide included not just physical destruction but also acts of cultural annihilation. For him, genocide included mass killings as well as actions to eliminate the "essential foundations of the life of national groups, things like purposeful destruction of language and traditions, as well more tangible forms of heritage like artworks, archives, libraries, monuments, universities and places of worship." Lemkin also believed that "physical and biological genocide are always preceded by cultural genocide or by an attack on the symbols of the group or by violent interference with religious or cultural activities." Linda Kinstler pointed out recently, "If Lemkin were alive today,

he would most likely recognize the Chinese effort to indefinitely detain, re-educate, imprison and torture Uyghurs, and to destroy their mosques, confiscate their literature and ban their language in schools, as precisely the kind of cultural and physical genocide that he hoped his convention would eliminate. While China is a party to the Genocide Convention, it has refused—like the United States, France and Russia—to recognize the jurisdiction of the I.C.J., shielding itself from the court's authority." That said, increasingly scholars and advocates believe cultural genocide should be a legal category too, but the bottom line is that states don't like to tinker with laws that might tie their hands during war, so cultural genocide is unlikely to be added to the Genocide Convention anytime soon. See A. Dirk Moses, "Raphael Lemkin, Culture, and the Concept of Genocide," in *The Oxford Handbook of Genocide Studies,* eds. Donald Bloxham and A. Dirk Moses (Oxford: Oxford University Press, 2010), 34. See also Samantha Power, *A Problem from Hell: America and the Age of Genocide* (New York: Basic Books, 2013), 17–73. See also Linda Kinstler, "The Bitter Fight over the Meaning of 'Genocide,' " *New York Times Magazine,* August, 20, 2024.

40. Timothy Grose, "China Is Trying to Remake Uyghur Kitchens," *Foreign Policy,* May 26, 2024.

41. Today the Bingtuan is less a paramilitary force and more a corporate juggernaut with billions of dollars in global assets. In 2020, it was sanctioned by the U.S. Treasury Department for its role in human rights abuses.

42. Ian Urbina, "How Uyghur Forced Labor Makes Seafood That Ends Up in School Lunches," *Politico,* November 11, 2023.

43. Christopher Knaus and Helen Davidson, "Thousands of Imports Enter Australia from Firms Blacklisted by US over Alleged Uyghur Forced Labour Links," *Guardian,* January 19, 2025.

44. Human Rights Watch, "China: Hundreds of Uyghur Village Names Change," June 18, 2024.

45. China Daily, "Booming Tourism Tells of a Flourishing, Stable, Open Xinjiang," July 5, 2022, YouTube video, 2:23, youtube.com/watch?v=fqOYUTvwKnA.

46. China Daily, "Booming Tourism."

47. China Daily, "Tourism Resurgence Tells of a Flourishing, Stable, Open Xinjiang," July 6, 2022.

48. Eva Xiao, "China Is Turning a Crushed Xinjiang into a Tourist Trap," *Foreign Policy,* May 24, 2023.

49. Wang Wei, "Tourism Officials: Xinjiang a Must-Visit Region in NW China," China.org.cn, July 11, 2023.

50. Vivian Wang, "Why Chinese Propaganda Loves Foreign Travel Bloggers," *New York Times,* July 31, 2024.

51. Sun Kissed Bucket List, "The Xinjiang China THEY Don't Want YOU to SEE (British Couple's SHOCKING EXPERIENCE)," May 2, 2024, YouTube video, 1:23:58, youtube.com/watch?v=6h_TAer0ScA. According to *The New York Times,* "the influencers have denied any ties to the

government." See also Wang, "Why Chinese Propaganda Loves Foreign Travel Bloggers."

52. For a particularly egregious example of this, see Sun Kissed Bucket List, "The Xinjiang China THEY Don't Want YOU to SEE."

53. "Mo's Delicacy Directory: Xinjiang Cuisine," CGTN, September 9, 2020.

54. Rian Thum, "The Spatial Cleansing of Xinjiang: *Mazar* Desecration in Context," *Made in China Journal,* August 24, 2020.

55. Simina Mistreanu, "The Capital of Xinjiang Is Now in Turkey," *Foreign Policy,* September 30, 2019.

56. Dake Kang points this out in "Terror & Tourism: Xinjian Eases Its Grip, but Fear Remains," Associated Press, October 10, 2021.

57. Author interviews. See also Kang, "Terror & Tourism."

58. The Communist Party in China views *supas* as antimodern, forcing Uyghurs to replace them with couches and coffee tables.

59. Safeguard Defenders, "Targeted in Türkiye: China's Transnational Repression Against Uyghurs" (report, August 10, 2023).

60. In 2017, Turkey signed an extradition treaty with China. But the deal is awaiting ratification by Ankara's parliament. That said, China has invested at least $4 billion in Turkey as part of its Belt and Road Initiative. And in July 2024, the Chinese electric vehicle manufacturer BYD agreed to build a $1 billion plant in Turkey. See Ceren Ergenç and Derya Göçer, "China's Response to Türkiye's Volatile Authoritarianism," Carnegie Endowment for International Peace, May 5, 2023. See also Laura He, "Chinese EV Giant BYD to Build $1 Billion Plant in Turkey," CNN, July 9, 2024.

61. Human Rights Watch, "China: Big Data Fuels Crackdown in Minority Region," February 26, 2018.

62. Uyghur Human Rights Project, "Kashgar Coerced: Forced Reconstruction, Exploitation, and Surveillance in the Cradle of Uyghur Culture" (report, June 2020).

63. United Nations Office of the High Commissioner for Human Rights, "OHCHR Assessment of Human Rights Concerns in the Xinjiang Uyghur Autonomous Region, People's Republic of China" (report, August 31, 2022).

64. Sigal Samuel, "China's Jaw-Dropping Family Separation Policy," *Atlantic,* September 24, 2018. See also Rushan Abbas, "The Uyghur Genocide Through the Lens of the Child," *Georgetown Journal of International Affairs,* August 17, 2021; and Emily Feng, "Uyghur Kids Recall Physical and Mental Torment at Chinese Boarding Schools in Xinjiang," NPR, February 3, 2022.

65. United Nations Office of the High Commissioner for Human Rights, "OHCHR Assessment."

Chapter 5: Bolivia and the Andes

1. In 2021, Marsia was voted Latin America's Rising Star Female Chef by Latin America's 50 Best Restaurants. In 2024, she was named Latin Amer-

ica's Best Female Chef also by 50 Best. See "Latin America's Best Female Chef 2024," 50 Best, accessed December 19, 2024.

2. Carolyn Kormann, "The Tasting-Menu Initiative," *New Yorker,* March 28, 2016.

3. Jason Palmer, "Coca Leaves First Chewed 8,000 Years Ago, Says Research," BBC, December 2, 2010.

4. Transnational Institute, "The WHO Cocaine Project," February 4, 2010, tni.org/en/article/the-who-cocaine-project.

5. Nicholas Yong, "Myanmar Overtakes Afghanistan as Top Opium Producer," BBC, December 12, 2023.

6. Gretchen S. Peters, "The Curse of the Shiny Object," *PRISM 7,* no. 1 (September 15, 2017).

7. Peters, "The Curse of the Shiny Object."

8. Catalina Oquendo, "Coca no es cocaína: Se saborea," *El País,* February 18, 2022; "Así defiende Leonor Espinosa el uso de la hoja de coca como ingrediente," *El Tiempo,* February 19, 2022.

9. In November 2024, Phayawi was ranked 69 on 50 Best's list of the top 100 restaurants in Latin America. See Josh Ong, "Latin America's 50 Best Restaurants 2024: the 51–100 list revealed," 50 Best, November 14, 2024.

10. Quoted in Clare Bucknell, "The Forgotten Drug Trips of the Nineteenth Century," *New Yorker,* April 17, 2023.

11. Quoted in Giorgio Samorini, "Paolo Mantegazza (1831–1910), Italian Pioneer in the Studies on Drugs," *Eleusis* 2 (1995): 14–20.

12. Quoted in Bucknell, "Forgotten Drug Trips."

13. Stuart Walton, "Vin Mariani: A Coca-Comeback," *World of Fine Wine,* April 12, 2023.

14. Walton, "Vin Mariani."

15. In 1906, Coca-Cola's official slogan was updated to "The Great National Temperance Beverage." See The Coca-Cola Company, "History of Coca-Cola Advertising Slogans," coca-colacompany.com/about-us/history/history-of-coca-cola-advertising-slogans. See also James Hamblin, "Why We Took Cocaine Out of Soda," *Atlantic,* January 31, 2013; Dominic Streatfeild, *Cocaine: An Unauthorized Biography* (New York: Picador, 2001), 81.

16. Paul Gootenberg, *Andean Cocaine: The Making of a Global Drug* (Chapel Hill: University of North Carolina Press, 2008), 22.

17. National Museum of American History, "Vin Mariani," americanhistory.si .edu/collections/nmah_1287058. See also Kat Eschner, "Coca-Cola's Creator Said the Drink Would Make You Smarter," *Smithsonian Magazine,* March 29, 2017.

18. D. G. Schuster, "Neurasthenia and a Modernizing America," *JAMA* 290, no. 17 (2003): 2327–28, doi.org/10.1001/jama.290.17.2327.

19. Amy Sue Biondich and Jeremy David Joslin, "Coca: The History and Medical Significance of an Ancient Andean Tradition," *Emergency Medicine International* (2016): doi.org/10.1155/2016/4048764.

20. Gootenberg, *Andean Cocaine.*

21. Some products sold with medicinal claims were benign, like the breakfast

cereal Grape-Nuts, which claimed in *The Atlantic* in 1905 that it could medicinally build brain muscle. Others, like Radithor, which claimed to cure impotence, killed people. See "Brains Rule This World," Grape-Nuts advertisement, *Atlantic*, November 1905, theatlantic.com/magazine/archive/1905/11/brains-rule-this-world-grapenuts-in-10-days/638039/.

22. Biondich and Joslin, "Coca."

23. Gootenberg, *Andean Cocaine*, 19.

24. Edward Huntington Williams, "Negro Cocaine 'Fiends' Are a New Southern Menace," *New York Times,* February 8, 1914.

25. Gootenberg, *Andean Cocaine*, 198–99.

26. Grace Elizabeth Hale, "When Jim Crow Drank Coke," *New York Times,* January 28, 2013.

27. The Stepan Company took over the Maywood facility in New Jersey in 1959. Stepan remains the only commercial entity allowed to import coca into the United States. The company imports an estimated 150 to 500 metric tons of coca a year primarily from Peru to produce extract for Coca-Cola. Stepan also sells coca leaf by-product to Mallinckrodt Pharmaceuticals, which uses the extracted cocaine for medicinal purposes. Mallinckrodt is just 50 miles down the road from Maywood, making New Jersey, in effect, the coca capital of the U.S. For more, see Jacob Geanous, "New Jersey Factory Imports Cocaine Plant That Flavors Coca-Cola Thanks to DEA Arrangement," *New York Post,* April 1, 2023, and James Hamblin, "Why We Took Cocaine Out of Soda," *Atlantic,* January 31, 2013.

28. Caroline S. Conzelman and Dawson M. White, "The Botanical Science and Cultural Value of Coca Leaf in South America," in *Roadmaps to Regulation: Coca, Cocaine, and Derivatives,* ed. Paul Gootenberg (Oxford: Beckley Foundation, 2016).

29. Conzelman and White, "The Botanical Science."

30. Gootenberg, *Andean Cocaine.*

31. Gootenberg, whose research I draw on here, points out that Pinto-Escalier's speech was a "forgotten precursor" to President Evo Morales's impassioned defense of decriminalizing coca at the 2006 UN General Assembly. It's worth noting that the American policy Pinto-Escalier was defending Bolivia against at the League of Nations—designating a benign raw material as a drug itself—is also a forgotten precursor to the militarized source-eradication campaign the United States would later fund in Bolivia. See Gootenberg, *Andean Cocaine,* 215.

32. Harry B. Fonda's comment was printed in the morning edition of *El Comercio,* a Peruvian newspaper, on September 12, 1949. A reprint of the article can be found in Annex 1 of *The Report of the United Nations Commission of Inquiry on the Coca Leaf: Communications from the Government of Bolivia and Peru,* February 28, 1952, digitallibrary.un.org/record/1640041?ln=en&v=pdf.

33. Raquel Gutiérrez Aguilar, *Rhythms of the Pachakuti: Indigenous Uprising and State Power in Bolivia* (Durham, NC: Duke University Press, 2014).

34. Aguilar, *Rhythms of the Pachakuti.*

35. There have been twenty-two coups since 1950, the start of Bolivia's modern democratic period. But if you go back to Bolivia's independence, the country has suffered nearly 190 coups, averaging more than one per year.

36. In October 2003, Lozada ordered the massacre of sixty-seven Aymara people in La Paz. Lozada is a staunch U.S. ally; he grew up in Iowa and reportedly speaks English better than Spanish. As planning minister in the 1980s, Lozada worked closely with Jeffrey Sachs on his "shock therapy" plan (discussed in the text on page 170). In 2002, the year before the October massacre, he used his connections to lure the high-profile American political consultant James Carville and his firm to La Paz to run his reelection campaign. Lozada's government was also the one that tried to frame Juana Quispe. After the massacre, Lozada fled to the United States, where he was granted asylum and protected against extradition, though in 2023 a U.S. federal court held him responsible for the killings, awarding the plaintiffs ten million dollars in compensation. See Paulina Villegas, "Bolivia's Ex-leader to Compensate Massacre Victims in Landmark U.S. Case," *Washington Post,* September 28, 2023.

37. The colonization scheme came at the expense of other Bolivian Indigenous peoples, like the Yuki, the Yuracaré, and others. Many are still there but have been pushed to the edges of society and the economy.

38. Thomas Grisaffi, *Coca Yes, Cocaine No: How Bolivia's Coca Growers Reshaped Democracy* (Durham, NC: Duke University Press, 2019).

39. Naomi Klein, *The Shock Doctrine: The Rise of Disaster Capitalism* (New York: Knopf, 2007).

40. James Painter, *Bolivia and Coca: A Study in Dependency* (Boulder: Lynne Rienner, 1993).

41. For more on this, see Kevin Healy, "The Cocaine Industry in Bolivia—Its Impact on the Peasantry," Cultural Survival, February 19, 2010.

42. Grisaffi, *Coca Yes, Cocaine No.*

43. Technically, the Narcotics Affairs Section (NAS) of the U.S. embassy in La Paz, not the Drug Enforcement Administration (DEA), was responsible for supporting U.S. eradication efforts in Bolivia. But the NAS and the DEA worked out of the same miliary base in the Chapare. For many Bolivians, the DEA versus the NAS is a distinction without a difference. Or as a drug policy analyst in Bolivia put it to me: "*La misma mierda.*" Same shit.

44. As Kathryn Ledebur points out, the five-year Plan Dignidad "proposed four pillars of action: alternative development, prevention and rehabilitation, eradication of illegal excess coca, and interdiction based on a 'shared responsibility' with the international community to reach these goals. In practice, the Bolivian government focused primarily on the forced eradication of 38,000 hectares of coca." Kathryn Ledebur, "Coca and Conflict in the Chapare," *WOLA Drug War Monitor,* July 2002.

45. Grisaffi, *Coca Yes, Cocaine No.* Washington also threatened to withhold desperately needed aid if the Bolivians didn't go through with the plan. See "Bolivia Under Pressure: Human Rights Violations and Coca Eradication," *Human Rights Watch/Americas* 8, no. 4 (D) (May 1996).

46. Aguilar, *Rhythms of the Pachakuti.*

47. Godofredo Reinicke, the *defenso del pueblo* (human rights ombudsman) in the Chapare at the time, said that the prosecutors told him they were Bolivians who worked for the NAS in La Paz. The NAS also had a satellite office in the Chapare on a Bolivian military base, which it shared with the DEA. The prosecutors who attempted to frame Juana were based in the Chapare office.

48. Grisaffi, *Coca Yes, Cocaine No.*

49. Transnational Institute, "The WHO Cocaine Project." A decision in 1995 by the UN's World Health Assembly banned the publication of the study. A significant part of the banned report is available on the Transnational Institute's website at tni.org/en/article/the-who-cocaine-project.

50. World Health Assembly, "Forty-eighth World Health Assembly," May 1995, iris.who.int/handle/10665/178304.

51. Jean Friedman-Rudovsky, "Bolivia to Expel U.S. Ambassador," *Time*, September 11, 2008; and "Bolivian President Evo Morales expels USAID," BBC, May 1, 2013.

52. Section II, article 384, of the Constitution of the Plurinational State of Bolivia.

53. Kathryn Ledebur and Coletta A. Youngers, "From Conflict to Collaboration: An Innovative Approach to Reducing Coca Cultivation in Bolivia," *Stability* 2, no. 1 (2013).

54. United Nations Office on Drugs and Crime, *Bulletin on Narcotics* 61 (2017).

55. Specifically, he said it took twenty-four *takis* of coca to produce five hundred bottles. A *taki* is roughly fifty pounds.

56. Paola Flores, "A Brew of Ancient Coca Is Bolivia's Buzzy New Beer. But It's Unclear If the World Will Buy In," Associated Press, June 11, 2024.

57. John Walsh and Martin Jelsma, "Coca Chronicles: Bolivia Challenges UN Coca Leaf Ban," Washington for Latin America, October 17, 2023.

Chapter 6: The Pueblo Nations

1. Santa Clara Pueblo clans are organized into two complementary units known as Summer People and Winter People. Marian is part of the Winter People clan, who are hunters. Summer People are associated with farming.

2. Some Native American nations and communities reserve the term "Fourth Sister" for other culturally important plants. For example, the Anishinaabeg around the Great Lakes may refer to *manoomin,* or wild rice, as the fourth sister.

3. Robin Wall Kimmerer, *Braiding Sweetgrass: Indigenous Wisdom, Scientific Knowledge and the Teachings of Plants* (Minneapolis: Milkweed Editions, 2013), 55.

4. Western taxonomy divides *Amaranthus* cultivars into dye amaranths and grain amaranths. The dye-grain distinction is based on each cultivar's primary uses, but it is not all that useful to everyday life, since both are edible.

5. For more on the amaranth's culinary uses in India, see Sonal Ved, "Everything You Need to Know About Rajgira, the Lesser-Known Indian Superfood," *Vogue India*, February 15, 2021.

6. For more on the history and meaning of the name "amaranth," see Mihai Costea and François J. Tardif, "The Name of the Amaranth: Histories of Meaning," *SIDA, Contributions to Botany* 20, no. 3 (2003): 1073–83, jstor.org/stable/41968150.

7. As early as the 1980s, amaranth was being called a superfood. See Jane E. Brody, "Ancient, Forgotten Plant Now 'Grain of the Future,'" *New York Times*, October 16, 1984. Cecilia Nowell has written more recently about the amaranth's superlative qualities as well as its resilience. See also Cecilia Nowell, "'It Could Feed the World': Amaranth, a Health Trend 8,000 Years Old That Survived Colonization," *Guardian*, August 6, 2021.

8. The name "Diné"—pronounced *di-nay*—is from their own language and means "the people," and it is increasingly preferred to "Navajo," though officially the tribe is still referred to as the Navajo Nation. Coincidentally, the word "Navajo" is a Spanish adaptation of a Tewa-Puebloan word *navahu'u*, which roughly means "place of planted fields."

9. Pueblo historians and archaeologists believe early Pueblo communities were using both wild and domesticated amaranth as early as the twelfth century.

10. Austin Fisher, "Ceremony in the Atomic Age," *Rio Grande Sun*, July 27, 2019. Updated March 12, 2020.

11. Ungelbah Dávila-Shivers, "Forgotten Superfood of the Americas," *Edible New Mexico*, March 2, 2021.

12. With regard to "virgin forests," Charles C. Mann suggests it was actually colonists who made them. He writes: "Throughout eastern North America the open landscape seen by the first Europeans quickly filled in with forest. According to William Cronon, of the University of Wisconsin, later colonists began complaining about how hard it was to get around. (Eventually, of course, they stripped New England almost bare of trees.) When Europeans moved west, they were preceded by two waves: one of disease, the other of ecological disturbance. The former crested with fearsome rapidity; the latter sometimes took more than a century to quiet down. Far from destroying pristine wilderness, European settlers bloodily *created* it. By 1800 the hemisphere was chockablock with new wilderness. If 'forest primeval' means a woodland unsullied by the human presence, William Denevan has written, there was much more of it in the late eighteenth century than in the early sixteenth." Charles C. Mann, "1491," *Atlantic*, March 2002. See also Roxanne Dunbar-Ortiz, *An Indigenous Peoples' History of the United States* (Boston: Beacon Press, 2014), 27–30.

13. The first quote in this paragraph is originally from Giovanni da Verrazano, cited by Charles C. Mann in *1491: New Revelations of the Americas Before Columbus* (New York: Alfred A. Knopf, 2005), and the second two are from David Wade Chambers, "Native American Road Systems and Trails,"

Udemy. I found these quotes in Dunbar-Ortiz, *An Indigenous Peoples' History*, 28–29.

14. Roxanne Swentzell and Patricia M. Perea, *The Pueblo Food Experience Cookbook: Whole Food of Our Ancestors* (Santa Fe: Museum of New Mexico Press, 2016).

15. Porter P. Swentzell, "A History of Pueblo Food," in Roxanne Swentzell and Patricia M. Perea, *The Pueblo Food Experience Cookbook*.

16. Jonathan Deininger Sauer, "The Grain Amaranths: A Survey of Their History and Classification," *Annals of the Missouri Botanical Garden* 37, no. 2684 (November 1950): 561–632.

17. Author interviews with academics and chefs, Mexico, January 2024. See also Bernardino de Sahagún, *General History of the Things of New Spain: The Florentine Codex* (Santa Fe: The School of American Research, 1982), 69–70.

18. Robert L. Myers, *Amaranth: An Ancient Grain and Exceptionally Nutritious Food* (Columbia, MD: Harvest Road, 2018), 12. See also Sauer, "The Grain Amaranths: A Survey of Their History and Classification." See also Jonathan Deininger Sauer, "The Grain Amaranths and Their Relatives: A Revised Taxonomic and Geographic Survey," *Annals of the Missouri Botanical Garden* 54, no. 2 (1967): 103–37.

19. Sophie D. Coe, *America's First Cuisines* (Austin: University of Texas Press, 1994), 91.

20. Ligaya Mishan, "Amaranto in Bushwick Is a Family Effort," *New York Times*, November 27, 2015.

21. Sauer, "The Grain Amaranths: A Survey of Their History and Classification."

22. Andrés Reséndez, *The Other Slavery* (Boston: Mariner Books, 2016).

23. Reséndez, *The Other Slavery*.

24. Reséndez, 10–11. Reséndez says he uses the phrase "the other slavery" in "the double sense that it targeted Native Americans rather than Africans and that it involved a range of forms of captivity and coercion." He acknowledges that "some scholars may object to this broad usage which glosses over conventional labor distinctions." But he has good reasons.

25. Reséndez, 4.

26. Reséndez, 4–5. The secrecy stems from the fact that African slavery was legal, whereas the Spanish Crown had largely outlawed Indian slavery in its colonies, although that didn't stop it in the least. It only pushed it underground. Because African slavery was legal and immensely profitable, its victims, as scholars point out, were often meticulously counted at almost every point in the transaction and are thus easy to find in the historical record. Indian slaves, however, did not cross oceans in the same numbers as enslaved Africans, so there are no ship manifests or port records or bills of sale. As the trade was largely illegal, its victims were literally kept off the books. In the past several years, however, historians have been able to piece together through old letters, judicial proceedings, and casual accounts of slaving

raids a clear picture of the magnitude. From the time of Columbus to the end of the nineteenth century, the estimate for the total number of Native Americans enslaved in the New World ranges from 2.5 million to 5 million.

27. Richard L. Garner, "Long-Term Silver Mining Trends in Spanish America: A Comparative Analysis of Peru and Mexico," *American Historical Review* 93, no. 4 (October 1988): 898–935, doi.org/10.2307/1863529. See also Reséndez, *The Other Slavery*, 66.

28. Cornell Botanic Gardens, "Amaranth Was First Cultivated Around 8,000 Years Ago," cornellbotanicgardens.org/wp-content/uploads/2018/11/history .panels.pdf. See also Kaufui V. Wong, "Amaranth Grain and Greens for Health Benefits," *Nutrition & Food Science International Journal* 2, no. 2 (January 2017): doi.org/10.19080/NFSIJ.2017.02.555584; and Coe, *America's First Cuisines*, 90–93 and 118.

29. Katarzyna Beilin, "The World According to Amaranth: Interspecies Memory in Tehuacán Valley," *Environmental Cultural Studies Through Time: The Luso-Hispanic World, Hispanic Issues On-line* 24 (Fall 2019): 144–67.

30. Reséndez, *The Other Slavery*, 118.

31. According to the archaeologist Matthew Liebmann, the colonial Spanish did this to differentiate the Pueblo from nomadic Indigenous people in the area at the time, the ancestors of today's Diné, Apache, and Ute people. See Matthew Liebmann, "Archaeology of the 1680 Pueblo Revolt," UNM-Taos Digital Media Services, YouTube video, September 29, 2016, 39:27, youtube .com/watch?v=wpP2h04ubLE.

32. Reséndez, *The Other Slavery*, 121.

33. Reséndez, 120. See also See Matthew Liebmann, *Revolt: An Archaeological History of Pueblo Resistance and Revitalization in 17th Century New Mexico* (Tucson: University of Arizona Press, 2012), 34.

34. By eating indigenous foods, the Spanish feared they would somehow degenerate to the level of their colonial subjects. As author and food historian Rebecca Earle points out, food helped create a caste system that defined European and Native American relationships then. For instance, the Spanish saw Native Americans as beardless and effete; their bodies were different because their diets were different. However, according to humoral theories pervasive at the time, these differences were by no means permanent. Bodies could be altered as easily as diets. Spaniards feared eating Native foods, say amaranth or corn, could turn a proud, bearded conquistador into a timid, beardless Native American—a transformation to be avoided at all costs. These claims were made even though, as Earle points out, Indigenous peoples' foods ironically formed much of the colonizers' diet. "Nonetheless, when illness struck," she writes, "settlers immediately blamed the New World diet." To an extent, this explains why the Spanish were so intent on shunning local foods, banning amaranth, and importing European crops and livestock like cows, pigs, and sheep, which forever changed the course of the Americas in countless ways. This went far beyond nostalgia for home, Earle points out. That European crops could grow in the Americas only signaled to the Spanish divine approval for colo-

nization. See Rebecca Earle, " 'If You Eat Their Food . . .': Diets and Bodies in Early Colonial Spanish America," *American Historical Review* 115, no. 3 (June 2010): 688–713, doi.org/10.1086/ahr.115.3.688.

35. Liebmann, *Revolt*.

36. Liebmann.

37. Colonial Santa Fe, the New Mexican capital, was a den of slavery. As the historian Andrés Reséndez points out, Santa Fe's earliest Spanish settlers had a habit of enslaving Pueblo Indians in their homes. "By 1630 Santa Fe's minuscule white population of about 250 held around 700 slaves; that is, every white man, woman, and child residing in the capital possessed between two to three Native servants on average." Reséndez, *The Other Slavery*, 122. For more on the connection between the Pueblo revolt and the founding of El Paso and Juárez, see Liebmann, "Archaeology of the 1680 Pueblo Revolt."

38. Malcolm Ebright, Rick Hendricks, and Richard Hughes, *Four Square Leagues: Pueblo Indian Land in New Mexico* (Albuquerque: University of New Mexico Press, 2014).

39. Margaret D. Jacobs, *After One Hundred Winters: In Search of Reconciliation on America's Stolen Lands* (Princeton, NJ: Princeton University Press, 2021), 153.

40. U.S. Department of the Interior, "Federal Indian Boarding School Initiative Investigative Report," May 2022, ia.gov/sites/default/files/dup/inline-files/bsi_investigative_report_may_2022_508.pdf. It should be noted that this report was a remarkable display of government accountability that is rarely seen these days. Its findings eventually led to a formal apology from President Joe Biden in October 2024 for the federal government's role in running boarding schools.

41. U.S. Department of the Interior, "Federal Indian Boarding School."

42. Andrea Freeman, "Unconstitutional Food Inequality," *Harvard Civil Rights–Civil Liberties Law Review* 55, no. 840 (2020). See also Anthony F. C. Wallace, *The Long, Bitter Trail: Andrew Jackson and the Indians* (New York: Hill & Wang, 1993).

43. Jacobs, *After One Hundred Winters*, 150.

44. Richard Henry Pratt, "The Advantages of Mingling Indians with Whites," *Proceedings of the National Conference of Charities and Correction*, June 1892, carlisleindian.dickinson.edu/teach/kill-indian-him-and-save-man-r-h-pratt-education-native-americans.

45. Quoted in Peter Nabokov, *Native American Testimony: A Chronicle of Indian-White Relations from Prophecy to Present, 1492–2000* (New York: Penguin, 1990), 222.

46. Statement of James "Jim" LaBelle, Sr., *Truth and Healing Commission on Indian Boarding School Policies Act: Hearing on H.R. 5444 Before the Subcommittee for Indigenous Peoples of the United States of the Committee on Natural Resources*, 117th Cong. (May 12, 2022).

47. Cody White and Rose Buchanan, "The Stories Behind the Names: Death at the Santa Fe Indian School, 1891–1909," *The Text Message* (blog of the Textual Records Division at the National Archives), May 11, 2022.

48. Jacobs, *After One Hundred Winters*, 156.

49. U.S. Department of the Interior, "Federal Indian Boarding School."

50. The 2014 edition of *Trends in Indian Health* is the latest edition. See U.S. Department of Health and Human Services, Indian Health Service, Office of Public Health Support, and Division of Program Statistics, *Trends in Indian Health: 2014 Edition*, March 2015, ihs.gov/sites/dps/themes/responsive2017/display_objects/documents/Trends2014Book508.pdf.

51. Nick Estes, "The Empire of All Maladies: Colonial Contagions and Indigenous Resistance," *Baffler*, July 2020.

52. Meir J. Stampfer and Walter C. Willett, "Rebuilding the Food Pyramid," *Scientific American*, December 1, 2006. It's worth pointing out that this happened at a time when the country was trying to address the growing problem of heart disease. Dietary fats were seen as the culprit. The solution was twofold: cut way back on fat—all kinds of fat, even the good kinds—and replace it with carbohydrates, like pasta, potatoes, and rice. To be fair, the USDA guidelines were pushing Americans to balance these carbs with others foods like whole grains, fruits, and vegetables. But that message never got through to the public. Instead, as the longtime food and health journalist Allison Aubrey points out, the public heard: "Fat is bad; carbs are good." In turn, she writes, "the food industry saw the low-fat, high-carb mantra as an opportunity to create a whole new range of products. Fat-free frozen yogurt, fat-free muffins and cookies—the formula was: Take out the fat; add lots of sugar." In trying to solve one problem—heart disease—we created other problems like diabetes and obesity. See Allison Aubrey, "Why We Got Fatter During the Fat-Free Food Boom," NPR, March 28, 2014.

53. The USDA defined one serving of grain products as one slice of bread, one small roll or muffin, half of a bagel or croissant, one ounce of ready-to-eat cereal, or half a cup of cooked cereal, rice, or pasta. See Linda E. Cleveland et al., "Pyramid Servings Data: Results from USDA's 1994 Continuing Survey of Food Intakes by Individuals," U.S. Department of Agriculture, March 1997, ars.usda.gov/ARSUserFiles/80400530/pdf/pynet_94.pdf.

54. Nancy M. Pindus et al., "Study of the Food Distribution Program on Indian Reservations (FDPIR): Final Report" (report prepared by the Urban Institute for the U.S. Department of Agriculture Food and Nutrition Services, June 14, 2016).

55. Janie Simms Hipp and Colby D. Duren, "Regaining Our Future: An Assessment of Risks and Opportunities for Native Communities in the 2018 Farm Bill" (report commissioned by Seeds of Native Health, a Campaign of the Shakopee Mdewakanton Sioux Community, June 2017).

56. Freeman, "Unconstitutional Food Inequality." See also *Hearing to Review the Food Distribution Program on Indian Reservations, Before the Subcommittee on Department Operations, Oversight, Nutrition, and Forestry of the Committee on Agriculture, House of Representatives*, 111th Cong. (June 23, 2010).

57. Amy Dillard, "Sloppy Joe, Slop, Sloppy Joe: How USDA Commodities Dumping Ruined the National School Lunch Program," *Oregon Law*

Review 87 (2008): 221, University of Baltimore School of Law Legal Studies Research Paper No. 2008-05.

58. Andi Murphy, "After a Fraught History, Some Tribes Finally Have the Power to Rethink 'Commodity Foods,'" *Civil Eats,* November 1, 2021, civileats.com/2021/11/01/after-a-fraught-history-some-tribes-finally-have-the-power-to-rethink-commodity-foods/.

59. Swentzell and Perea, *Pueblo Food Experience Cookbook.*

60. It is worth pointing out, as Andi Murphy does, artists like Daniel McCoy, Jr., a Muscogee Creek/Citizen Band Potawatomi painter whose works incorporate images of canned commodity foods as a form of "commentary on the addictive nature of highly processed American foods and its effect on Indigenous people." See Murphy, "After a Fraught History."

61. Ungelbah Dávila, "The Indigenous Taco's Origin Story," *New Mexico Magazine,* May 8, 2024.

62. Dávila, "The Indigenous Taco's Origin Story."

63. Dávila.

64. *Hearing Before the Select Committee on Hunger, House of Representatives,* 101st Cong., 2nd Sess. (February 26, 1990).

65. Kalen Goodluck, "This Pilot Program Is Supporting Tribal Food Sovereignty with Federal Dollars," *Civil Eats,* July 5, 2022. The current program functions under the Agriculture Improvement Act of 2018 (also called the 2018 Farm Bill) which was extended in December 2024 with the American Relief Act of 2025. Future drafts propose expanding the FDPIR Self-Determination Demonstration Project to additional tribes. For more, see the 2024 Farm Bill at agriculture.house.gov/farmbill/.

66. Quoted in Freeman, "Unconstitutional Food Inequality." See also *Hearing to Review the Food Distribution Program.*

67. Swentzell and Perea, *Pueblo Food Experience Cookbook,* xiii.

68. Ellise Pierce, "Native Artist Roxanne Swentzell Embarked on a Mission to Improve Her Community's Health Through Pre-colonial Foods," *Cowboys & Indians,* November 5, 2017.

69. Cecilia Nowell, "'It Could Feed the World': Amaranth, a Health Trend 8,000 Years Old That Survived Colonization," *Guardian,* August 6, 2021.

Epilogue: The United States

1. Sara Sinclair, ed., *How We Go Home: Voices from Indigenous North America* (Chicago: Haymarket Books, 2020), 185.

2. Myrriah Gómez, *Nuclear Nuevo México: Colonialism and the Effects of the Nuclear Industrial Complex on Nuevomexicanos* (Tucson: University of Arizona Press, 2022).

3. Advisory Committee on Human Radiation Experiments, *Final Report* (Washington, DC: U.S. Government Printing Office, October 1995). On January 15, 1994, President Clinton appointed the Advisory Committee on Human Radiation Experiments. The president created the committee to investigate reports of possibly unethical experiments funded by

the government. The report covers the RaLa experiments at Los Alamos, where lab scientists, for nearly two decades, tested explosives incorporating radioactive lanthanum. Test protocols required wind to be moving away from Los Alamos and over Española and three Pueblo nations, San Ildefonso, Santa Clara, and Pojoaque.

4. Advisory Committee on Human Radiation Experiments, *Final Report*.
5. Joseph Masco, *The Nuclear Borderlands: The Manhattan Project in Post–Cold War New Mexico* (Princeton, NJ: Princeton University Press, 2020), 26.
6. National Cancer Institute's fact sheet on iodine 131, cancer.gov/about -cancer/causes-prevention/risk/radiation/i-131.
7. Nikk Ogasa, "Nuclear Fallout Is Showing Up in U.S. Honey, Decades After Bomb Tests," *Science,* April 20, 2021.
8. Masco, *Nuclear Borderlands*. See also Pueblo Alliance, "Los Alamos National Lab's Flanged Tritium Waste Container (FTWC) Venting in Pueblo Communities," n.d., Pueblo Action Alliance.
9. Robert E. Kelley, "Starve Nuclear Weapons to Death with a Tritium Freeze," Stockholm International Peace Research Institute, August 28, 2020.
10. Masco, *Nuclear Borderlands*.
11. Alicia Inez Guzmán, "LANL Plans to Release Highly Radioactive Tritium to Prevent Explosions. Will It Just Release Danger in the Air?," *Searchlight New Mexico,* June 12, 2024.
12. Jennifer McKee, "Waste Found in Water: Tritium Traces in LANL Well," *Albuquerque Journal,* February 8, 2001.
13. Guzmán, "LANL Plans to Release."
14. Tewa Women United, "Protect Vulnerable NM Communities: Halt Radioactive Tritium Release from LANL," July 27, 2023, change.org/p/protect -vulnerable-nm-communities-halt-radioactive-tritium-release-from-lanl -2ed0dbb5-2b94-4f76-9156-a66e679d1e4d.
15. Guzmán, "LANL Plans to Release."
16. Masco, *Nuclear Borderlands,* p. 150.
17. P. R. Fresquez et al., "Radionuclide Concentrations in Pinto Beans, Sweet Corn, and Zucchini Squash Grown in Los Alamos Canyon at Los Alamos National Laboratory" (Los Alamos National Laboratory report LA-13304-MS, May 12, 1997).
18. Los Alamos National Laboratory, "Los Alamos Lab Continues to Protect Water Quality amid Changing Regulations" (press release, December 19, 2023).
19. New Mexico Environment Department v. United States Department of Energy and Los Alamos National Security, LLC, No. HWB 07-27 (CO), (2007), env.nm.gov/wp-content/uploads/sites/12/2019/10/LANL_2015-6-14 _ChromiumSttlmtAgrmt.pdf.
20. Department of Energy officials say the chromium plume does not threaten Los Alamos's drinking water supply. Los Alamos County, however, shut down its main groundwater well in 2023 because of its proximity to the

plume. See Danielle Prokop, "Lawmakers Request Feds and State Officials Find Third Party in Chromium Plume Fight," *Source New Mexico,* August 22, 2023.

21. Gómez, *Nuclear Nuevo México.*
22. Lesley M. M. Blume, "Collateral Damage: American Civilian Survivors of the 1945 Trinity Test," *Bulletin of the Atomic Scientists,* July 17, 2023.
23. Los Alamos Historical Document Retrieval and Assessment Project, "Final Report of the Los Alamos Historical Document Retrieval and Assessment (LAHDRA) Project," Centers for Disease Control and Prevention, November 2010.
24. Los Alamos Historical Document Retrieval and Assessment Project, "Final Report."
25. Steven Simon, André Bouville, and Charles Land, "Fallout from Nuclear Weapons Tests and Cancer Risks," *American Scientist* 94, no. 1 (January–February 2006): 48.
26. J. D. Boice, Jr., et al., "Mortality Among Workers at the Los Alamos National Laboratory, 1943–2017," *International Journal of Radiation Biology* 98, no. 4 (2022): 722–49. See also Rebecca Moss, "Half-Life," ProPublica, in partnership with *Santa Fe New Mexican,* October 26, 2018.
27. New START treaty caps the number of strategic nuclear warheads that the United States and Russia can deploy. It was signed by former U.S. President Barack Obama and his Russian counterpart Dmitry Medvedev in 2010.
28. Stockholm International Peace Research Institute, *SIPRI Yearbook 2024* (Oxford, UK: Oxford University Press, 2024).
29. Hans M. Kristensen, Matt Korda, Eliana Johns, and Mackenzie Knight, "United States Nuclear Weapons, 2024," *Bulletin of the Atomic Scientists,* May 7, 2024. See also W. J. Hennigan, "The Staggering Price You're Paying for America's Nuclear Makeover," *New York Times,* October 10, 2024.
30. "National Security Council Senior Director Speaks at Arms Control Conference," C-SPAN, June 7, 2024, C-SPAN video, 41:04, c-span.org/video/?536232-3/national-security-council-senior-director-speaks-arms-control-conference. See also Alicia Inez Guzmán, "The Reawakening of America's Nuclear Dinosaurs," *Searchlight New Mexico,* February 28, 2024.
31. W. J. Hennigan, "In the Lab Oppenheimer Built, the U.S. Is Building Nuclear Bomb Cores Again," *Time,* July 24, 2023.
32. Hennigan, "The Staggering Price You're Paying for America's Nuclear Makeover."
33. Here I focus only on the contamination of the plateau and its potential victims. But it must be said that the entire state of New Mexico is affected by the toxic consequences of the larger U.S. nuclear weapons complex. On July 16, 1979, a dam failure at the United Nuclear Corporation's uranium mill near Gallup, New Mexico, released more than 1,100 tons of radioactive waste and approximately ninety-four million gallons of acidic radioactive tailings into the Puerco River, deeply affecting the Navajo Nation. It was the largest accidental release of radioactive material in U.S. history, larger than the more familiar Three Mile Island leak. No one can

agree where this sits on the global blacklist. But all agree it was bigger than Three Mile Island. Yet because it mostly affected Indigenous people, it didn't get nearly the same attention or funding for a cleanup.

34. The citations were issued in 2023, but the incidents took place in 2021. See U.S. Department of Energy, "Preliminary Notice of Violation, Triad National Security, LLC," May 18, 2023; and Alicia Inez Guzmán, "Safety Lapses at Los Alamos National Laboratory: A History of Flooding, an Earthquake and Little Fires in the Belly of the Beast," *Searchlight New Mexico,* July 13, 2023.

35. Guzmán, "Safety Lapses."

36. Sharon LaFraniere, Minho Kim, and Julie Tate, "DOGE Cuts Reach Key Nuclear Scientists, Bomb Engineers, and Safety Experts," *New York Times,* March 17, 2025.

37. See Maire O'Neill, "Los Alamos National Laboratory Monitors Emerging Issue of PFAS," *Los Alamos Reporter,* March 15, 2021. See also Laura Paskus, "'Forever Chemicals' Found at Los Alamos," New Mexico PBS and *Frontline,* April 26, 2021. See also Laura Paskus, "LANL Continues Search for 'Forever Chemicals,'" New Mexico PBS and *Frontline,* April 26, 2021.

38. Amy Linn, "'This Has Poisoned Everything'—Pollution Casts Shadow over New Mexico's Booming Dairy Industry," *Guardian,* February 20, 2019. See also State of New Mexico Environment Department, "New Mexico Assists Clovis Family Dairy Farm with PFAS Contamination" (news release, May 19, 2022).

39. The DOE's budget and timeline are referenced in *Nuclear Waste Cleanup: DOE Needs to Address Weaknesses in Program and Contractor Management at Los Alamos,* U.S. Government Accountability Office (report to congressional committees, July 2023), gao.gov/assets/gao-23-105665.pdf. See also Hennigan, "The Staggering Price You're Paying for America's Nuclear Makeover."

40. *Nuclear Waste Cleanup.*

BIBLIOGRAPHY

This was truly a multidisciplinary research project. Here you will find many of the principal books that supplied me with facts or influenced my thinking about the complexity of culture. I also drew inspiration from *Whetstone Magazine,* the food writing in *The Juggernaut* and *Freeman's, The Best American Food Writing,* and The Ark of Taste database. Ligaya Mishan's essays, Alicia Katz Kennedy's Substack, Ungelbah Dávila and Cecilia Nowell's writing about food culture in New Mexico and the Southwest, and the informal book reviews posted by food studies professor Krishnendu Ray on Instagram were also invaluable resources.

Abdurraqib, Hanif. *They Can't Kill Us Until They Kill Us: Essays.* Columbus, OH: Two Dollar Radio, 2017.

Akins, Damon B., and William J. Bauer, Jr. *We Are the Land: A History of Native California.* Oakland: University of California Press, 2021.

Anti Mani. *A Taste of Jaffna.* Published by the author.

Arudpragasam, Anuk. *A Passage North: A Novel.* London: Hogarth, 2021.

Assmann, Aleida. *Cultural Memory in Western Civilization: Functions, Media, Archives.* New York: Cambridge University Press, 2013.

Ayubi, Durkhanai. *Parwana: Recipes and Stories from an Afghan Kitchen.* Northampton, MA: Interlink Books, 2021.

Bittman, Mark. *Animal, Vegetable, Junk: A History of Food, from Sustainable to Suicidal.* Boston: Mariner Books, 2021.

Buford, Bill. *Among the Thugs.* New York: Vintage, 1993.

———. *Dirt.* New York: Vintage, 2021.

———. *Heat.* New York: Vintage, 2007.

Byler, Darren. *In the Camps: China's High-Tech Penal Colony.* New York: Columbia Global Reports, 2021.

———. *Terror Capitalism: Uyghur Dispossession and Masculinity in a Chinese City.* Durham, NC: Duke University Press, 2022.

Chin, Josh, and Liza Lin. *Surveillance State: Inside China's Quest to Launch a New Era of Social Control*. New York: St. Martin's Press, 2022.

Cho, Grace M. *Tastes Like War: A Memoir*. New York: Feminist Press, 2021.

Chowdhary, Zara. *The Lucky Ones: A Memoir*. New York: Crown, 2024.

Collingham, Lizzie. *Curry: A Tale of Cooks and Conquerors*. Oxford: Oxford University Press, 2006.

———. *The Taste of War: World War II and the Battle for Food*. New York: Penguin Press, 2012.

Cwiertka, Katarzyna J. *Cuisine, Colonialism and Cold War: Food in Twentieth-Century Korea*. London: Reaktion Books, 2012.

———. *Modern Japanese Cuisine: Food, Power and National Identity*. London: Reaktion Books, 2006.

Daniel, E. Valentine. *Charred Lullabies: Chapters in an Anthropography of Violence*. Princeton, NJ: Princeton University Press, 1996.

De las Casas, Bartolomé. *An Account of the Destruction of the Indies*. London: Penguin Books, 1992.

Deloria, Vine Jr. *Custer Died for Your Sins: An Indian Manifesto*. Norman: University of Oklahoma Press, 1988.

Demetz, Peter. *Prague in Black and Gold: The History of a City*. New York: Penguin Books, 1997.

Demick, Barbara. *Eat the Buddha: Life and Death in a Tibetan Town*. New York: Random House, 2021.

———. *Nothing to Envy: Ordinary Lives in North Korea*. New York: Spiegel and Grau, 2010.

Drakulić, Slavenka. *Café Europa: Life After Communism*. New York: Penguin Books, 1999.

———. *Café Europa Revisited: How to Survive Post-Communism*. New York: Penguin Books, 2021.

Duguid, Naomi. *Burma: Rivers of Flavor*. New York: Artisan Books, 2012.

Dunbar-Ortiz, Roxanne. *An Indigenous Peoples' History of the United States*. Boston: Beacon Press, 2014.

Ebright, Malcolm, Rick Hendricks, and Richard W. Hughes. *Four Square Leagues: Pueblo Indian Land in New Mexico*. Albuquerque: University of New Mexico Press, 2014.

Eden, Caroline. *Black Sea: Dispatches and Recipes*. London: Quadrille, 2018.

Eliezer, Nesa, and Anjali Roberts. *Handmade: Stories of Strength Shared Through Recipes from the Women of Sri Lanka*. Edited by Jessica Perini. Sydney: Palmera Projects, 2015.

Estes, Nick. *Our History Is the Future: Standing Rock Versus the Dakota Access Pipeline, and the Long Tradition of Indigenous Resistance*. New York: Verso, 2023.

Foster, Kim. *The Meth Lunches: Food and Longing in an American City*. New York: St. Martin's Press, 2023.

García, María Elena. *Gastropolitics and the Specter of Race: Stories of Capital, Culture, and Coloniality in Peru*. Oakland: University of California Press, 2021.

Ghosh, Amitav. *The Nutmeg's Curse: Parables for a Planet in Crisis*. Chicago: University of Chicago Press, 2021.

Gold, Jonathan. *Counter Intelligence: Where to Eat in the Real Los Angeles.* New York: St. Martin's Press, 2000.

Goldstein, Darra. *The Kingdom of Rye: A Brief History of Russian Food.* Oakland: University of California Press, 2022.

Gómez, Myrriah. *Nuclear Nuevo México: Colonialism and the Effects of the Nuclear Industrial Complex on Nuevomexicanos.* Tucson: University of Arizona Press, 2022.

Gootenberg, Paul. *Andean Cocaine: The Making of a Global Drug.* Chapel Hill: University of North Carolina Press, 2008.

Gopal, Anand. *No Good Men Among the Living: America, the Taliban and the War Through Afghan Eyes.* New York: Picador, 2014.

Gowrinathan, Nimmi. *Radicalizing Her: Why Women Choose Violence.* Boston: Beacon Press, 2021.

Grisaffi, Thomas. *Coca Yes, Cocaine No: How Bolivia's Coca Growers Reshaped Democracy.* Durham, NC: Duke University Press, 2019.

Gustafson, Bret. *Bolivia in the Age of Gas.* Durham, NC: Duke University Press, 2020.

Gutiérrez Aguilar, Raquel. *Rhythms of the Pachakuti: Indigenous Uprising and State Power in Bolivia.* Durham, NC: Duke University Press, 2014.

Harjo, Joy, and Gloria Bird, eds. *Reinventing the Enemy's Language: Contemporary Native Women's Writings of North America.* New York: W. W. Norton, 1997.

Harris, Jessica B. *High on the Hog: A Culinary Journey from Africa to America.* New York: Bloomsbury, 2012.

Higgins, Noelle. *The Protection of Cultural Heritage During Armed Conflict: The Changing Paradigms.* New York: Routledge, 2020.

Hoja, Gulchehra. *A Stone Is Most Precious Where It Belongs: A Memoir of Uyghur Exile, Hope, and Survival.* New York: Hachette Books, 2023.

Hrabal, Bohumil. *I Served the King of England.* New York: New Directions, 2007.

Ibrahim, Azeem. *The Rohingyas: Inside Myanmar's Genocide,* revised and updated edition. London: Hurst, 2018.

Izgil, Tahir Hamut. *Waiting to Be Arrested at Night: A Uyghur Poet's Memoir of China's Genocide.* New York: Penguin Press, 2023.

Jacobs, Margaret. *After One Hundred Winters: In Search of Reconciliation in America's Stolen Lands.* Princeton, NJ: Princeton University Press, 2021.

Jaffrey, Madhur. *An Invitation to Indian Cooking.* New York: Vintage, 1973.

Kassis, Reem. *The Palestinian Table.* London: Phaidon, 2017.

Kimmerer, Robin Wall. *Braiding Sweetgrass: Indigenous Wisdom, Scientific Knowledge, and the Teaching of Plants.* Minneapolis: Milkweed Editions, 2013.

Kurlansky, Mark. *The Food of a Younger Land.* New York: Riverhead Books, 2009.

———. *Milk! A 10,000-Year Food Fracas.* New York: Bloomsbury, 2018.

———. *Salt: A World History.* New York: Penguin Books, 2002.

LaDuke, Winona. *Recovering the Sacred: The Power of Naming and Claiming.* Chicago: Haymarket Books, 2005.

Levi, Primo. *The Drowned and the Saved.* New York: Simon & Schuster, 2017.

Lewis, Edna. *The Taste of Country Cooking*. New York: Knopf, 2020.

Liebmann, Matthew. *Revolt: An Archaeological History of Pueblo Resistance and Revitalization in 17th Century New Mexico*. Albuquerque: University of Arizona Press, 2012.

MacMillan, Margaret. *War: How Conflict Shaped Us*. New York: Random House, 2020.

Malhotra, Aanchal. *Remnants of a Separation: A History of the Partition Through Material Memory*. Noida, Uttar Pradesh: HarperCollins India, 2017.

Masco, Joseph. *The Nuclear Borderlands: The Manhattan Project in Post–Cold War New Mexico*. Princeton, NJ: Princeton University Press, 2020.

McDonell, Nick. *The Bodies in Person: An Account of Civilian Casualties in American Wars*. New York: Blue Rider Press, 2018.

Millward, James. *Eurasian Crossroads: A History of Xinjiang*. New York: Columbia University Press, 2021.

Murray, Sarah. *Moveable Feasts: From Ancient Rome to the 21st Century, the Incredible Journeys of the Food We Eat*. New York: Picador, 2008.

Myint-U, Thant. *The Hidden History of Burma: Race, Capitalism, and the Crisis of Democracy in the 21st Century*. New York: W. W. Norton, 2021.

———. *The Making of Modern Burma*. Cambridge University Press, 2001.

———. *The River of Lost Footsteps: A Personal History of Burma*. New York: Farrar, Straus and Giroux, 2006.

———. *Where China Meets India: Burma and the New Crossroads of Asia*. New York: Farrar, Straus and Giroux, 2011.

Ortiz, Alfonso. *The Tewa World: Space, Time, Being, and Becoming in a Pueblo Society*. Chicago: University of Chicago Press, 1969.

Ostler, Jeffrey. *Surviving Genocide: Native Nations and the United States from the American Revolution to Bleeding Kansas*. New Haven, CT: Yale University Press, 2019.

Perlin, Ross. *Language City: The Fight to Preserve Endangered Mother Tongues in New York*. New York: Atlantic Monthly Press, 2024.

Pinker, Steven. *The Better Angels of Our Nature: Why Violence Has Declined*. New York: Penguin Books, 2012.

Pollan, Michael. *The Botany of Desire: A Plant's-Eye View of the World*. New York: Random House, 2002.

Power, Samantha. *A Problem from Hell: America and the Age of Genocide*. New York: Basic Books, 2013.

Ray, Krishnendu. *The Ethnic Restaurateur*. London: Bloomsbury, 2016.

Reséndez, Andrés. *The Other Slavery: The Uncovered Story of Indian Enslavement in America*. New York: Mariner Books, 2016.

Roberts, Sean R. *The War on the Uyghurs: China's Internal Campaign Against a Muslim Minority*. Princeton, NJ: Princeton University Press, 2020.

Rohingya Women's Development Network. *The RWDN Cookbook: Recipes and Stories from Our Kitchens to Yours*. Kuala Lumpur, Malaysia: RWDN Enterprise, 2019.

Saladino, Dan. *Eating to Extinction: The World's Rarest Foods and Why We Need to Save Them*. New York: Farrar, Straus and Giroux, 2021.

Sen, Mayukh. *Taste Makers: Seven Immigrant Women Who Revolutionized Food in America*. New York: W. W. Norton, 2022.

Shanmugalingam, Cynthia. *Rambutan: Recipes from Sri Lanka*. London: Bloomsbury, 2022.

Sheldrake, Merlin. *Entangled Life: How Fungi Make Our Worlds, Change Our Minds & Shape Our Futures*. New York: Random House, 2021.

Sherman, Sean, and Beth Dooley. *The Sioux Chef's Indigenous Kitchen*. Minneapolis: University of Minnesota Press, 2017.

Sifton, John. *Violence All Around*. Cambridge, MA: Harvard University Press, 2015.

Sinclair, Sara, ed. *How We Go Home: Voices from Indigenous North America*. Chicago: Haymarket Books, 2020.

Stewart, Amy. *The Tree Collectors: Tales of Arboreal Obsession*. New York: Random House, 2024.

Swentzell, Rina. *Children of Clay: A Family of Pueblo Potters*. Minneapolis, MN: Lerner Publications, 1992.

Swentzell, Roxanne, and Patricia M. Perea, eds. *The Pueblo Food Experience Cookbook: The Whole Food of Our Ancestors*. Santa Fe: Museum of New Mexico Press, 2016.

Templer, Robert. *Shadows and Wind: A View of Modern Vietnam*. New York: Penguin Books, 1998.

Thomson, Sinclair, Rossana Barragán, Xavier Albó, Seemin Qayum, and Mark Goodale, eds. *The Bolivia Reader: History, Culture, Politics*. Durham, NC: Duke University Press, 2018.

Tipton-Martin, Toni. *Jubilee: Recipes from Two Centuries of African American Cooking*. New York: Clarkson Potter, 2019.

Tursun, Perhat. *The Backstreets: A Novel from Xinjiang*. New York: Columbia University Press, 2022.

Twitty, Michael. *The Cooking Gene: A Journey Through African American Culinary History in the Old South*. New York: Amistad, 2017.

———. *Koshersoul: The Faith and Food Journey of an African American Jew*. New York: Amistad, 2022.

Vaněk, Roman, and Jana Vaňková. *Velká kuchařka Čech a Moravy*. Prague: Prakul Productions, 2021.

Van Oudenhoven, Frederik, and Jamila Haider. *With Our Hands: A Celebration of Food and Life in the Pamir Mountains of Afghanistan and Tajikistan*. Utrecht: Stichting LM, 2015.

Von Bremzen, Anya. *Mastering the Art of Soviet Cooking: A Memoir of Food and Longing*. New York: Crown, 2013.

ABOUT THE AUTHOR

MICHAEL SHAIKH is a writer and human rights investigator who has worked for twenty years in areas marred by political crisis and armed conflict. He has worked at Human Rights Watch, International Crisis Group, the Center for Civilians in Conflict, the UN's Office of the High Commissioner for Human Rights, and the New York City Mayor's Office of Climate and Environmental Justice. Shaikh is on the board of *Adi Magazine*. Originally from Cleveland, Ohio, he lives in New York City.